WELLS FARGO & CO. IN IDAHO TERRITORY

W. Turrentine Jackson

IDAHO STATE HISTORICAL SOCIETY

Boise 1984

This publication was made possible, in part, through the assistance of Wells Fargo & Company.

The cover photograph of the Wells Fargo office in Silver City, Idaho, is from the collection of the Idaho State Historical Society. Color tinting is by Bennett Hall, San Francisco.

Illustrations for chapter openings are used with the kind permission of the following institutions: Special Collections and Archives, Utah State University, for the drawing of coaches in the Bear River Valley, north of Corinne (from J. H. Beadle, *The Undeveloped West* [Philadelphia, 1873]), on p. 1; the Oregon Historical Society, for the photographs of The Dalles, Oregon, in 1864 on p. 21 and of Celilo, Oregon (a Carlton Watkins photograph), in 1867 on p. 43; the History Department, Wells Fargo & Company, for the printer's cut of a Wells Fargo stagecoach on p. 62 and a check on Wells Fargo on p. 103; and to Stanford University, for the photograph of the Golden Spike on p. 85.

ISNB: 0-931406-05-6

CONTENTS

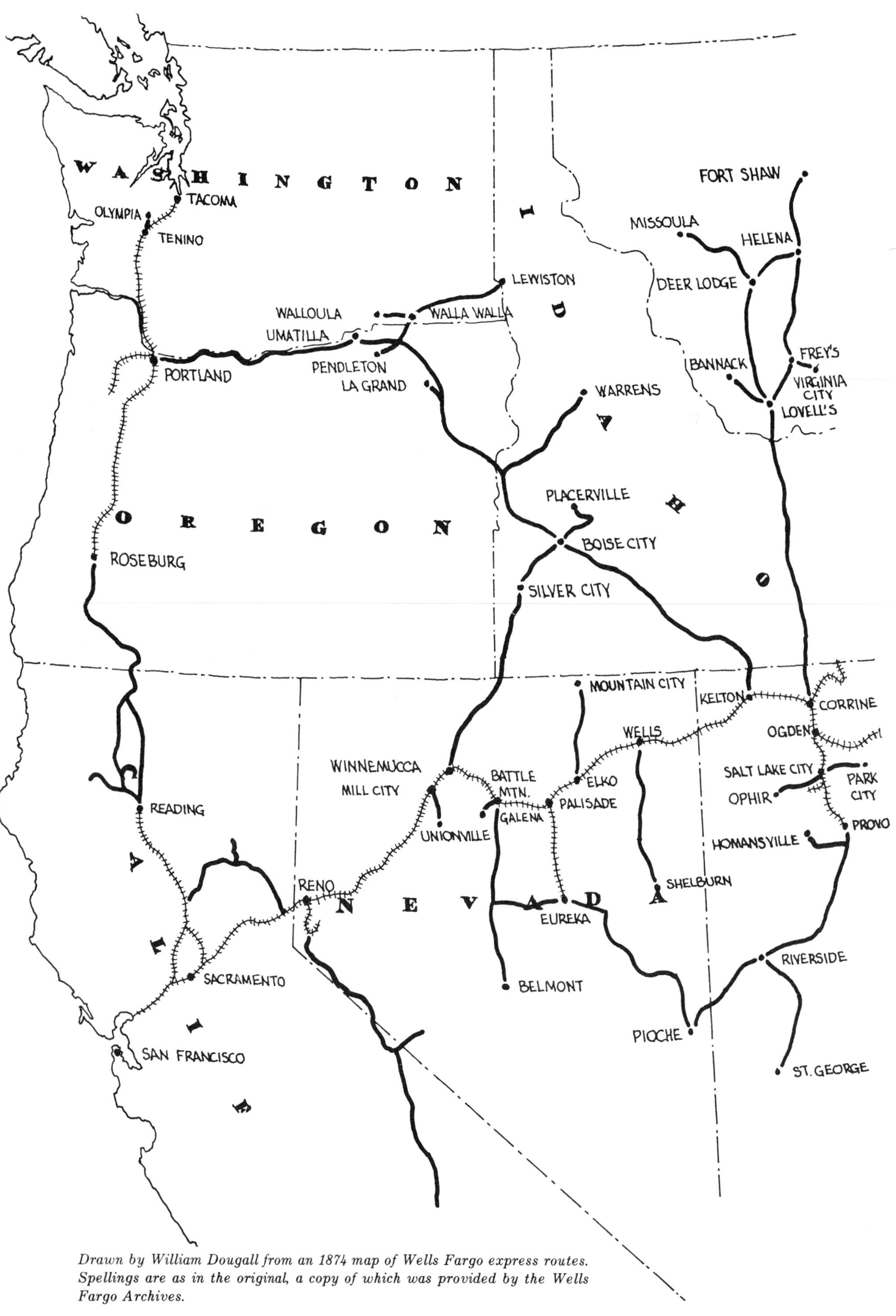

Drawn by William Dougall from an 1874 map of Wells Fargo express routes. Spellings are as in the original, a copy of which was provided by the Wells Fargo Archives.

INTO THE INLAND EMPIRE AND IDAHO TERRITORY

WELLS FARGO & CO. was established as a joint stock association in New York in March, 1852, chiefly to take advantage of business opportunities in California. Within two months the company had completed its organization, which provided for conveyance of specie, mails, packages, and freight of all kinds between the eastern seaboard and San Francisco and thence to the mining camps of California. Gold dust was gathered from prospectors and, along with bullion, shipped from San Francisco to the East and Europe.[1] Business got under way in California in July, 1852.[2] Within three months, Wells Fargo & Co. had announced the establishment of an office in Portland.[3] Slowly but surely, transportation and communication facilities radiated out of Portland, and Wells Fargo seized every opportunity to receive and deliver letters, packages, and precious cargo.

The waterways of Oregon provided the first avenues of transportation. Navigation of the Columbia River above the mouth of the Willamette was complicated by natural obstructions that divided the river into three sections: between Portland and the lower Cascades, from the Cascades to the Dalles rapids, and the upper river. On the upper reaches, R. R. Thompson and L. W. Coe carried supplies to Walla Walla by using small scow-like boats rigged with sails. In 1858, they built the *Colonel Wright*, a sternwheeler, at the mouth of the Deschutes River; it made regular trips between Celilo and Wallula. Many well-known small steamers churned the waters of the Columbia River in the 1850's.[4]

The Fraser River and succeeding gold rushes had a tremendous impact on the economic development of both the Pacific Northwest and Wells Fargo & Co. News of the discovery in British Columbia reached San Francisco in April, 1858.[5] Scarcely had the Fraser River rush collapsed the next season when the discovery of gold elsewhere further stimulated Portland's growth as a trading and transportation center. Miners who has been disappointed in the Fraser River country had turned toward the south and east to prospect along the tributaries of the Snake River. Gold was discovered in the summer and fall of 1860 in the region drained by the Clearwater and its smaller tributaries, such as Orofino Creek. During the winter of 1860-61 many miners assembled at the frontier outfitting town of Walla Walla in eastern Washington Territory, while others founded an advance supply depot

[1] *New York Times*, May 20, 1852, p. 4, c. 5; *New York Herald*, May 22, 1852, p. 1, c. 3. Both newspapers published detailed articles on the organization of Wells Fargo.

[2] *Daily Alta California* (San Francisco), July 1, 1852, p. 3, c. 2; *San Francisco Herald*, July 2, 1852, p. 2, c. 3. According to the *California Directory of 1861*, compiled by Henry F. Langley, the San Francisco office was officially opened on July 13, 1852 (p. 493).

[3] James Henry Gilbert, *The Development of Banking in Oregon*, University of Oregon Bulletin, New Series, Vol. 9, No. 1 (Eugene: The University, 1911), 7. Gilbert based his information on advertisements in the Portland *Oregonian*.

[4] The primary source of information on Columbia River steamboats is Edgar W. Wright, editor, *Lewis & Dryden's Marine History of the Pacific Northwest* (Portland: Lewis & Dryden Printing Co., 1895). See also Fred W. Wilson, "The Lure of the River," *Oregon Historical Quarterly* (March, 1933), 34:1-18; Earle L. Stewart, "Steamboats on the Columbia: The Pioneer Period," *Oregon Historical Quarterly* (March, 1950), 51:20-42. The studies by Wilson and Stewart have been republished in *Steamboat Days on the Rivers* (Portland: Oregon Historical Society, 1969).

[5] Margaret A. Ormsby, *British Columbia; A History* (Toronto: The Macmillan Co., 1958), 138-140; T. A. Rickard, *Historic Backgrounds of British Columbia* (Vancouver, B.C.: The Author, 1948), 298-299.

Stagecoaches were used in Idaho well into the twentieth century. Clarence Bisbee photographed this coach on the road into the Snake River Canyon near Twin Falls in the 1910's.

at the town of Lewiston on the Snake River at the mouth of the Clearwater. The usual stampede occurred in the spring of 1861, and several thousand miners established the towns of Oro Fino City and Pierce City. A nearby discovery on the south fork of the Clearwater resulted in the founding of Elk City. Miners continued to head southward, and soon news filtered back to the Clearwater camps that gold had been located on another tributary of the Snake, the Salmon River. Here the population concentrated at Florence. In the summer and fall of 1862, the great placer mines of the Boise Basin were discovered. Miners came in from all directions and the towns of Boise City, Idaho City, Centerville, Placerville, and Pioneer City emerged. The Boise Basin became the center of mining activity in Idaho, which was made a territory in 1863.[6] The mining regions of Idaho Territory were isolated, and access to them was exceptionally difficult. Transportation of supplies and food, the delivery of express and mails, and the removal of gold dust became, in many ways, the major problems that had to be dealt with.

In 1860, the Oregon Steam Navigation Company was organized to consolidate all the various steamboat and portage interests along the Columbia River into a single company. It was established just in time to take advantage of the Idaho gold rush, the biggest boom that ever struck in the Oregon country.[7] Wells Fargo & Co. assigned messengers to every steamer. When the *Tenino* left Lewiston on August 1, 1862, the editor of that town's newpaper, *The Golden Age*, reported:

> Upwards of two hundred thousand dollars in treasure went down yesterday . . . . Of this amount, one hundred and fifty thousand dollars, which came through from Florence on Thursday, in charge of Mr. Getzler, was shipped by Wells, Fargo & Co.[8]

Although the earliest express service into the Inland Empire from Portland is difficult to document, Ika V. Mossman probably started operating an express early in the summer of 1861 and was the first expressman into the diggings known as the Nez Perces or Clearwater District.[9] He had organized his company in April, 1861; the initial issue of *The Golden Age* carried an advertisement indicating that his service had been expanded from Lewiston to the Elk City, Salmon, and Powder River mines by July, 1862.[10] Right on the heels of Mossman & Co.'s express, E. W. Tracy, Wells Fargo & Co.'s agent in Oregon and Washington since 1861, established an express company that extended its lines and those of Wells Fargo into the Clearwater and Salmon River districts. Tracy and Co. ran a pony express into the Salmon River District as early as August, 1861, charging $1.00 for delivery from Lewiston. Wells Fargo & Co. opened its first express office in Lewiston in the summer of 1861; envelopes marked "And to Salmon River and Nez Perces Mines" and bearing the date of September 27, 1861, are extant. Letter envelopes purchased in San Francisco, addressed to Elk City, Washington Territory, were delivered for $1.00. Early in 1862, Wells Fargo & Co. established a second office in the Clearwater District at Orofino. An envelope cover, dated August 21, 1862, stamped from Orofino and bearing a "Salmon River & Nez Perces Express" imprint with a surcharge of fifty cents, has been preserved.[11]

Wells Fargo & Co.'s "Banking, Exchange and Express Company" advertised that it was the "Only Safe and Responsible Express." In addition to express offices in Vancouver,

[6]General accounts of the rush to the Inland Empire can be read in LeRoy R. Hafen and Carl Coke Rister, *Western America*, first edition (New York: Prentice-Hall Co., 1941), 462-466, and Ray Allen Billington, *Westward Expansion: A History of the American Frontier*, fourth edition (New York: The Macmillan Co., 1974), 539-543. More detailed accounts appear in Oscar Osburn Winther, *The Great Northwest* (New York: Alfred A. Knopf, 1950), 222-223; Rodman W. Paul, *Mining Frontiers of the Far West, 1840-1880* (New York: Holt, Rinehart & Winston, 1963; reissued, Albuquerque: University of New Mexico Press, 1974), 133-140; and William J. Trimble, *The Mining Advance into the Inland Empire . . .* (Madison: University of Wisconsin, 1914; reissued, New York: Johnson Reprint Corp., 1972).

[7]Irene L. Poppleton, "Oregon's First Monopoly—The Oregon Steam Navigation Company," *Quarterly of the Oregon Historical Society* (September, 1908), 9:274-304; Dorothy O. Johansen, "The Oregon Steam Navigation Company: An Example of Capitalism on the Frontier," *Pacific Historical Review* (June, 1941), 10:179-188.

[8]*Golden Age* (Lewiston), August 2, 1862, p. 2, c. 5.

[9]Mossman Collection, Idaho State Historical Society, 32, 37.

[10]*Golden Age*, August 2, 1862, p. 1, c. 5. Newspaper citations in the indices of the Idaho State Historical Society, Boise, indicate that Mossman & Co. advertised in the *Statesman* as early as September 27, 1862. The earliest extant advertisement found in the *Statesman* is in the issue for November 22, 1862, p. 3, c. 7.

[11]The earliest history of the express business must be ascertained from the covers, or envelopes, of letters. The Idaho Express folder, Art Ferrell Collection, Idaho State Historical Society (hereafter cited Ferrell Collection), is invaluable for this purpose.

Cascades, The Dalles, Wallula, and Walla Walla and all the mining towns of the Inland Empire, the company had opened an office at Auburn in the Powder River mines of eastern Oregon. The express from Lewiston to Walla Walla and the Powder River mines left tri-weekly and returned on alternate days.[12] Wells Fargo's personnel followed the practice in Lewiston, as elsewhere, of delivering newspaper exchanges and assisting the local newspaper editors whenever possible. "We are under special obligations to Mr. Watkins, Mr. Getzler, and other gentlemen connected with Wells, Fargo & Co.'s Express, for courtesies extended while preparing our next issue," noted the editor of *The Golden Age.*[13] Wells Fargo opened another agency in Florence in November, 1862; but just as that mining camp proved transitory, so did Wells Fargo's service: declining business forced the closure of the office in November, 1864.[14]

Walla Walla had become a transportation hub before the end of 1862. A stage service operated by J. F. Abbott to Wallula, on the bank of the Columbia River, was integrated with the arrival and departure of steamers. No postmaster had been appointed for Wallula, and Wells Fargo's express carried the bulk of the mail in the interim. In Walla Walla, E. L. James served as agent for both Wells Fargo & Co. and E. W. Tracy's Express. Other express services shared the same office, including Shepard, Cooper & Co., which ran to the Powder River and John Day mines with a terminus in Auburn, Oregon. Messrs. Thatcher & Rickey, operating Concord coaches between Walla Walla and Lewiston, advertised that all inquiries should be addressed to Wells Fargo & Co. When winter came on, travel and communication either ceased or slowed. Navigation on the Columbia River closed down at Wallula because of the ice and steamboats came up the river only as far as The Dalles. Messrs. Greathouse & Co. immediately introduced stagecoach service from Walla Walla to The Dalles.[15]

Among the many developments in transportation in 1862 was a projected pony express from Lewiston to Fort Benton on the Missouri River. Mason J. Haggard, a former messenger of Wells Fargo & Co., expected to cover the nine-hundred-mile distance in fifteen days. "Hurrah for the Pony!" exclaimed the Lewiston editor in August.[16] During the winter of 1862-63, Haggard, Dennee & Co., connecting with Wells Fargo, succeeded in lauching its promised pony express service to the Montana country, where gold discoveries had just been made. The route ran to Bitter Root, American Fork, Deer Lodge, Hell Gate, Prickly Pear, Horse Prairie, Bog Hole, Beaver Head, and all the known mining camps, finally terminating at Fort Benton on the Missouri River. Thus Wells Fargo & Co. was able to deliver express from Portland into these mining settlements ever before the establishment of Montana Territory.[17]

The Lewiston newspaper also noted that E. W. Tracy had instructed the traveling agent for both his express service and that of Wells Fargo & Co. to proceed to the Boise mines for the purpose of establishing an office. "We presume Placerville will be the point selected," announced *The Golden Age.* "Mr. Tracy with his usual shrewdness and sagacity predicts that Lewiston will be the principal point for the Boise Express, as it is much less by distance than any other point, and the more feasible route at all seasons of the year." Success to the enterprise."[18] E. W. Tracy did establish Wells Fargo & Co. and Tracy & Co. offices in the Boise Basin on February 27, 1863, at Placerville, Centerville, Bannock City (later Idaho City), and Pioneer. John Todd was named district agent and J. M. Shepherd the first rider.[19]

Apparently Wells Fargo & Co.'s service on the Lewiston-Boise route did not last long: in April the *Statesman* of Walla Walla reported, "Wells, Fargo & Co. have stopped sending

[12]*Golden Age*, August 2, 1862, p. 3, c. 6.

[13] *Ibid.*, p. 3, c. 1.

[14]Ferrell Collection.

[15]*Golden Age*, August 2, 1862, p. 3, c. 2; *Statesman*, November 22, 1862, p. 1, c. 2, p. 3, c. 1, 2; December 13, 1862, p. 3, c. 3, p. 4, c. 6.

[16]*Ibid.*, August 2, 1862, p. 3, c. 6.

[17]*Ibid.*, February 5, 1863, p. 4, c. 3.

[18]*Ibid.*, p. 4, c. 2.

[19]Ferrell Collection.

Pioneers of Placerville, photographed in 1894.

their express by way of Lewiston to the Boise mines, and will in the future, until further notice, send their express matter from this place by Grande Ronde."[20] The Walla Walla newspaper reported that a Wells Fargo messenger had attempted to deliver the express from Lewiston to Boise in the early spring and had been forced to turn back because of heavy snowstorms after traveling three hundred fatiguing miles. Competition among the various routes to the Boise mines and the resulting impact on competing communities brought forth tirades from rival newspaper editors. The Lewiston-Boise route was by no means permanently closed, for Charles Woodward continued to advertise his tri-weekly express lines of stages between the two points.[21]

CHARLES T. BLAKE, who had served as Wells Fargo & Co.'s agent in Folsom, California, was soon on his way to the Boise Basin to represent the company there. He explained that the conflict over the competing routes resulted, in part, from a break in the relationship between the company and its agent, E. W. Tracy. Tracy had appointed the agent to go from Lewiston to Placerville in the Boise Basin with express which failed to get through. Tracy resigned as Wells Fargo's representative to avoid being dismissed, and many of the agents appointed by him had to go. Blake was rushing to the Boise Basin to fill the void.

Blake traveled from Portland to Walla Walla in the company of Sam Knight and Tom Cole, employees of Wells Fargo & Co. in the Northwest. In Walla Walla, the three met with Charles Woodward, now the traveling agent of Wells Fargo & Co. for Oregon and Washington Territory, to plan the move into the Boise Basin. "I start from here in the lightest possible trim as to Express apparatus," Blake wrote his family. "A small forwarding receipt book, a check book, a lot of way bills, and an agency appointment, with a few franks, are all my stock in trade."[22] He joined a mule train that expected to make the distance of three hundred miles in ten days, paying $75 for his passage and baggage and $30 more for his meals.

Blake expressed reservations about Wells Fargo & Co.'s decision to move into the Boise Basin in 1862.

It seems the strangest thing to me that Wells Fargo & Co. should start an office in such an out of the way place. They literally know nothing about the country except that it was

[20]*Statesman*, April 18, 1863, as quoted in newspaper index, Idaho State Historical Society.

[21]*Ibid.*, May 9, 1863, p. 2, c. 2, p. 3, c. 2.

[22]Anson S. Blake, "Working for Wells Fargo—1860-1863: Letters of Charles T. Blake," *California Historical Society Quarterly* (June, 1937), 16:172.

reported rich last year, and that all the rush is that way this year. About all the instructions I go in with now are, write every chance you get, write fully.[23]

On April 27, 1863, after nine days on the road from Walla Walla, Blake arrived in Placerville. "We had a high old trip, camping out nights, cooking our own grub, bacon, bread baked in a frying pan, and coffee, and standing guard nights the last half of the way to keep the mules from being stampeded by the Indians," he recalled. Blake has left a record in vivid detail of Wells Fargo & Co.'s entry into the town.

We had hardly cleared the snow before we saw signs of mining in prospect holes sunk here and there. Very soon we came on miners at work, men whipsawing and making shingles, etc., and very soon came out on a little flat ridge and, riding down a street still filled with stumps and tops of trees lined on each side with newly built houses, came into a little square about as big as our garden at home and were in the town of Placerville. As we rode through the square to a hay yard beyond, quite a crowd followed us to learn the news we brought. . . . One of the crowd that followed us in said to our guide "Can you tell us anything about Wells Fargo and Co.? We understand that they were going to establish an agency here." "Yes" says the guide "they are, and that man in spectacles is the agent." The next instant I heard a shout taken up and repeated through the whole town "Wells Fargo have come." In less than three minutes I was surrounded by an excited crowd of two or three hundred men, who hardly allowed me time to get my saddle off from my mule before they almost dragged me into a large unfinished building on the Plaza, as they called the square. The carpenters were at work, but were stopped at once, the shavings were cleaned out, a couple of boards put on tressels were fixed up for a counter, one man ran for a whiskey keg to make a stool and another brought in a pair of scales and a yeast powder box to put gold dust in and installed himself to weigh for me. I had brought in with me about 400 letters, and now proceeded to call them over. As the news of my arrival spread, the crowd increased and for eight mortal hours my tongue had to wag without cessation. I disposed of a great many letters though at a dollar apiece and about eight o'clock at night broke up business in spite of the crowd, being very hungry and tired and started out to get something to eat. This was my introduction to Placerville. . . .

Soon Blake had time to move about the Boise Basin and prepared a description of what he saw:

This town lies in one edge of a sort of Basin surrounded by snowy mountains. Looking back there are three or four main creeks running through this basin, which is about 40 miles long by 15 broad in the widest part. These creeks all unite at the lower end of the basin and run off into Boise River. Every one of these creeks and the gulches leading into them and the whole hillsides between them seem to be rich in gold. Men working with cradles on little points in the hills take out $100.00 a day to the man. The whole country is claimed up though by the first comers, some men holding 15 or 20 claims, and it is difficult for those that come in now to find ground that isn't claimed. As the emigration comes in this will be remedied and men cut down to what they can legally hold. The dust here is poor, a rough quartzy looking gold . . . fineness ranging from 750 to 850. It is almost the only currency here and is paid out full of sand as it was in old California times, at $16.00 per oz. Hard show for gold dust buying as $13.50 to $14.50 is all that W. F. & Co. want to pay. . . .

Blake described the appointments and method of operation of his express office:

There are very few houses yet finished here. I have rented one of the best fronting on the plaza at $150.00 a month. It is yet a mere shell, but I have a board fixed up in one corner for a counter and take in letters and packages. I have no office furniture, no blanks or anything. The stuff which was to start this office was sent out by the way of Lewiston and was shut in in the snow. I am in hopes it will be in soon for I am almost run ashore. My stock in trade consists of about 50 envelopes, two or three quires of paper, a forwarding receipt book, some pens, ink, a stock of sealing wax, and some way bills. Envelopes for this coast we sell at 50 cts. apiece. States do. 75 cts. We get letters from Oregon P. Offices for 50 cts. apiece. I should judge from appearances that the letter business alone would reach $1,000.00 a month. We charge 5 per cent on treasure to Portland, and merchants think it quite reasonable. I am going into the newspaper business here. Sacramento Weekly Unions sell for $1.50 apiece. Other papers in proportion. . . . As soon as I have a settlement with W. F. & Co. I can remit you some coin. I have been pretty busy since coming in — have written up two or three quires of paper — all on business. I send out my first Express day after tomorrow and expect then to have two or three days of leisure. . . .

Placerville was a lively mining camp.

I found my hands full as long as I staid. I was busy from morning till night and very soon began to see that there was a great deal of money in the country and that the office, when fairly established would do a tremendous business. Everything reminded me of '49 times in California. Money was easily made and recklessly spent. Nearly every finished house in the town was a gambling saloon and all were crowded every night. Fighting, shooting, etc., were every day occurrences. On Sundays there would be two or three thousand people in the town. Sometimes it would be almost impossible to elbow your way across the plaza for the crowd. During the day there would probably be half a

[23] *Ibid.*, 173.

dozen fights and two or three shooting scrapes, and as all the gambling houses kept a band of music in each in full blast, the uproar and confusion would be perfectly deafening, about as strong a contrast to a quiet New England Sunday as you could well find. . . .[24]

Blake received one express about a week after he arrived in Placerville and immediately dispatched another for Walla Walla. The second express did not come in as soon as he had expected, so he dispatched a messenger with the accumulated dispatches. Two or three days later, after he had gone, the long delayed express arrived. To Blake's astonishment there was a letter from Samuel Knight stating that he had concluded that the route was too dangerous and long to run and that he had decided to withdraw. The letter was written the day before Blake had arrived in Placerville. Blake recalled,

I hardly arrived here and begun to get things arranged before I received notice to close out the business here and go below to Auburn and do the same thing there, and instead of the quiet office life which I had expected to lead during the summer, I was travelling through this wild country all the time, mostly on horseback. . . .[25]

Wells Fargo & Co.'s first service in the Boise Basin was unquestionably a short one. Another authority has stated that the date of the temporary withdrawal of the company's express was on May 17, 1863, and suggests that potential trouble with Indians and highway robbers was the cause. W. H. Rockefellow immediately established a pony express from Walla Walla to Boise with offices at E. W. Tracy's Express.[26] Further evidence indicates that C. B. Austin and William A. Yates, who had served as messengers for both Wells Fargo & Co. and E. W. Tracy's Express, were employed by Rockefellow. Wells Fargo & Co. instructed their new agent in Walla Walla to entrust the delivery of express for the Boise Basin to Rockefellow, who made weekly trips to Placerville and Idaho City during the spring and summer.[27]

Upon leaving Placerville, Charles T. Blake went to Auburn to buy gold dust for Wells Fargo & Co.

I stayed there about a week to get acquainted with the people and the diggings. When I first got into the town I wrote to [the] Portland office to send up some coin and some little fixtures that I wanted for dust buying. After staying in Auburn about a week I left for Walla Walla to get my coin. I had to wait at that place a week before it arrived. I then went back to Auburn, turned it all into dust and then rode down to the Umatilla Landing on the Columbia River and took the steamer. . . .

Blake reported that passage down the Columbia River on the steamers was free, including meals, because he was introduced to the officers as an express agent.[28]

In Portland, Blake learned that the conflict between Wells Fargo & Co. and its former agent, E. W. Tracy, had become serious and was a factor in the company's withdrawal from the Idaho Territory.

I find on my arrival here that W. F. & Co. have established an assay office here, and are going to try and run Tracy and King off the track. There is a good deal of feeling about it, and it can't be denied that W. F. & Co. are somehow very unpopular here. But the chief item in the count against them is the closing of that Boise route. Two-thirds of all the business done with the mines this summer is with Boise and almost all of the gold comes from there and the business men are very indignant with W. F. & Co. for withdrawing, saying that if they can't run that route they had better withdraw from every other. The boys in this office say it was the greatest mistake that was ever made and are looking anxiously for orders to start again.

While the difficulties were being ironed out, Blake was charged with continuing to buy gold dust in the Auburn District. He wrote to a former California associate:

What do you think of the idea of buying dust one day in the week and then spending six in the saddle to get it into the hands of the Express? That seems to be about the way of it now, and I have to ride 50 miles a day on the average to make the trip down and back in six days. If it should continue I shall have a change of horses and make it in two days for I think I could ride 100 miles a day without fatigue. I am getting used to it. . . .[29]

[24] *Ibid.*, 174-177.

[25] *Ibid.*, 178.

[26] Ferrell Collection.

[27] *Statesman*, May 23, 1863, p. 2, c. 1; May 30, 1863, p. 3, c. 2, as cited in newspaper index, Idaho State Historical Society.

[28] Blake, "Letters," 177.

[29] *Ibid.*, 178.

MAIL CARRIERS and expressmen sought to serve as many routes as possible in Idaho Territory during the summer of 1863. Geo. F. Thomas and Co. ran a line of stages from Wallula and Walla Walla, usually three times a week on the arrival of steamers. The express services from Florence in the Salmon River District and from Walla Walla to Lewiston were integrated with that stage schedule.[30] Among the more far-flung changes was the establishment of a pony express service between Salt Lake City and Bannock City, Idaho, by Messrs. Davis, Patterson & Co., initiated in September. Eastern newspapers delivered by this route contained far more recent news than that provided by the California and Oregon papers arriving by the Columbia River route.[31]

Wells Fargo & Co. announced on June 20, 1863, that it was establishing an assay office in its Portland office in competition with Tracy and King and other assayers. The company promised to receive gold and other ores and to make returns in bars or coins within six hours.[32] The *Statesman* reported that gold dust was coming into the Wells Fargo & Co. office in Walla Walla at the rate of $12,000 a week; if the flow continued, the total amount for 1863 would be twenty times that of the previous year.[33] Wells Fargo & Co. also continued to bring gold dust from Lewiston into Walla Walla, one shipment at the end of

[30]*Statesman*, August 22, 1863, p. 3, c. 2; *Golden Age*, August 8, 1863, p. 3, c. 1.
[31]*Statesman*, August 8, 1863, p. 2, c. 1; September 5, 1863, p. 2, c. 3.
[32]*Ibid.*, June 20, 1863, p. 2, c. 7; *Golden Age*, August 8, 1863, p. 1, c. 2.
[33]*Statesman*, June 27, 1863, p. 2, c. 5.

Wells Fargo building, Idaho City.

July amounting to one hundred seventy-five pounds.[34] As might be expected, express services delivering gold dust were occasionally robbed. Charles Frush, a pony express rider from Fort Benton, while on his way from the Beaverhead mines (in Idaho Territory but in the area later to be incorporated into Montana Territory) to Walla Walla was attacked in the mountains by road agents and robbed. Wells Fargo's agent in Walla Walla confirmed that $3,850 worth of gold dust had been lost.[35]

On August 29, 1863, Wells Fargo & Co., noting the rapidly increasing business, announced that the company would resume express service to the Boise Basin, running directly from Walla Walla about the first of September. Thus, the decision of May 17 was reversed. However, the express to Florence in the Salmon River District and Orofino along the Clearwater was to be drawn off.[36] Immediately a new partnership of Durkee & Crampton announced that it would run Concord stages on the road from Lewiston to Florence as far as Mountain House and from there use horses to deliver the express on the trail to the Salmon River District.[37] Charles Woodward connected with Durkee & Crampton stages in Lewiston and delivered both the United States mails and Wells Fargo's express into Walla Walla. There the mails and express were entrusted to Thomas's Wallula line of stages to make connections with the steamers headed down river to The Dalles and Portland.[38]

Tracy & King continued to operate an assay office opposite Wells Fargo & Co. in Portland. Messrs. E. W. Tracy & Co. announced a new express service in competition with Wells Fargo & Co. into the Boise Basin.[39] With the establishment of Idaho's first newspaper in Bannock City, *The News*, in September, 1863, detailed information about the status of the express lines was provided. In addition to Wells Fargo's express, Rockefellow & Co., Mossman & Co., and Tracy & Co. were actively engaged in the business. Early in October, Wells Fargo & Co. moved their express office from the old stand on Main Street next door to the Idaho Saloon.[40]

On August 6 Blake had arrived back in San Francisco, supposedly to stay. Within four days, he was on his way back up the Sacramento River on the way to Oregon and Idaho Territory. By October 1, 1863, the Bannock office was permanently established.

Blake left his impressions of Bannock.

> As for the town itself, it would be difficult to give you any idea of it. There is nothing in New England that I could compare it with. The smallest village there would cover twice the ground that this occupies and yet even now our population would number 3000 and in busy days in the best part of the mining season it would be safe to say that 10,000 people were in the town at one time. At the last election we polled 2700 votes. . . .
>
> . . . Considering the age of the place (not quite one year since the first house was built) we are improving very rapidly. We have two theatres in operation with performances every night, a weekly newspaper and three daily stage lines running from here to different points. A company has been organized (of which I am one) to build gas works and also to supply the town with water. We hope to have everything in operation by the 1st of July. We expect to manufacture it out of pitch pine of which there is abundance in the neighborhood.[41]

Wells Fargo & Co. soon launched a program of consolidating the various express lines. The interests of Mossman & Co. in the Nez Perces and Salmon River districts were purchased and their own service introduced.[42] From the company's Boise Basin headquarters at Bannock City, Charles Woodward, now the company's superintendent, advertised that it had offices not only in Bannock but in Placerville, Centerville, Hogem, and Auburn and was prepared to conduct a general express business to all points in the Pacific and Atlantic states and in Europe. As an initial banking service, Wells Fargo, long a financial power in the Far West, offered a secure

[34] *Ibid.*, August 1, 1863, p. 2, c. 4; reprinted in *Golden Age*, August 8, 1863, p. 3, c. 1.

[35] *Statesman*, June 27, 1863, p. 2, c. 5.

[36] *Ibid.*, August 29, 1863, p. 2, c. 6.

[37] *Golden Age*, September 5, 1863, p. 3, c. 6; see also p. 4, c. 2.

[38] *Statesman*, August 8, 1863, p. 2, c. 7.

[39] *Ibid.*, p. 2, c. 5, 6.

[40] *Boise News*, September 29, 1863, p. 3, c. 1; October 6, 1863, several items.

[41] Blake, "Letters," 178.

[42] *Boise News*, October 6, 1863, p. 3, c. 1.

depository for the Idaho miners in all the company's offices in the Boise Basin.[43] On October 1, 1863, Rockefellow & Co.'s express sold out to Wells Fargo, transferring its entire business between Walla Walla and the Boise Basin.[44] In northern Idaho, the Express Stage Line continued to carry Wells Fargo & Co.'s express directly from Lewiston to Walla Walla. A new company, Bradley & Co., was handling Wells Fargo's express from Lewiston via the Salmon River to Florence and Warren's Diggings. The two firms occupied joint offices in Lewiston. During the last weeks of October and early November, 1863, Wells Fargo & Co. was engaged in a vigorous competition with E. W. Tracy & Co. in seeking the good will of both the press and the public in Idaho. Then came the news that Wells Fargo had purchased Tracy & Co.'s Portland and Boise Express.[45]

WELLS FARGO'S EXPRESS and banking services in Idaho Territory had reached maturity by the end of 1863. Major competition from Portland into the Inland Empire had been eliminated and a stage and express line between the Columbia River depot and the Boise mines had been purchased. Wells Fargo thus possessed a through route and would contract with other express companies to deliver express and treasure to outlying communities when desirable and economically beneficial. The company advertised that it would run a weekly express between Portland and the Boise mines, which would arrive every Sunday and leave every Monday morning: "Treasure and Small Parcels carried to and brought from any point, and insured. Collections made. Drafts procured, &c. Letters forwarded to all parts of the world, and procured from any post or express office on the Pacific Coast." In addition, the company planned to run a daily express between the Basin towns of Placerville, Centerville, and Bannock.

Agents were named: W. A. Atlee, Placerville; P. W. Johnson, Centerville; A. Slocum, Pioneer; and C. T. Blake in Bannock. Simultaneously it was announced that Wells Fargo's express wagon had made its last trip of the season directly from Walla Walla to Boise. Hereafter it would run to and from Umatilla City, downstream on the Columbia and more likely to be free of ice in the winter.[46]

The company was busy furnishing its new offices in Bannock City in November, 1863. *The Boise News* noted, "Wells, Fargo & Co. have received a fine, large pair of gold-scales for their Bannock office that will be an ornament to the place and a convenience to parties in doubt as to the correctness of their scales. The bearings work in the finest of jewels and with perfect correctness."[47] Company employees continued to favor the editor with exchanges, a courtesy that was repeatedly acknowledged.

> We are under renewed, continued and continuing obligations to Wells, Fargo & Co. for bundles of Oregon, California and Eastern papers and magazines. They have furnished us this week with an immense bundle. Beautifully bound sample copies of the Waverly, Frank Leslie's Magazine were found among the lot.[48]

However, Wells Fargo was forced to give up deliveries in Idaho on a weekly basis during December and managed to make only three trips a month: the California Stage Company, under contract to bring the United States mails from Sacramento to Portland in seven days, was allowed a winter schedule of twelve days beginning November 15 and came into Portland only three times a month, making connections there with the Columbia River steamers.[49]

The geographic location of the Boise Basin was such that residents continued to debate whether it was better to look to the Columbia River route and Portland or to Salt Lake City for transportation and communication

[43] *Ibid.*, p. 3, c. 1, 3; Thomas G. McFadden, "Banking in the Boise Region: The Origins of the First National Bank of Idaho," *Idaho Yesterdays* (Spring, 1967), 11/1:4.

[44] *Statesman*, October 17, 1863, p. 3, c. 2; *Golden Age*, October 24, 1863, p. 3, c. 2.

[45] *Golden Age*, October 24, 1863, p. 2, c. 5; *Boise News*, October 27, 1863, p. 2, c. 2; November 3, 1863, p. 2, c. 3, 4, November 10, 1863, p. 2, c. 2; *Statesman*, November 14, 1863, p. 2, c. 2.

[46] *Boise News*, November 10, 1863, p. 3, c. 4; *Statesman*, November 14, 1863, p. 2, c. 3.

[47] *Boise News*, November 14, 1863, p. 2, c. 1.

[48] *Ibid.*, November 21, 1863, p. 2, c. 1. See also the issues for November 14 and 28.

[49] *Ibid.*, December 5, 1863, p. 3, c. 1.

services. D. C. Patterson's Salt Lake City express continued to bring in eastern newspapers, but by now not with as recent dates as Wells Fargo delivered from California and Oregon. Patterson's pony express rider was attacked by Indians and the service disrupted in late November.[50]

Agent Blake commented on the isolation of the Boise Basin and the expanding discussion over the most logical patterns of communication and transportation.

> ...Our means of communication with the outer world have been hitherto almost exclusively by way of the Columbia River (about 300 miles distant) and through Oregon. There has been an express for the last three or four months between here and Salt Lake, but as it has to come over four hundred miles through an unsettled country inhabited by hostile Indians and in winter across a country deeply covered with snow without any trail, it has been very irregular in its arrivals. Since the new discoveries in Owyhee, however, new routes have been projected and charters have been obtained from the Idaho legislature now in session to open roads between here and Red Bluff on the head of navigation on the Sacramento River, and also between here and Humboldt City in Nevada Territory. It is said to be only 300 miles to this latter place from here and once there you can go through by stage to San Francisco in five days. To Red Bluffs [sic] it is said to be only 450 miles and a good route the whole way.[51]

As usual, transportation services experienced serious difficulties during the winter months. Patterson's pony express service was overdue for almost a month in January, 1864, and when the messager finally arrived during the third week of the month he had been twenty-eight days on the route from Salt Lake.[52] The following month the pony express from Salt Lake was again delayed and D. C. Patterson personally left Bannock City for the Utah community to ascertain the trouble.[53] In mid-March, the Salt Lake express finally arrived in the Basin. It "brought us a large bundle of exchanges that have been accumulating at Salt Lake City all winter," commented the editor of *The Boise News*. "The dates are old, yet they are quite acceptable." All things considered, the service to Salt Lake City was unreliable and unsatisfactory. In addition to problems with winds and snow, the Snake Indians had been troublesome, driving off stock at river crossings and continuously threatening the pony express messenger. The press expressed the opinion that the military at Fort Boise should do something about it.[54]

Throughout the winter, Wells Fargo & Co. continued to deliver express, including letters and newspapers, to the mining camps of the Boise Basin. The Columbia River was often clogged with ice or frozen over; when river steamers were forced to stop at The Dalles, messengers continued on foot. *The Weekly Oregonian* reported in January, "Mr. Henderson, of Wells, Fargo & Co.'s Express, informs us that navigation is still closed above the Dalles, and is likely to be so for some time. He learned from a man who came on foot from Umatilla that the river was frozen from Grande Ronde Landing to the mouth of the Des Chutes."[55] Simultaneously the Bannock City newspaper was reporting, "The arrival of Johnny Enright [of Wells Fargo] on Monday with a sleigh load of express matter made times lively during the day and until late in the night in the vicinity of their office. No communication with the outside world had been held [sic] for seventeen days, and people were becoming anxious to hear the news." Wells Fargo kept the exchanges coming. "Thanks—Wells, Fargo & Co., as usual, have been generous with bundles of papers from East and West," noted the editor of the *News*.[56] The company also continued to move treasure and gold dust down the Columbia River to Portland for re-shipment to San Francisco. On January 22, the steamer *Julia* arrived in Portland from the Cascades with sixty passengers and about three hundred pounds of treasure in care of Wells Fargo.[57] Every steamer brought in some gold dust. "Mr. West arrived in charge of Wells, Fargo & Co.'s Express from the upper country, last evening, with $20,000 in dust and $10,000 in coin," reported the Portland *Oregonian* on February

[50] *Ibid.*, November 14, 1863, p. 2, c. 3; November 28, 1863, p. 2, c. 5.

[51] Blake, "Letters," 180.

[52] *Boise News*, January 2, 1864, p. 3, c. 1; January 16, 1864, p. 3, c. 1; January 23, 1864, p. 1, c. 4.

[53] *Ibid.*, February 27, 1864, p. 2, c. 3.

[54] *Ibid.*, March 12, 1864, p. 2, c. 1.

[55] *Weekly Oregonian* (Portland), January 23, 1864, p. 3, c. 2.

[56] *Boise News*, January 16, 1864, p. 2, c. 4; February 13, 1864, p. 3, c. 3.

[57] *Weekly Oregonian*, January 23, 1864, p. 3, c. 1.

27, 1864. "The day before $25,000 in dust came down on the *Hunt.*"[58] The "Heavy Treasure Express" continued to arrive in Portland in March. "Messenger Burke, of Wells, Fargo & Co.'s Express, came down the Columbia yesterday with a very heavy treasure express, amounting to about three hundred pounds in gold. The connection was through Boise."[59]

Within the Boise Basin local expressmen continued service during the winter months. E. Lee operated a daily express service between Bannock City, Centerville, and Placerville and carried passengers between these mining camps. Hillhouse & Co. announced an express that would run from the Owyhee District of southwestern Idaho, specifically the towns of Boonville and Ruby City, to Boise City, Bannock, Centerville, and Placerville three times a month, connecting with Wells Fargo & Co. for Portland and San Francisco.[60] In Lewiston, *The Golden Age* continued to advertise Charles Woodward's Express Line of Stages between that point and Walla Walla. When the steamers reached Wallula, the stages departed for Lewiston and Wells Fargo & Co.'s express was aboard. "We are indebted to Wells, Fargo & Co., of this place, and several messengers on the boats below, for papers," the editor wrote.[61] Lewiston residents were not completely satisfied with Charles Woodward's stage service.

> Arrangements are about to be made to establish a line of stages between this place and Walla Walla. This line will be owned and controlled in this place; and hence will not be at the mercy of the people below, who seem to use every endeavor to discourage travel in this direction. In this respect we have suffered long enough, and it is high time our citizens take active measures to check this power used against us.[62]

Lewiston citizens were dependent upon the express services because the delivery of the United States mails carried by Woodward continued to be a chronic problem. The editor of the Bannock City paper commented:

> The people of Lewiston are in a pack of trouble concerning the carrying of the mail between Walla Walla and that point. It seems that the contractor has failed to come on time, consequently our Lewiston friends are not much better off in that respect than the inhabitants of our own beautiful city who have never been blessed with the sight of one of Uncle Sam's mail carriers.[63]

On February 10, 1864, the ice went out of the Columbia River, and four days later the Oregon Steam Navigation Company sent one of its steamboats from The Dalles to Umatilla.[64] Soon thereafter boats reached Wallula. Wells Fargo immediately made arrangements to deliver express from these via Walla Walla into the Boise Basin on the tri-weekly stages to be jointly operated by George F. Thomas & Co. and Henry Greathouse & Co. On February 20, 1864, the *News* revealed:

> Today, according to announcement, the first coach of a tri-weekly line will leave Walla Walla for this city. Messrs. Thomas, Greathouse and others are proprietors, and have been for the last three or four weeks supplying the road with feed. Men are busily engaged along Burnt river and elsewhere, repairing the road, bridging streams, &c. Wells, Fargo & Co., we understand, will carry their express on the stages so that by Wednesday we may expect the first arrival of stage and express, and every alternate day thereafter throughout the season.[65]

In February, 1864, the legislature of Idaho Territory changed the name of Bannock City to Idaho City to avoid confusion with a Montana mining community with the same name (though usually spelled Bannack). For a time, the post office and express companies had attempted to make the distinction by designating the first significant mining community in the Boise Basin West Bannock, but confusion continued until the name change by the legislature.[66] Somewhat earlier, Charles Blake had been troubled by the confusion.

> On the eastern side of the Salmon River Mts. between them and the main range of Rocky Mts. lies what is called the Beaverhead country on the headwaters of the Missouri

[58] *Ibid.*, February 27, 1864, p. 3, c. 3.

[59] *Ibid.*, March 26, 1864, p. 3, c. 3.

[60] *Boise News*, January 30, 1864, p. 2, c. 4; February 6, 1864, p. 3, c. 4.

[61] *Golden Age*, March 12, 1864, p. 1, c. 1, p. 3, c. 4.

[62] *Ibid.*, p. 3, c. 1.

[63] *Boise News*, February 20, 1864, p. 3, c. 1.

[64] John Hailey, *The History of Idaho* (Boise: Syms-York Co., 1910), 95.

[65] *Boise News*, February 20, 1864, p. 2, c. 2.

[66] *Weekly Oregonian*, March 19, 1864, p. 1, c. 2. The news of the change of the name of West Bannock to Idaho City was reprinted in many newspapers. See, for example, the *Semi-Weekly British Colonist* (Victoria, B.C.), March 29, 1864, p. 6, c. 3.

River. There is another Bannack [sic] City about as large as this and as they are both in Idaho Territory it creates considerable confusion—people being very apt to get the two places confounded with each other. Our Bannack [sic] we distinguish by adding to it Boise.[67]

THE BIGGEST NEWS of March, 1864, was that Ben Holladay had obtained a contract to carry the mail between Salt Lake City and Walla Walla, effective July 1.[68] Holladay, who operated the Overland Mail from the Missouri border into Salt Lake City, had submitted a bid of $156,000 for this service. The Sacramento *Union* published the details on March 11, commenting: "Our Oregon neighbors will, by this arrangement, find themselves in receipt of Eastern mails as early as the people of California, and the California mails will be greatly relieved by the diversion of Oregon."[69] The news dispatch was reprinted by the press in Oregon, eastern Washington, and Idaho. No one was certain just what route Holladay's line would traverse. The contract stated the mails would be delivered via Fort Hall, and the *Statesman* of Walla Walla expected the service to be via Idaho City and Auburn.[70]

Before the summer of 1864 there had been no United States mail service in the Boise Basin. The bulk of the letters had been entrusted to Wells Fargo, which in turn had made arrangements with various carriers.[71] Far-flung changes and additions to the United States mail service in addition to the Holladay contract were being proposed during the spring of 1864. Resolutions had been introduced in Congress by Oregon representatives requesting the House Post Office Committee to introduce a bill to establish a postal service from Fort Bridger, in Utah Territory, via the Boise River, in Idaho Territory, to Auburn and Dalles City, Oregon.[72] A contract for carrying the mail from Salt Lake City to Bannack, Montana, had been awarded to E. S. Alvord to begin on July 1. "If the mail from here to Hellgate [Missoula, Montana] gets into operation again," suggested the *Statesman* of Walla Walla, "we will have mail communication from the States both by way of 'Boise' and 'Beaver Head'."[73] Since the contractor who was responsible for delivering the mails between Walla Walla and Lewiston had failed to fulfill the terms of his contract, the Post Office Department made a new contract with Captain John Mullan, the builder of the famous Mullan Road from the headwaters of the Missouri River at Fort Benton to the Columbia River at Fort Walla Walla or Wallula, to deliver the mails from Walla Walla to Lewiston, Orofino, and Florence along the Salmon River, to Colville in Washington Territory, and to the Hellgate in Montana Territory.[74]

In the spring of 1864 there was keen competition between Umatilla and Wallula, each community hoping to obtain a monopoly of the passenger, express, and freight business. As soon as the first steamboat arrived in Umatilla, the passengers urged Ish & Hailey, a saddle-train company, to transport them to the Boise Basin. Although their saddle horses were still out on the winter range, William Ish and John Hailey soon had a saddle train organized to transport sixteen men to the mines.[75] Thereafter, Ish & Hailey sent out saddle trains every time a steamboat came up the Columbia River—about three times a week. In mid-March the partners began to run a stagecoach from Umatilla to the foot of the Blue Mountains, a distance of about fifty miles and about as far as the stage could run because of the poor conditions of the road beyond. The rest of the route was by pack saddle train. Stations had been established from twenty to twenty-five miles apart on this portion of the route so the horses could be changed and passengers could obtain meals or sleep. In April, Ish & Hailey advertised their "New Line of Coaches and Passenger Trains" to run between Placerville and Umatilla in six days. "On and after the 20th of April, our Passenger

[67]Blake, "Letters," 180.

[68]*Statesman*, March 19, 1864, p. 3, c. 1.

[69]Reprinted in *Weekly Oregonian*, April 23, 1864, Supplement, p. 2, c. 5.

[70]*Statesman*, March 19, 1864, p. 3, c. 1; *Boise News*, May 7, 1864, p. 1, c. 5.

[71]Hiram T. French, *History of Idaho* (Chicago and New York: Lewis Publishing Co., 1914), 1:405-406.

[72]*Boise News*, March 12, 1864, p. 1, c. 5.

[73]*Statesman*, March 26, 1864, p. 2, c. 3.

[74]*Ibid.*, p. 3, c. 1.

[75]Hailey, *Idaho*, 95; French, *Idaho*, 405.

Trains will leave the Empire Hotel, (Placerville), for Umatilla, every other day, connecting with our Line of Coaches at the Blue Mountains." The fare to Umatilla was $40, and express freight was carried for 30 cents a pound.[76] During this period the mountains were crossed by what was designated the Meacham route, but by May the road from La Grande, on the east side of the Blue Mountains, to the Express Ranch on Burnt River was ready for travel. By the first of June the entire distance between Umatilla and Placerville, 283 miles, was opened for stages that made the journey in four days of daylight travel.[77]

Early in March, 1864, Idaho residents learned what Walla Walla citizens had known at least two weeks earlier: that the initial departure of the Walla Walla and Boise Stage Company of Thomas and Greathouse had been delayed.[78] The *Statesman* finally confirmed that the first stage for Boise had left Walla Walla on March 11; after the following week tri-weekly trips would be made.[79] By the end of the month, the editor of *The Boise News* reported,

Henry Greathouse called upon us a day or two since, after an absence of several months, during which time he has perfected and has in operation his long line of stages from Boise Basin to Wallula on the Columbia. They are now arriving and departing every other day at and from Placerville, and will, after this week, come straight through to this city, bringing in Express and passengers. An express manager will come through once, and letter bags three times a week.[80]

While Greathouse worked on locating and stocking the road out of Placerville, George F. Thomas & Co., already operating between Wallula and Walla Walla, located a new route across the Blue Mountains about twelve miles north of where the Ish & Hailey road ran, known locally as the Thomas and Ruckles road. The road was stocked, stations established, barns built, and hay and grain purchased to feed the horses all the way to the Express Ranch on the Burnt River, a little more than halfway to the Boise Basin. Here Greathouse & Co. assumed responsibility for the route into Placerville.[81]

There was great rivalry between the Ish & Hailey and Thomas & Greathouse lines. Thomas & Greathouse advertised that they carried Wells Fargo & Co.'s express, and Hailey admitted that it gave that firm something of an advantage. He wrote:

Mr. Thomas having had experience in the stage business with the California Stage Company, seemed to be a favorite with Wells, Fargo & Co. managers, who had established an express for carrying treasure, fast freight, letters, newspapers, etc. all over the route and they entered into a contract with the Wallula company to haul on their stages all of their treasure, freight and other matter at a stated price per pound for the year, at a high price. The express company in this contract obligated the stage company to receive no freight or anything for transportation except the passengers and their baggage. This was to give the express company a monopoly of the carrying of all treasure, fast freight, letters, newspapers, etc. At first it seemed that this might freeze out the Umatilla line, as the Wallula company predicted. In fact, all the circumstances seemed to be in their favor. Even the navigation companies' employees sent all the passengers they could up the river to Wallula to have them go on that line.[82]

Ish & Hailey challenged Thomas & Greathouse, thus favored by Wells Fargo & Co. and the Oregon Steam Navigation Company, by cutting rates for fast freight, carrying gold at freight rates with the owner assuming all risks, and delivering copies of the Portland newspapers a day early and selling them at half price. By May, Wells Fargo & Co.'s express was arriving and departing in Idaho City regularly every other day on Greathouse's stages.[83]

James M. Wood stocked a stage line between Idaho City and the Owyhee country in May, 1864. Initially he used pack trains on the route between Idaho City and Boise and stages the rest of the distance, but in the summer he

[76] *Boise News*, April 30, 1864, p. 2, c. 1.

[77] Hailey, *Idaho*, 95; French, *Idaho*, 405.

[78] *Boise News*, March 5, 1864, p. 2, c. 3; March 19, 1864, p. 2, c. 2.

[79] *Statesman*, March 12, 1864, p. 3, c. 1.

[80] *Boise News*, March 26, 1864, p. 2, c. 2. Thomas & Greathouse's stages left from the International Hotel in Placerville, while Ish & Hailey used the nearby Empire: *ibid.*, p. 2, c. 4.

[81] Hailey, *Idaho*, 96.

[82] *Ibid.*, 98; *Boise News*, March 26, 1864, p. 2, c. 4.

[83] French, *Idaho*, 406; *Boise News*, May 7, 1864, p. 2, c. 1, 2; May 21, 1864, p. 2, c. 2; *Statesman*, May 6, 1864, p. 3, c. 4.

operated stages all the way.[84] The Owyhee District was becoming a more important producer of precious metal, and the express companies served the role of explorer in seeking a more direct route from these to California. Two rival expresses dispatched parties early in May to go through to Sacramento, California, by way of the Humboldt and Washoe mining districts. A pony express route between Idaho City and Star City, Nevada, was also located. The first pony left Star City on May 4, 1864, traveling to the vicinity of Winnemucca, thence north through Paradise Valley on the Little Humboldt, over Paradise Hill to Quinn River, and from there into Idaho City by way of the Owyhee River crossing, Ruby City, and Boise City. This six-day trip each way, scheduled for every week, called for two riders who would use a total relay of twelve horses. The pony express rider headed north expected to reach Paradise Valley the first day; the head of Quinn River the second day; the Owyhee River crossing on the third; Boonville, near Ruby City and Silver City, on the fourth; Boise City on the fifth; and Idaho City on the final day. Apparently the service was tremendously successful: riders delivered 1,000 to 1,200 papers per trip and as many as 200 letters.[85]

The citizens of Lewiston, somewhat bypassed since the discovery of gold in the Boise Basin, managed in June, 1864, to obtain a more reliable stage line than that previously operated by Charles Woodward. Hill Beachey assumed responsibility for the service. The *Statesman* advertised that the Walla Walla and Lewiston Stage Line left Walla Walla every Monday morning and returned on Friday. Passengers were carried for $15 and allowed forty pounds of baggage. Extra baggage and freight was transported at ten cents a pound. Most important, the Beachey line carried the United States mails and Wells Fargo & Co.'s express.[86]

WALLA WALLA
AND
LEWISTON
STAGE LINE!
Carrying U. S. Mails and Wells, Fargo & Co.'s Express.
THROUGH IN ONE DAY!
Leaves WALLA WALLA and LEWISTON every other day, connecting with stages to
WALLULA, BOISE AND FLORENCE,
AND EXPRESSES TO
ORO FINO AND ELK CITY.
PASSENGERS Leaving LEWISTON in the Morning reach the Steamers at WALLULA the SAME DAY.
Passengers' Fare, $15.00.
TWENTY-FIVE pounds of BAGGAGE allowed each passenger. EXTRA baggage, on freight, 12 cents per pound.
STAGE OFFICES:
In Lewiston, at - - - - - - - - - - - - - HILL BEACHY'S

Within the Boise Basin there were continual changes among the local stage and express services. Goodrich & Enright operated between Idaho City and the South Boise communities, integrating their service and schedule with that of the Wells Fargo & Co. messenger from the Columbia River. Communication between Idaho City and the Owyhee District was improved when C. T. Blake and J. J. McCommons, former Wells Fargo employees, connected with the latter company's express in Idaho City and carried it on to the Owyhee District.[87]

AMIDST ALL THESE changes in transportation and communication, Wells Fargo & Co. systematically delivered the express throughout Idaho Territory and carried the treasure produced in the various mining camps down the Columbia River in charge of messengers into Portland. Each issue of *The Weekly Oregonian* in April, 1864, reported that the "Boise Express" was arriving regularly in Wallula and that large amounts of

[84] *Boise News*, April 30, 1864, p. 3, c. 3.

[85] *Ibid.*, May 14, 1864, p. 2, c. 1; May 28, 1864, p. 2, c. 1; Victor Goodwin, "William C. (Hill) Beachey: Nevada-California-Idaho Stagecoach King," *Nevada Historical Society Quarterly* (Spring, 1967), 10:22.

[86] *Statesman*, June 3, 1864, p. 2, c. 6.

[87] *Boise News*, May 14, 1864, p. 2, c. 1, 3, 4; June 11, 1864, p. 3, c. 2; June 18, 1864, p. 2, c. 2, 4; *Statesman*, June 24, 1864, p. 2, c. 5.

treasure were aboard the *Wilson G. Hunt* each time it arrived from the Cascades. Each shipment of gold dust was estimated to be worth from $50,000 to $60,000—sometimes described in terms of pounds, usually one hundred to one hundred fifty pounds. The express from Lewiston took five days to reach Portland; from the Boise Basin, ten days. At times Wells Fargo & Co.'s messenger brought down as much as three hundred pounds in gold dust.[88] These regular shipments continued throughout June, with the *New World* making the deliveries. Like the *Wilson G. Hunt*, this 220-foot-long sidewheeler had been built in New York, came to California in the summer of 1850, and had worked on the Sacramento River for the California Steam Navigation Company before the Oregon Steam Navigation Company purchased her in 1864. It was reported that on one trip from the Cascades she carried a ton of gold and made the round trip between Portland and the Cascades in six hours and fifty-seven minutes, a record.[89]

Most Wells Fargo agents in the Boise Basin remained at their posts: W. A. Atlee in Placerville, P. W. Johnson in Centerville, A. Slocum in Pioneer. Charles Blake retired to the Owyhee District and went into the express business; his replacement was J. L. Smith.[90]

Meanwhile, everyone awaited news of Holladay's plans. The Walla Walla *Statesman*, full of enthusiasm for the new service, reported in mid-June that he was expected in town to make final arrangements for his mail stage line to Salt Lake and the east. The first stage and mail was expected to leave Walla Walla on July 4.[91] Idaho City residents were doomed to disappointment: plans called for the main line to run from Boise City to Payetteville, bypassing the Boise Basin, with only a branch line between the Basin and Boise carrying the mail.[92] At the time there was no indication that Holladay intended operating beyond Boise City, because he had contracted with Thomas & Co.'s line to carry the mail from that community to Walla Walla.[93] Meanwhile, *The Boise News* reported that D. C. Patterson's express was still bringing in letters and newspapers awaiting Holladay's initial run.[94]

The Salt Lake City *Telegraph* reported on July 5 that Holladay had notified his agents that he had obtained the contract for carrying the Overland Mail from Atchison, Kansas, to Folsom, California. Two days later the paper carried two separate advertisements, one for the Central Overland Mail Route of the Overland Mail Company and a second for the Overland Stage Line that was to operate out of Salt Lake City to Virginia City, Montana, and to Walla Walla via Boise.[95] In spite of all the advertising, there was a delay in starting the service into the Northwest. Wells Fargo & Co., meanwhile, had put two additional messengers on the stages of Thomas & Greathouse to insure delivery of express more often than once a week. Now shippers could have the assurance that their packages would go forward almost immediately upon being deposited in the Wells Fargo & Co. office. The delivery of newspapers to the Idaho editors also became more frequent.[96]

No Holladay stage had arrived in Boise as late as July 16. "No stages from Salt Lake yet," reported the *News* on July 23. "It is understood, upon what authority we know not, that Holladay & Co. have got an extension of 20 days time in which to start."[97] The Holladay Overland Stage Co. brought the first mail into Walla Walla on August 8, with dates from Denver, Colorado, to July 20; by this time the overland mail was in regular operation throughout the West.[98] When Holladay & Co. released the rates to be charged for stage passage, they were far higher than the $150 to Missouri and Nebraska that had been

[88] *Weekly Oregonian*, April 2, 1864, p. 3, c. 3; April 9, 1864, p. 3, c. 4; April 16, 1864, p. 3, c. 3; April 23, 1864, p. 3, c. 3; April 30, 1864, p. 3, c. 3; May 7, 1864, p. 3, c. 1; May 14, 1864, p. 3, c. 1, 2, 3; May 28, 1864, p. 3, c. 3.

[89] Randall V. Mills, *Stern-Wheelers Up Columbia: A Century of Steamboating in the Oregon Country* (Palo Alto, California: Pacific Books, 1947), 46-47.

[90] *Boise News*, April 16, 1864, p. 2, c. 3.

[91] *Statesman*, June 17, 1864, p. 2, c. 6.

[92] *Boise News*, June 25, 1864, p. 2, c. 2.

[93] *Statesman*, July 1, 1864, p. 2, c. 1.

[94] *Boise News*, July 2, 1864, p. 2, c. 1, 2.

[95] *Daily Telegraph* (Salt Lake City), July 5, 1864, p. 2, c. 1; July 7, 1864, p. 2, c. 4.

[96] *Boise News*, July 9, 1864, p. 2, c. 2.

[97] *Ibid.*, July 16, 1864, p. 2, c. 1. See advertisements, p. 2, c. 4, and p. 3, c. 5; July 23, 1864, p. 2, c. 1.

[98] *Statesman*, August 12, 1864, p. 3, c. 2.

predicted: from Boise City to Salt Lake, the charge in gold or its equivalent was $75; to Omaha or Atchison, $480. Each passenger was to be allowed only twenty-five pounds of baggage rather than the customary forty pounds.[99]

Once the Holladay stages ran, the old pony express between Salt Lake City and Idaho City ceased operation. D. C. Patterson had terminated his service as early as July 1, 1864, in anticipation of the starting of Holladay's mail line. W. H. Bennett kept the pony express in operation during the period of delay, bringing six hundred letters that had accumulated in Salt Lake through on at least one occasion.[100]

Toward the end of July, 1864, *The Boise News* of Idaho City described the various stage and express lines that converged on Boise City and somewhat reluctantly recognized that the town would become the transportation, economic, and political center of the Idaho Territory by 1865. Ward & Co. had been pioneers in staging in and out of Boise City to all the communities in the Basin. Jo. Leach had established a line to Boonville and Ruby City, with a schedule closely integrated with Ward & Co.'s service. Charley Barnes was preparing to run a tri-weekly line from Boise to the various camps in Alturas County. Preparations were afoot to extend the line from The Dalles to Canyon City and on to Boise. Most important, Holladay & Co. would pass through the town tri-weekly. By the end of the summer some eighteen stages a week would be arriving and departing from Boise City. The editor concluded, "Boise has a mighty future in store. All the wire-working that can be brought to bear against it, will hardly prevent the location of the capital there next Winter."[101] In August, 1864, a new newspaper known as the *Idaho Tri-Weekly Statesman* was launched in Boise City. Ben Holladay advertised his Overland Stage Line; B. M. DuRell & Co., his agents in the community, announced that they were dealers in exchange and gold dust and would receive money on deposit and sell sight drafts on Portland and San Francisco.[102]

In Idaho City, the most exciting development of August, 1864, was the establishment of the Humboldt Express Co., formed by a consolidation of Cutler & Westerfield and Blake & McCommons, running from Idaho City to San Francisco in seven days. Initially they continued pony express service into Star City, connecting there with Wells Fargo & Co., and also operated a tri-weekly express between Boise City and Owyhee.[103] In short order the pony express service had more business than it could handle, and the new company put passenger wagons on the route to cover the distance between Idaho City and Star City in four days. Wells Fargo & Co. was very supportive of the service on this route. The company not only carried letters and small packages by express from the connection in Star City but continued to bring in California and eastern newspapers for the Idaho press. The files of Oregon newspapers came in to Boise City from the opposite direction, Walla Walla. The Humboldt Express Co. continued operation for about a year, until the Paiute-Bannock uprising put the company out of business.[104]

Wells Fargo & Co. also turned its attention to another area in August, 1864, establishing an express office at Canyon City in the John Day mines. "Letters and packages and treasure will be forwarded and received by this company from that section, with the regularity for which they are noted," the *Oregonian* commented.[105] James A. Henderson was named agent. In Walla Walla, there was great concern with this route between The Dalles and Canyon City. "The stages are now making regular trips between Dalles and Canyon City—the John Day mines," the *Statesman* noted. "They have made one trip between the points in thirty-six hours, being the quickest time on record. The road is again free from Indian depredations and

[99] *Boise News*, August 20, 1864, p. 2, c. 1.

[100] *Ibid.*, July 30, 1864, p. 2, c. 1.

[101] *Ibid.*, July 23, 1864, p. 2, c. 4.

[102] *Idaho Tri-Weekly Statesman* (Boise), August 2, 1864, p. 3, c. 3.

[103] *Boise News*, August 6, 1864, p. 2, c. 3.

[104] *Idaho Tri-Weekly Statesman*, August 6, 1864, p. 2, c. 3; August 20, 1864, p. 2, c. 3; August 27, 1864, p. 1, c. 4. See also Goodwin, "Beachey," 23.

[105] *Weekly Oregonian*, August 6, 1864, p. 3, c. 2.

annoyances."[106] At the end of the month, the Walla Walla newspaper reported, "Wells, Fargo & Co. have armed their messengers, on the Dalles and Canyon City road, with double barrelled shot guns. The guns have been furnished the messengers in order that they may protect themselves from Indian attacks."[107]

Thus, Wells Fargo & Co., recognizing that Ben Holladay's Overland Stage Company had gained control of the Boise and Walla Walla route and favored competitors like DuRell & Co. in the transport of treasure and the exchange business, made a decision to favor The Dalles, Walla Walla's competitor on the Columbia River, and encourage the connection thence to the John Day mines in eastern Oregon. "The steamer Wilson G. Hunt arrived from the Cascades last evening with about 100 passengers, representatives in all parts of the upper country, from Kootenai to John Day's river," the *Oregonian* noted. "They all appeared well provided with *filthy lucre*, and took lodgings at hotels. Wells, Fargo & Co.'s Messenger had charge of $60,000."[108] The decision of Wells Fargo & Co. to provide its messengers on the Canyon City road with double-barrelled shotguns proved wise, for during October the Indians began to attack prospectors and break into the corrals of the stage company, running off all the horses. Military patrols along the route were only available on occasion, and army commanders regularly dispatched Indians scouts to assess the situation among the raiding parties.[109]

Wells Fargo & Co. continued to use the stages of Thomas & Greathouse to transport treasure and express—the same stages that carried the United States mail under subcontract with Holladay. In Portland, the "Treasure Drift" also continued through September. "Mr. West [Wells, Fargo & Co.'s messenger] had in charge over eight hundred pounds in bullion," the *Oregonian* noted on one arrival of the *Wilson G. Hunt.*[110] At the end of September the steamer *New World* arrived from the Cascades, bringing $38,000 in gold bullion to Wells Fargo & Co. and 100 passengers.[111]

On October 1, 1864, Wells Fargo & Co. lowered its charges for letters on a nationwide basis.

This morning Wells, Fargo & Co. put down the price of carrying letters to all parts of the United States to one bit a piece, or ten cents each where envelopes are bought in large quantities. . . . Everybody can now write to his gal and enclose an envelope for an answer, all for two bits, no matter whether she be in Webfoot, Maine or New Orleans—everywhere within the limits of the Universal Yankee Nation; and creditors who expect no answers from their correspondents can dun for bit. Mighty nice arrangement, this cheap postage.[112]

The *Idaho Tri-Weekly Statesman* complained that the Walla Walla stages of Thomas & Greathouse and the Umatilla stages of Ish & Hailey continued to make Placerville their Idaho headquarters and warned that if they did not move to Boise, they could expect Ben Holladay to extend his line from there on to Walla Walla. The editor explained the problem:

Many passengers are now traveling direct through, and to compel them to travel sixty-five miles over the Boise Mountains in order to secure a passage is too intolerable to be borne. Every morning passengers are wanting to go west from this city, but can't secure seats except to go to Placerville, sixty-five miles out of the way.[113]

The Boise newspaper continued its crusade, pointing out that the stage lines charged $60 to go from Boise to either Walla Walla or Umatilla but only $40 from Placerville. The usual fare between Boise and Placerville, or Idaho City, was $5 or at the most $10, and the $20 additional was considered excessive. The editor concluded his observations:

This city is already the greatest staging thoroughfare north of California, and destined to be largely improved by an honorable course of business stage men. We are anxious

[106] *Statesman*, August 12, 1864, p. 3, c. 2.

[107] *Ibid.*, August 26, 1864, p. 3, c. 2.

[108] *Weekly Oregonian*, August 27, 1864, p. 3, c. 2.

[109] *Ibid.*, October 15, 1864, p. 3, c. 6.

[110] *Weekly Oregonian*, September 17, 1864, p. 3, c. 1.

[111] *Ibid.*, October 1, 1864, p. 3, c. 1.

[112] *Boise News*, October 1, 1864, p. 2, c. 2. Early in October, the *Boise News* ceased publication in Idaho City. It was replaced by the *Idaho World*, which published its initial issue on October 29, 1864. *Ibid.*, p. 2, c. 3; *Idaho World* (Idaho City), October 29, 1864, p. 1, c. 4, 5.

[113] *Idaho Tri-Weekly Statesman*, October 29, 1864, p. 2, c. 3.

to see this business conducted with profit to the stage men, and with advantages to the public, and shall take pleasure in recommending them when we can do so in good conscience.[114]

By the end of November, winter weather conditions developed. "Passengers from Walla Walla by the last stage state there was a foot and a half of snow on the Blue Mountains and the sleighing good," reported the *Idaho Tri-Weekly Statesman.* "Thomas & Co.'s line is making good time. On the Umatilla route there is less snow and more mud."[115] No matter the snow, Wells Fargo & Co.'s express was on every stagecoach running between Idaho City and Walla Walla. "Mr. Bledsoe, W. F. & Co. messenger, informs us that the snow has been about two feet deep on the Blue Mountains for some time," noted the *Idaho World.* "It was snowing when he crossed them last week, and probably the late storm has largely increased its depth."[116] Howard Bledsoe continued to cross the Blue Mountains on horseback or foot even when the snow was six feet deep and still falling. On his last trip of the year, Bledsoe arrived in Placerville after six days on the road from Walla Walla.[117]

Even though the mining season had closed, the flow of treasure into Portland continued. "The treasure box of Wells, Fargo & Co.'s express by the steamer *Wilson G. Hunt* last evening, contained nearly $80,000 in gold and silver bullion," reported the *Oregonian* on November 24, 1864. "The season of mining has closed for some time, but the flow of treasure does not seem to close with the season."[118] When the Columbia River froze, Wells Fargo's employees resorted to stagecoaches or horses to deliver the treasure. "Last evening, Messrs. Cann, Edgar, and Austin, Messengers of Wells, Fargo & Co.'s express, arrived from The Dalles, with one of Geo. Thomas & Co.'s coaches on Sunday, and bring to this city letters and papers of late date from Walla Walls," reported the Portland newspaper. "The party report having a very pleasant trip of it, and bring about $60,000 in treasure, besides forty or fifty pounds of letters, etc. Their animals stood the jaunt very well, for traveling on sleet and ice."[119]

When the first *Idaho Directory* was published in 1864, the appointment of J. L. Smith as Wells Fargo & Co. agent on Main Street in Idaho City was confirmed. W. A. Atlee remained agent in Placerville at the company offices on Granite Street. There had been a change in Pioneer City by the end of the year, for W. W. Chapman, a Main Street banker, was Wells Fargo agent, having replaced Slocum.[120]

Throughout the winter, Wells, Fargo & Co. continued to advertise its Portland assay office in the Idaho newspapers.

ASSAY OFFICE
WELLS, FARGO & CO.,
ASSAYERS,
Portland, Oregon

WE ARE NOW PREPARED to receive Gold and Ores of every description for Assay, at our office in Portland.

BARS AND COIN within Six Hours. Bars Discounted at the Very Lowest Rates.

Wells, Fargo & Co.[121]

Winter weather made communication exceeding difficult. As the snows fell, sleighs were resorted to. The fierce competition between Ish & Hailey and Thomas & Greathouse came to a close on December 1, 1864, when Ish & Hailey withdrew their service; Thomas & Greathouse apparently continued to operate throughout the winter months. John Hailey recalled, "Of course, when the Umatilla line stopped for the winter, the other company had everything its own way. However, the business was over for the season. There was no travel, but little express, yet the mail had to be carried."[122]

[114] *Ibid.*, November 1, 1864, p. 2, c. 2.

[115] *Ibid.*, November 26, 1864, p. 2, c. 1.

[116] *Idaho World*, December 3, 1864, p. 2, c. 4.

[117] *Ibid.*, December 31, 1864, p. 2, c. 1.

[118] *Weekly Oregonian*, November 26, 1864, p. 2, c. 4.

[119] *Ibid.*, December 24, 1864, p. 3, c. 2.

[120] *Idaho Directory Including the Pinciple* [sic] *Towns in Boise, Owyhee and Alturas Counties, I. T.* (N.p.: Published by Geo. Owens, 1864), 18, 40, 45.

[121] *Golden Age*, November 19, 1864, p. 3, c. 4.

[122] Hailey, *Idaho*, 99.

GREAT OVERLAND
MAIL ROUTE.

PACIFIC AND ATLANTIC STATES.

WELLS, FARGO & CO.

SOLE PROPRIETORS.

FARE REDUCED! TIME SHORTENED!

On and after the 1st day of April, 1867, passengers will be forwarded through at the following reduced rates, viz:

Sacramento to Omaha	$300.
Virginia City to Omaha	275.
Austin to Omaha	225.
Sacramento to Cheyenne	250.
Virginia City to Cheyenne	225.
Austin to Denver	175.
Salt Lake to Bannock, Montana	120.
" *Virginia*	120.
" *Helena*	145.
" *Fort Benton*	175.

ALL LEGAL TENDERS OR THEIR EQUIVALENT.

12

Time from Sacramento to Omaha, 15 Days.

First class conveyances, careful and experienced drivers and attentive agents are employed, and every possible arrangement has been made for the comfort and safety of passengers.

The route passes through the celebrated silver regions of Nevada, the valley of Great Salt Lake, the beautiful scenery of the Rocky Mountains and the GREAT PLAINS, and is the cheapest and most expeditious route to the Atlantic States.

Good meals at reasonable prices will be furnished passengers at convenient distances.

Passengers may lay over at any home station and renew their journey whenever there are vacant seats in stages, by notifying the local agent immediately on arrival.

At Morrow's Station, the cars of the Union Pacific Railroad Company will afford direct communication with Railroads at Omaha for all Eastern cities and towns. Wells, Fargo & Co., are also sole proprietors of connecting Stage Lines at Salt Lake City, for the Mining regions of Montana and Idaho, and at Denver with the mining regions of Colorado.

Express packages taken to any of the above named points at low rates

Tickets may be purchased at the offices of Wells, Fargo & Co., on the route.

Persons desiring to secure passage for their friends in the States, can do so by making application to the Agents of the Company. No seat secured until paid for.

Twenty-five (25) pounds of baggage allowed each passenger, but they will not be permitted to carry valuables as baggage or extra baggage

For further particulars enquire at any of the offices of the Company on the line, or of

WELLS, FARGO & CO.
Stage Department, San Francisco.

San Francisco, April 1st, 1867.

13

OLD AND NEW ROUTES, 1865

THE PROVISION OF communication and transportation in the Idaho Territory in 1865 was largely a process of sustaining old routes and pioneering new ones. During the midwinter months, a major concern, as always, was keeping Idaho residents in touch with the outside world. The firm of Thomas & Greathouse bridged the gap between Walla Walla and Idaho communities, taking nine days to make the trip. Ben Holladay's Overland Stage Line adjusted its schedule in January, 1865, to every-other-day service out of Salt Lake City rather than a tri-weekly schedule. As a rule, the run from Salt Lake City into Boise took seven to seven and a half days. Between Boise City and Idaho City, Cornish & Co.'s stages made the trip in six hours, a good time on a newly built road. Charley Barnes carried passengers, express, and mail from Boise City to the Owhyee District in southwestern Idaho.[1] In the Lewiston area, local stage men made every effort to carry letters and treasure back and forth to the mining camps. Bacon's Express ran from Lewiston to Elk City, Newsome Creek, and Clearwater Station and promised prompt attention to all letters forwarded through Wells Fargo & Co. E. K. Davidson delivered express to Oro Fino and Pierce City and on to the Bald Mountain Diggings. Dwight Brothers Express bridged the gap to the Salmon River District, going to Warren's Diggings and Florence.[2]

Throughout the winter, stage and express services dealt with a triumvirate of problems: bad weather, highwaymen, and Indian depredations. More often than not, the severe winter weather or Indian disturbances resulted in an irregular arrival of the mail. The *Idaho Tri-Weekly Statesman,* reduced to a single sheet in the winter, reported:

[1] *Idaho Tri-Weekly Statesman* (Boise), January 10, 1865, p. 2, c. 1, January 17, 1865, p. 2, c. 1.

[2] *North-Idaho Radiator* (Lewiston), January 28, 1865, p. 1, c. 4, February 4, 1865, p. 4, c. 5, February 11, 1865, p. 1, c. 1.

The Overland Mail started for Salt Lake yesterday morning. A large mail came in on Sunday, but brought nothing east of Salt Lake due to Indian troubles on the plain. The last storms have been severe between Salt Lake and Fort Hall, and would have closed the route entirely but for the determination and perseverance of Holladay's agents and drivers.

In spite of problems, Holladay's service often appeared more reliable than that between Walla Walla and Boise.[3] Ice was a problem in the Walla Walla area in all directions by both land and river. Not only did the stages and wagons on the Boise road have to cross the Snake River on ice for fifteen days, but along the Columbia River at the rapids between Wallula and The Dalles the ice was banked up to a height of eight or ten feet.[4]

Between Walla Walla and The Dalles all communication was by land: the Columbia was closed. Thomas & Co.'s stages ran the route, carrying the U.S. mail and Wells Fargo's express on a trip that usually took four to four and a half days. However, the Wells Fargo messenger on the stages reported unusually heavy rains in The Dalles area. From The Dallas on to Portland, the river was open but land routes operated as well. Thomas & Co. had competition on the river road from a line of passenger wagons operated by a Mr. Chiles. Whenever the stages arrived in Walla Walla from Boise or Lewiston (or for that matter whenever a wagonload of passengers was ready) he made the trip at reduced rates—usually about twice a week.[5]

In addition to problems with the weather, stages had to be on the lookout for highwaymen. Wells Fargo & Co.'s expressman on the Walla Walla-Umatilla Road, en route to The Dalles, reported that a passenger on the stage had discovered that a package of gold dust belonging to him was missing. A search of the personal belongings of all travelers revealed that another one had lost $1,200 and a third $6,200; it was agreed that the robbery must have occurred while the owners were at dinner at one of the way stations.[6]

Serious problems developed on the mail route between The Dalles and Canyon City, in the John Day District of eastern Oregon, in February of 1865. For the previous eight months the mail had been carried by The Dalles and Canyon City Stage Company with no remuneration. The Post Office Department had designated this a "special route" not qualifying for financial support, so nothing but the proceeds from the Canyon City office could be used to defray the carrying costs. The stage company, concluding that the job did not pay, discontinued the service. Wells Fargo & Co. immediately announced that all persons sending letters to Canyon City could forward them by that company's express, which left The Dalles once a week, and promised twice-a-week service in the spring. The Portland *Weekly Oregonian* noted: "They charge a dime, and offer the only sure means of sending letters regularly."[7]

Such conditions led to frustration with the federal mail service. The *Idaho Tri-Weekly Statesman* editor in Boise City complained that there were no post offices established on the Overland Mail route through the Boise and Payette valleys. He urged that three new offices be established between Boise and the crossing of the Snake River and others on the route down the Boise Valley and by way of Canyon City to The Dalles. He urged citizens to petition Idaho's Territorial Delegate in Washington, D.C., William H. Wallace, to come to their aid. The Boise editor was also annoyed that the overland mail service between Walla Walla and Boise went by way of Placerville, Centerville, and Idaho City in the Boise Basin rather than coming direct into Boise.[8] There were even more serious concerns about the mails in Walla Walla: the Columbia River, which had been opened between The Dalles and Portland in January, was blocked in many places by ice the next month, and week after

[3] *Idaho Tri-Weekly Statesman*, January 17, 1865, p. 2, c. 3, January 30, 1865, p. 2, c. 1.

[4] *Statesman* (Walla Walla), January 6, 1865, p. 2, c. 4, and p. 3, c. 1 and 2, January 20, 1865, p. 3, c. 2.

[5] *Ibid.*, January 6, 1865, p. 2, c. 6, and p. 3, c. 1, January 13, 1865, p. 2, c. 2, January 20, 1865, p. 3, c. 2, January 27, 1865, p. 3, c. 1.

[6] *Idaho World* (Idaho City), February 4, 1865, p. 2, c. 1.

[7] *The Weekly Oregonian* (Portland), February 18, 1865, p. 2, c. 3.

[8] *Idaho Tri-Weekly Statesman*, January 21, 1865, p. 2, c. 1, January 25, 1865, p. 2, c. 1.

week the stage came in with no news from the outside.[9]

Toward the end of February, stagecoach operators looked forward to improved weather conditions in the spring and began to restock their routes. But early in March heavy snow slides completely blocked the road between Boise City and Idaho City. No teams could get through. Men shoveled out the road as fast as possible, but stages were not expected to attempt the trip for several days. Twenty to thirty men were hired to try to keep the road open; with the aid of volunteers they almost succeeded, but snow slides again closed the road. After ten days of closure, Nat Cornish left Boise on March 18, 1865, determined to get through unless he were caught in a slide. The *Idaho Tri-Weekly Statesman* commented:

> Mr. Cornish has rendered to the people of Idaho City efficient service this winter in carrying the mails and express. He has several times packed both on his back a great portion of the way. It ought to be remembered at the same time that not a dollar has yet [been] received from the Post Office Department for his service.[10]

The South Boise Express that had been running since 1863 announced in March that it would operate in the coming season between the Boise Basin, Boise City, and the South Boise and Yuba mining towns, connecting with Wells Fargo & Co. The line ran to Red Rock City and Rocky Bar. The firm advertised that goods purchased for "ladies and others" in the

[9] *Statesman*, February 3, 1865, p. 3, c. 1, February 10, 1865, p. 2, c. 5, February 24, 1865, p. 2, c. 3, and p. 2, c. 6.

[10] *Idaho Tri-Weekly Statesman*, March 7, 1865, p. 2, c. 1, March 11, 1865, p. 2, c. 1, March 18, 1865, p. 2, c. 5, March 30, 1865, p. 2. c. 2. At the end of March, David Updyke invested in a partnership with Cornish & Co. to run the Boise and Idaho City Stage Line.

Ruby City, Idaho Territory, as shown in an 1865 woodcut.

Reproduction courtesy Wells Fargo Co.

Boise Basin would be delivered C.O.D. by Wells Fargo & Co.'s Express.[11]

News finally came through from Salt Lake City at the end of March that the Overland Mail would soon be running regularly again. The United States Army was sending an escort with the stagecoaches through the hostile Indian country on the plains to prevent Indian attacks from disrupting the delivery of the United States mails.[12] The Overland Mail Company, according to David Street, Ben Holladay's agent and paymaster, had again made a contract with Geo. F. Thomas & Co. to carry the mails between Boise City and Walla Walla, while Ben Holladay's stages could carry the passengers, mail, and express through from Boise City to Salt Lake and the east. Thomas & Co. also assumed the responsibility for delivering the mails between Walla Walla and The Dalles. This new contract was for three years and three months—the remainder of the unexpired term of Holladay's own contract.[13]

The firm of Ish & Hailey, which had closed down its Umatilla-Placerville route during the winter, was back on the road placing stock and wagons at the stations and was in business by April. The *Idaho World* reported, "The stages are running crowded with passengers. Very many are also coming in on foot packing their blankets."[14] Ish & Hailey's competitors from the Columbia River, Thomas & Greathouse, reported that mud and water had become as great an obstacle on the Walla Walla-Placerville route as the snow had been a few months earlier.[15] Thomas & Co. was working to improve the service out of Walla Walla and had ordered five new "Concord coaches." By the end of May, Howard Bledsoe, Wells Fargo & Co.'s messenger, came into Walla Walla on the stage and reported that the snow was all gone in the Boise Basin and the miners were busy sluicing, ditching, and fluming.[16]

On June 17, 1865, came the surprise announcement that the rival lines from Walla Walla and Umatilla had consolidated their interests and that their Idaho headquarters would be transferred from Placerville to Idaho City.[17] In Boise, the *Idaho Tri-Weekly Statesman* printed the rumor that Ish & Hailey and Thomas & Ruckle had formed a co-partnership to run their stages into Boise, leaving on alternate days from Umatilla and Walla Walla. The editor admitted that he was unable to obtain positive information about the arrangement. It was further reported that Greathouse was withdrawing from participation in the overland route to Walla Walla. He was expected to operate a branch line from Payette to Placerville, one between Boise and Idaho City, and one to Ruby City.[18]

[11] *Idaho World*, March 18, 1865, p. 3, c. 2. C. L. Goodrich was the superintendent in Idaho City.

[12] *Statesman*, March 25, 1865, p. 2, c. 1, March 30, 1865, p. 2, c. 2.

[13] *Ibid.*, April 4, 1865, p. 2, c. 1, April 14, 1865, p. 2, c. 6; *Idaho World*, April 29, 1865, p. 2, c. 1. It is not clear whether Thomas & Co. had a single contract for the entire distance from Boise to The Dalles, via Walla Walla, or two separate contracts.

[14] John Hailey, *The History of Idaho* (Boise, Idaho: Syms-York Company, 1910), 99; *Idaho World*, April 1, 1865, p. 2, c. 1.

[15] *Statesman*, May 5, 1865, p. 2, c. 2.

[16] *Ibid.*, May 26, 1865, p. 3, c. 2.

[17] *Idaho World*, June 17, 1865, p. 2, c. 1.

[18] *Idaho Tri-Weekly Statesman*, June 17, 1865, p. 2, c. 1. The *Daily Mountaineer* (The Dalles, Oregon) for June 23, 1865, included advertisements for the stage lines from the Columbia River.

John Hailey states that Ish sold out his interest in the partnership that had run the stage line to Umatilla to him and in turn bought a half interest in the Thomas & Co. stage line that ran from Walla Walla to the Express Ranch.[19] In mid-July, The *Weekly Oregonian* confirmed: "The different lines of stages running to the Columbia river, have combined for the purpose of more effectively accommodating the travel, and a daily line now runs from Idaho City to Wallula or Umatilla."[20] Poujade House, on the corner of Main and Commercial streets in Idaho City, must have been a busy place: the offices of the consolidated stage lines to Umatilla and Walla Walla were there as well as those of the South Boise Express and Wells Fargo & Co. C. L. Goodrich was the agent of all three companies.[21]

Cornish & Co., who had been operating the Boise and Idaho City Stage Line for many months, also sold out to Greathouse & Co., who planned to commence a daily line between the two Idaho communities at the end of June. According to Hailey, Greathouse & Co. operated twice daily on the twelve-mile route from Placerville via Centerville into Idaho City.[22] Charley Barnes's service between Boise and Owyhee was expanded by Jos. Leach & Co., in which Barnes and William A. Yates were also partners. They sent out stages on a tri-weekly basis over the 65-mile route.[23]

Several new express services advertised early in the season. F. McKay announced that he would run a pony express service between Boise and Yuba City and Rocky Bar once a week, carrying the U.S. mails. Rigg & Kane organized an express service from Idaho City to Warren's Diggings, in northern Idaho, expecting to bridge the distance in two days and delivering San Francisco newspapers to Warren's Diggings within nine days.[24]

Reproduction courtesy Wells Fargo Co.

THE INCREASING IMPORTANCE of the Owyhee District in the mid-1860's as a producer of silver shifted the attention of Idaho communities to the possibility of finding a more convenient and direct route for supplies and shipping out treasure directly to California rather than going northward to the Columbia River, on to Portland, and south by steamer to San Francisco. During the winter of 1865, travelers continued to experiment with the opening of a route from Idaho City, via Owyhee, through Nevada and into northern California. In February, the Walla Walla *Statesman* reported:

Stage Line to Owyhee—Mr. Hill Beachy left San Francisco in the latter part of January for Star City, Nevada Territory, with stages and teams, to start a stage line from

[19]Hailey, *History of Idaho*, 123. No additional source has been found to confirm Hailey's statement.

[20]*Weekly Oregonian*, July 15, 1865, p. 2, c. 5.

[21]*Idaho World*, June 24, 1865, p. 3, c. 1.

[22]*Idaho Tri-Weekly Statesman*, June 24, 1865, p. 2, c. 1. Reports in the Idaho newspaper contradict the testimony of John Hailey. He states that Ward & Co. operated the line between Idaho City and Boise City, thirty-six miles, on a tri-weekly basis and it was this partnership that sold to Greathouse. The newspapers repeatedly said that service had been operated by Cornish & Co. See Hailey, *History of Idaho*, 123.

[23]*Idaho Tri-Weekly Statesman*, May 25, 1865, p. 3, c. 5; *Weekly Oregonian*, July 15, 1865, p. 2, c. 5; Hailey, *History of Idaho*, 213.

[24]*Idaho Tri-Weekly Statesman*, May 27, 1865, p. 2, c. 4; *Idaho World*, May 27, 1865, p. 2, c. 1.

Star City to Owyhee. If such a line can be made a permanent institution, Mr. Beachy is the man to do it.[25]

The news item was reprinted in Lewiston's *North-Idaho Radiator*, whose editor added, "We acquiesce in the opinion of Beachey and we go futher—we think the new stage line will succeed and will be a paying thing. But it will strike deep at the Columbia River travel." Plans called for running the coaches over the 240-mile route between Silver City and Star City on a tri-weekly basis until travel warranted a daily service.[26] Hill Beachey was advertising in the Virginia City, Nevada, newspapers that he would start his line of stages on April 7 or 8 and that the fare would be $75. The start must have been delayed; it was reported on April 8 that the stages would not take off until the following week. More authoritative evidence suggests a June, 1865, date for the first departure.[27]

Beachey had scarcely started his line in June when Indians attacked his stock along the Owyhee River and elsewhere, taking with them horses estimated from thirty-seven to fifty-seven in number. Beachey withdrew the balance of the stock from the road. The *Idaho World* bristled: "Closed, we become the victims of Oregon monopolies." The editor insisted that the military were needed to patrol the route.[28] The Humboldt Express arrived in Boise from the Owyhee District for the last time during the third week in June, and the messenger reported that he had to run the gauntlet of two hundred miles of hostile Indians.[29]

By the end of July, Beachey had definitely given up on his plans for the season, although in August rumors again circulated that he would put a line of stages on the Humboldt road. One of his associates arrived in Boise City from Unionville and reported that the road was at last cleared of Indians.[30] However, it was too late in the season to try again. Beachey was severely hurt financially by the collapse of his plans, but he did not give up the idea of running stages from southwest Idaho to the Humboldt District. He had abandoned the plan of going as far as Virginia City, realizing he could not compete with the east-west overland line subsidized by a government contract.[31] But in anticipation of stagecoach service in the season of 1866, a list of stations along the route and distances between them was published.

From Star City to Dundan	20
Humboldt bridge	22
Paradise Valley	24
Hooker Creek	16
Buffalo Springs	8
Willow Creek	16
Queene River	23
Ten Mile Creek	10
Summit Springs	18
Desert Wells	23
Owyhee River	20
Boonville	60

Whole distance from Star City to Boonville 260 miles.[32]

A second route from Idaho to California, known as "The Chico and Red Bluff Route," was much in the news in the season of 1865. The proposal for this route had largely grown out of extreme rivalry between the Oregon Steam Navigation Company on the Columbia River and the California Steam Navigation Company on the Sacramento River. People in southwestern Idaho often felt victimized by the inadequate communication network in the Pacific Northwest, and they blamed the high cost of transportation on the Oregon Steam Navigation Company's monopoly. During the winter months, the Boise Basin was largely isolated when the Columbia River froze and heavy snows fell in the Blue Mountains. During the winter of 1863-64 both the California Steam

[25] *Statesman*, February 24, 1865, p. 2, c. 5.

[26] *The North-Idaho Radiator*, March 11, 1865, p. 4, c. 2; *Idaho World*, March 25, 1865, p. 3, c. 2.

[27] *Idaho Tri-Weekly Statesman*, April 18, 1865, p. 2, c. 1, quoting the (Virginia City, Nevada) *Virginia Union*. This item also appeared in the *Statesman*, April 28, 1865, p. 3, c. 2. See Victor Goodwin, "William C. (Hill) Beachey: Nevada-California-Idaho Stagecoach King," *Nevada Historical Society Quarterly* (Spring, 1967), 10:23. Goodwin is following the suggestion of James F. Abel, a resident of Paradise Valley who had known Beachey and who prepared a manuscript about him for the Nevada Historical Society in 1952. Goodwin is more certain of the June, 1865, date. The present author is of the opinion that some stagecoaches may have started out during the season of 1865 but that because of Indian resistance none got through.

[28] *Idaho World*, June 17, 1865, p. 2, c. 2. The *Daily Mountaineer* reprinted portions of the article from the *World* on June 28, 1865.

[29] *Idaho Tri-Weekly Statesman*, June 24, 1865, p. 2, c. 1.

[30] *Idaho World*, July 22, 1865, p. 3, c. 1, August 5, 1865, p. 2, c. 1.

[31] Goodwin, "Beachey," 24.

[32] *Idaho Tri-Weekly Statesman*, September 7, 1865, p. 2, c. 3.

The Idaho Hotel, Wells Fargo office, and courthouse, Silver City, in July of 1867.

Navigation Company and the California Stage Company had dispatched agents to explore a practicable route inland. As the topography became better known, cattle drives and the pack trains of freighters crossed the land successfully.

In California, the two communities of Chico and Red Bluff constructed roads in hopes of controlling the traffic to the Owyhee District. With the leadership of John Bidwell, the citizens of Chico had raised $40,000 in 1862 to build a road across the Sierra to Susanville, northwest of Honey Lake. Here the route met the federal wagon road that had been improved from Honey Lake to the Humboldt District. This route, known as the Nobles Road, ran west to Lassen Meadows. In 1863 the residents of Red Bluff, also at a cost of $40,000, constructed the Tehama County Wagon Road over the Sierra to join the Chico-Owyhee Road at Mountain Meadows west of Susanville.

In 1864-1865, four well-known Idaho men pioneered the organization of a stage service between northern California and Idaho. They were J. B. Francis, who had earlier explored the route; E. D. Pierce, who had discovered gold on the Clearwater and was hostile to the Oregon Steam Navigation Company, which had reaped the harvest from his discovery without sharing; G. C. Robbins, superintendent of the Owyhee Gold and Silver Mining Company at Silver City in the Owyhee District; and Hill Beachey. The first three partners favored the route from either Chico or Red Bluff; Beachey preferred to operate from Idaho southward to the Humboldt District, expecting to make connections with the Overland Line that ran to Hunter's Station on the Truckee River and there to meet the Pioneer Stage Company that ran on into Virginia City and to the railhead of the Central Pacific.

It is not clear why the promoters of the Idaho Stage Company chose Chico rather than Red Bluff for the western terminus. The latter town was the head of navigation on the Sacramento River and a more important shipping point; the road from there to Susanville was superior because of the lower grade and pass through the mountains, with less snow. Apparently citizens of Red Bluff hesitated to make the expenditures to keep their road improved. In contrast, John Bidwell and his wealthy ranching associates near Chico promised support with livestock, hay, harness, and coaches; and Bidwell, who had just been elected to the United States Congress, was in a position to work for a mail contract.[33]

The *Semi-Weekly Independent* of Red Bluff announced on March 6, 1865, that the first saddle train of the Idaho Stage Company would depart on March 20, 1865: "Ho! for Owyhee and Boise." The editor asked, "What will our Portland friends say now?"[34] Portland's *Oregonian* expressed great concern about this development, but in Boise the *Idaho Tri-Weekly Statesman* took the position that the goal was the opening of all practical routes—not the case of Red Bluff vs. Chico or the Columbia River route vs. the Sacramento River route to San Francisco.[35]

George F. Nourse, a forwarding and commission merchant at Chico Landing, traversed the route with a saddle train belonging to Messrs. Pierce, Francis & Co. in the spring of 1865. Once in Boise, he went immediately to see the editor of the *Idaho Tri-Weekly Statesman* and reported on the glories of the journey. Nourse placed a large "Notice to Shippers: New Road from Chico to Idaho!" in the Boise newspaper, launching a vigorous campaign for freight business. Wells Fargo & Co. was included in the plans: "Bills not paid at the Landing will be sent by Wells, Fargo & Co. for collection at the expense of the shipper." Apparently some packers did get through this first season from Chico, exploring as they came, reporting on the difficult sections of the route, and taking from twenty-six to twenty-nine days to make the journey.[36]

Captain John Mullan, who had held a mail contract in the northern part of the region, found himself back in the stage business in late May in Walla Walla, working with the Idaho Stage Company. He was soon a major partner in a reorganized Idaho and California Stage Company. The citizens of Boise signed a petition addressed to Lieutenant Colonel John M. Drake, in command at Fort Boise, urging him to provide an escort for Mullan's party, which planned to explore in hopes of locating still a better route. Caleb Lyon, governor of Idaho Territory, also urged the commander at Fort Boise to provide an escort.[37] Mullan left Boise on July 3, 1865, with a military escort that was to accompany him from Ruby City to Surprise Valley; from there his party was to be provided with an escort of California cavalry to complete the survey into Susanville. The army had also resolved to establish a military post in Surprise Valley.[38] J. B. Francis reported that tri-weekly stages were running on the road from Chico Landing to Susanville, a distance of ninety-five miles, and weekly stages from Susanville to Deep Hole Springs, about that much further. From there, saddle trains headed for Ruby City. Francis again left the impression that a mail contract had been obtained for the Chico route, because the Boise City newspaper entitled his report "New Mail Route" and concluded, "as soon as the route can be freed from hostile Indians, the mail will be regular and coaches will run all the way."[39]

The *Weekly Oregonian* published an extensive comment on the Chico route, suggesting that it had been a promotional scheme, that it was not a viable route, and that teamsters starting out on it left just seeking to find Idaho. "Nevertheless there has been a most unhappy termination of the matter," wrote the editor. "We now see freight coming to our wharves which has been a part of the

[33]Clarence F. McIntosh, "The Chico and Red Bluff Route: Stage Lines from Southern Idaho to the Sacramento Valley, 1865-1867," *Idaho Yesterdays* (Fall, 1962), 6/3:12-14; Goodwin, "Beachey," 17-20. Goodwin follows McIntosh's evidence closely. McIntosh relies heavily on California newspapers, including the *Semi-Weekly Independent* of Red Bluff, the *Chico Weekly Courant*, and the *Weekly Union Record* of Oroville, for this early information. He also uses some issues of the *Idaho World* and the *Owyhee Avalanche*.

[34]The article in the *Red Bluff Independent* was reprinted in the Idaho newspapers. See the *North-Idaho Radiator*, March 25, 1865, p. 4, c. 1, and the *Idaho Tri-Weekly Statesman*, April 4, 1865, p. 2, c. 1.

[35]*Idaho Tri-Weekly Statesman*, April 25, 1865, p. 2, c. 1.

[36]*Ibid.*, May 9, 1865, p. 2, c. 1, May 16, 1865, p. 2, c. 4, May 18, 1865, p. 2, c. 1, May 23, 1865, p. 2, c. 2.

[37]*Ibid.*, May 30, 1865, p. 2, c. 1, June 10, 1865, p. 2, c. 3, June 15, 1865, p. 2, c. 1.

[38]*Ibid.*, July 4, 1865, p. 2, c. 1; *Daily Mountaineer*, July 12, 1865, p. 3, c. 1.

[39]*Idaho Tri-Weekly Statesman*, July 18, 1865, p. 2, c. 1.

way to Idaho by the new route, unable to get through. It now becomes us to profit by the experience of the past."[40] In contrast, the *Daily Mountaineer* at The Dalles expressed alarm at the potential competition from the California route.

On more than one occasion, when we have urged interested parties to take measures to head off the Chico and Red Bluff routes, we have been met with the reply that the routes named existed only in the imagination, and that neither freight nor passengers would ever succeed in getting through that way. We were only too willing to believe that the routes we feared so much were myths but such has not proved to be the facts.[41]

In addition to concern with preserving communication and trade along the Columbia River, there was never-ending interest at The Dalles in sustaining the line to Canyon City. The Dalles & Canyon City Stage Company advertised that it was running Concord stages tri-weekly between The Dalles and Canyon City by way of Todd's Bridge, Cross Hollows, Bridge Creek, Alkali Flat, Camp Watson, Rock Creek, Cottonwood, and John Day's River and that the trip was being made in three days.[42] More important, plans were being made to extend the line to the Owyhee District.

By mid-June the road from The Dalles to Canyon City appeared safe, the Indians having moved farther south. However, pack trains were being attacked in the Burnt River area and animals driven off. Isolated parties of miners were fired upon and some were dangerously wounded. The Wells Fargo & Co. messenger reported that Indians in the neighborhood of Auburn were frightening the residents and the area was considered dangerous to travelers.[43] In reality, none of the routes from Idaho to the south, southwest, or west in either eastern Oregon or Nevada seemed safe from Indians harassment in June and July, 1865. Even so, the residents of The Dalles still longed for a land route via Canyon City to Boise to bring the treasure and trade of Idaho directly to that community rather than waiting on it to come down the Columbia River from upstream depots.

AMIDST ALL THE exploration for new routes of communication and transportation in the Pacific Northwest and the changes in the ownership and operations of older ones in the season of 1865, the management of Wells Fargo & Co. in San Francisco and Portland seized every opportunity to transport express, letters, and treasure at profit to the company and service to the region. *A Directory of the Principal Towns East of the Cascades* published in 1865 listed the Wells Fargo & Co. agents as follows:

IDAHO TERRITORY.

J. L. SMITH	Main Street, Idaho City.
W. A. ATLEE	Granite Street, Placerville.
W. W. CHAPMAN	Main Street, Pioneer City.
R. B. WALLACE	Washington Street, Centerville.

WASHINGTON TERRITORY.

J. B. CONDON	Main Street, Walla Walla.

OREGON.

A. W. BUCHANAN	Main Street, Dalles City.
T. L. BRADBURY	Front Street, Umatilla City.[44]

Wells Fargo & Co. was listed in each of the communities under "Express Companies" and "Gold Dust Dealers." Boise City was conspicuously absent from the list. In contrast, company personnel were extremely active in Idaho City. Messengers Edgar and Bledsoe brought in not only the express but newspaper exchanges, and company agent J. L. Smith was responsible for numerous courtesies noted by the editor of the *Idaho World.* In turn the newspaper reminded its readers, "Remember the South Boise Expresses envelopes are only fifty cents. For sale by Wells, Fargo & Co. at all of their offices in the Basin."[45]

In Boise City, plans were under way to establish a Wells Fargo agency by the end of

[40] *The Weekly Oregonian*, July 15, 1865, p. 3, c. 2.

[41] *Daily Mountaineer*, June 20, 1865, p. 2, c. 1.

[42] *Ibid.*, June 23, 1865, p. 1, c. 4.

[43] *Idaho World*, June 17, 1865, p. 2, c. 2, July 8, 1865, p. 2, c. 2; *Idaho Tri-Weekly Statesman*, June 24, 1865, p. 2, c. 1.

[44] *A General Directory and Business Guide to the Principal Towns East of the Cascade Mountains for the Year 1865*, compiled by George Owens (San Francisco: Towne and Bacon, 1865). Each of the agents listed in Idaho, Washington, and Oregon was located in the directories of the separate communities.

[45] *Idaho World*, April 1, 1865, p. 2, c. 1, April 8, 1865, p. 3, c. 1, April 15, 1865, p. 2, c. 1, April 22, 1865, p. 3, c. 1.

April. Thomas Cole, Jr., a representative of the company from San Francisco, and Charles Woodward of Walla Walla, who was the superintendent of the company in Idaho and Washington territories, were in town making preparations. The *Idaho Tri-Weekly Statesman* noted:

It is their purpose we understand to establish an office here immediately. Glad of it. Wells, Fargo & Co. are an indispensible institution on this coast. Be the mail facilities ever so good, business men send their letters by them; and as to shipping treasure, no one thinks of any other method where their route is in operation.[46]

"Wells, Fargo & Co. are on hand and Wm. Yates is their agent," the Boise City paper noted further on May 1, 1865.

They have opened their office next door below the Stage House, and are ready for business. Mr. Yates is an old expressman, thoroughly competent, and obliging in manners. Business men will be glad to learn that they have commenced business and Yates is their agent.[47]

Wells Fargo & Co. had followed the custom practiced elsewhere of planting a pole at their office where a flag was displayed on the arrival of the express. It was thrown to the breeze in Boise for the first time on June 26, 1865.[48] Wells Fargo employees on the stage line from Walla Walla always remembered the Boise editor. Thomas H. Cann brought in the latest Oregon newspapers, and he and Agent Yates tried to outdo each other in bestowing favors on the local newspaper.[49] At the same time, Wells Fargo moved into a new office in Idaho City, on the corner of Main and Commercial streets. Howard Bledsoe, the faithful Wells Fargo messenger, brought news that an enormous amount of goods, particularly provisions, was on the road from Walla Walla and Umatilla for the Boise Basin early in June.[50]

During the first week in July, Wells Fargo & Co. dispatched General Agent Charles Woodward to Rocky Bar in the South Boise District to establish an agency there with Messrs. Dilly & Dover as agents. The company had temporary difficulty because the stage company withdrew from that route, but it was expected to be running again soon.[51] The *Owyhee Avalanche* commented on August 19:

We learn that the stage line between South Boise and Boise City has been discontinued on account of the scarcity of travel on the route. Wells, Fargo & Co. recently established an office in South Boise, and this stage arrangement must necessarily affect that institution very seriously.[52]

The company opened a third new office in Idaho during 1865, in Silver City, on July 22. On August 7 a new safe was received at that office, having come through from Chico via the Humboldt River route. J. L. Browne, the company agent in Owyhee, operated in both Silver City and Ruby City.[53]

Wells Fargo had continuously expressed great interest in the route between The Dalles and Canyon City. In June of 1865, the company advertised that it had established an office in Canyon City and was running a Canyon City Express to and from The Dalles. James A. Henderson served as agent for the express company and for The Dalles and Canyon City Stage Company, and the two firms shared an office. Henderson was prepared to forward letters, packages, and treasure on the stages and be responsible for making collections, procuring drafts, and attending to commissions.[54]

In the same month, New York newspapers were suggesting that the United States government would be well advised to give up the postal service and turn it over to the express companies. The *Idaho World* agreed with the suggestion of the *New York Post* that the express companies should be given the privilege of carrying everything sent by mail for a bonus of one cent on each letter. By doing so, the government could get rid of twenty thousand postmasters and make money in the

[46] *Idaho Tri-Weekly Statesman*, April 29, 1865, p. 2, c. 1.

[47] *Ibid.*, May 1, 1865, p. 2, c. 1.

[48] *Ibid.*, June 26, 1865, p. 2, c. 1.

[49] *Ibid.*, June 1, 1865, p. 2, c. 1, June 3, 1865, p. 2, c. 1, June 6, 1865, p. 2, c. 1.

[50] *Idaho World*, June 10, 1865, p. 3, c. 2.

[51] *Idaho Tri-Weekly Statesman*, August 22, 1865, p. 3, c. 2.

[52] *Owyhee Avalanche*, August 19, 1865, p. 3, c. 3.

[53] *Ibid.*, August 19, 1865, p. 3, c. 3, August 26, 1865, p. 2, c. 4, and p. 3, c. 1.

[54] *Weekly Mountaineer*, June 16, 1865, p. 4, c. 3; *Daily Mountaineer*, June 23, 1865, p. 1, c. 4.

process. After indicting the western postmasters and postal agents for incompetence, the Idaho City editor commented:

> Nearly all business men now transact their business through the expresses for both safety and speed. There is no doubt that were the expresses substituted for the present postoffice system their requirements would be as fully met as they are now, and probably much more so; . . . We never could see why the government should carry the letters of an individual and leave his trunk.[55]

WHILE WELLS FARGO was interested in delivering letters and express packages throughout Idaho, it found its most profitable business in handling the "Treasure Drift" that continued down the Columbia River. At The Dalles, the *Weekly Mountaineer* noted that Thomas H. Cann brought down $74,000 in treasure from the Idaho mining camps on June 15, 1865. The next week he delivered three hundred pounds in treasure equal to $60,000 in value. As of July 15, Wells Fargo & Co. was continuing to bring down $72,700 a week. A week later, The Dalles paper noted:

> Despite the complaint of hard times, the flow of treasure through our town is immense. For the month of June the treasure shipped by Wells, Fargo & Co., footed up to within a fraction of $2,000,000. . . . The business of shipping dust is more systemized than in former years, and as a consequence, it attracts less attention although constantly increasing in amounts.[56]

By August, Wells Fargo & Co. was moving gold dust and treasure down the Columbia River on every steamer that arrived in Portland. "There was a heavy treasure by the steamer *Cascade*, from the upper Columbia country last evening; $100,000 was received from the Boise region through Wells, Fargo & Co.'s express," the *Oregonian* reported on August 12. And again, "Messenger West, of Wells, Fargo & Co.'s express last evening delivered $80,000 to the Portland office—one shipment from east of the mountains."[57]

Following the discoveries of gold along the Fraser River and in the Cariboo region, a third British Columbia mining district had developed along the Big Bend of the Columbia River and in the Kootenay District. Immediately the question arose as to whether the trade would be moving between this new mining district into Portland or Victoria. F. J. Barnard, an experienced stage proprietor, notified the colonial government of British Columbia that he proposed to operate an "interior" route rather than using the "boundary route" where he would have to compete with an opposition express from Portland. The latter would be a mistake, according to Barnard, because his service would be in competition with "parties on whom we depend for California and United States business—I mean Wells, Fargo & Co."[58]

An express service—Waldron's Kootenay Express—was also established between the Kootenay District and Walla Walla. The service was to make two trips a month, leaving Walla Walla on the 1st and 15th. In July, 1865, the Walla Walla *Statesman* announced its departure and added, "Mr. W. has established his office at Wells, Fargo & Co.'s where Mr. [J. B.] Condon will act as agent." As Condon also served as agent for Wells Fargo, that company's sponsorship of Waldron's service was obvious.[59]

Everywhere the newspaper editors continued to comment on the courtesies extended by Wells Fargo & Co. In the Owyhee District, company personnel provided exchanges for the newspapers and general news. The *Avalanche* editor reported that a safe brought through for Wells Fargo's office in Ruby City arrived one day sooner than a similar safe shipped the same day from San Francisco, via Portland and the Columbia River, had arrived at the Boise office.[60] At The Dalles, the *Mountaineer* inserted the standard statement in issue after issue, "Thanks to Wells, Fargo & Co. for very many express favors." The company employees also

[55] *Idaho World*, June 24, 1865, p. 2, c. 1.

[56] *Weekly Mountaineer*, June 16, 1865, p. 2, c. 4, July 21, 1865, p. 1, c. 6; *Daily Mountaineer*, June 23, 1865, p. 2, c. 1, July 16, 1865, p. 2, c. 1.

[57] *The Weekly Oregonian*, August 12, 1865, p. 3, c. 1, and p. 3, c. 2.

[58] F. J. Barnard to Hon. Arthur N. Birch, Colonial Secretary, February 21, 1865, F. J. Barnard Papers, Provincial Archives of British Columbia, Victoria.

[59] *Statesman*, July 7, 1865, p. 2, c. 6, and p. 3, c. 2.

[60] *Owyhee Avalanche*, September 2, 1865, p. 3, c. 1 and 2, September 30, 1865, p. 1, c. 2.

ARTER'S
GRAPH GALLERY.
WALLACE & EVANS
GROCERS & CONFECTIONERS
OASIS
SALOON.

The photograph at left, often reproduced, shows a Wells Fargo stage pulling up in front of C. W. Carter's photo gallery on Main Street in Salt Lake City. It was taken—probably by Carter—in 1866 or earlier. Photo courtesy Special Collections and Archives, Utah State University.

performed many public services, some of which were unusual. Thomas H. Cann, the express messenger, brought down a prisoner charged with burglary to The Dalles. "We have heard of a good many strange things passing through the express," observed the local editor, "but this is the first time we have known a prisoner to be forwarded 'C.O.D.' "[61] In Boise, the *Idaho Tri-Weekly Statesman* commented toward the end of September, "Wells, Fargo & Co.'s agents in this city and on the road, one and all, will accept thanks of this office for favors this week." In Portland, the *Oregonian* depended on Wells Fargo to deliver the newspapers that provided information for a weekly column entitled "From Idaho."[62]

Important changes in the express and staging business outside the Pacific Northwest were also reported in the regional newspapers. In September, 1865, it was noted that Wells Fargo & Co. had established an agency in Salt Lake with H. S. Rumfield, also Ben Holladay's representative, as agent.[63] The Pioneer Stage Co., operating across the Sierra to the south of Lake Tahoe, purchased the right, franchises, and appurtenances of the California Stage Co. on the Dutch Flat route running across the Sierra to the north of Lake Tahoe. The company would thus control the two principal routes across the Sierra Nevada.[64] This change of ownership was to be of tremendous importance to Wells Fargo & Co., which owned the Pioneer Stage Line, when Hill Beachey succeeded in reopening his stage line from the Idaho mining camps to Nevada and California the next year.

THROUGHOUT THE SUMMER, Holladay's Overland Stage Line continued to make trips from Boise to Salt Lake City in four days, apparently so effectively that there was little comment in the Idaho newspapers.[65] Wells Fargo & Co.'s interest in the Overland Mail route across the transMissouri West, particularly the section west of Salt Lake into California, increased with each passing year. Louis McLane, the long-time superintendent of Wells Fargo's express, made a speedy transit of the route from San Francisco to Salt Lake City to prove the fine condition of the road: 850 miles in 3 days, 12 hours, and 10 minutes.[66]

Efforts to improve the service and reduce the fares on the overland route were not fully appreciated in the Pacific Northwest—particularly in Portland, which felt neglected by the United States mail. The Oregon newspapers began to push for a through mail from Salt Lake City all the way to the lower Columbia River towns and into Portland, insisting that it would be more convenient than the "overland route" from the Sacramento Valley. For example, in Portland, the *Oregonian* noted the improvement in the east-west Overland Mail route between Salt Lake and Denver but, with a tone of bitterness over the temporary cancellation of the mail contract on "California-Oregon Overland Mail" in September, 1865, commented:

> This arrangement will be an excellent one for our California neighbors, but as we of Oregon are to have no mail connections whatsoever with the rest of the country hereafter, it makes very little difference to us whether the mails are continued elsewhere or not.[67]

The communities in eastern Oregon and Washington were temporarily inconvenienced by the suspension, but soon the *Mountaineer* at The Dalles announced a better arrangement for the mails:

> Our postmaster informs us that since the stoppage of the California Overland Mail, all letters deposited in the office for the Eastern States have been forwarded by way of Boise and Salt Lake City. So far as eastern correspondence is

[61] *Daily Mountaineer*, September 7, 1865, p. 2, c. 1.

[62] *Idaho Tri-Weekly Statesman*, September 30, 1865, p. 2, c. 1; *Weekly Oregonian*, September 9, 1865, p. 3, c. 2, September 16, 1865, p. 3, c. 2.

[63] *Statesman*, September 26, 1865, p. 2, c. 2.

[64] *Idaho World*, September 16, 1865, p. 2, c. 1; *Owyhee Avalanche*, September 23, 1865, p. 1, c. 2.

[65] *Idaho Tri-Weekly Statesman*, July 20, 1865, p. 2, c. 1.

[66] *Ibid.*, October 17, 1865, p. 2, c. 3; *Daily Mountaineer*, October 29, 1865, p. 2, c. 1.

[67] *Weekly Oregonian*, September 16, 1865, p. 2, c. 2, October 21, 1865, p. 1, c. 3.

John Hailey

concerned, our people are the gainers rather than otherwise by the breakdown of the California mail.[68]

October brought the resumption of the overland mails from California to Portland and the impact was felt both east and west of the Cascades. "The daily mail service between Portland and Lincoln, California [the new southern terminus], has been resumed by the California Stage Company," the *Daily Mountaineer* reported on October 12. Later in the month, the *Idaho World* revealed that the overland mail service between California and Portland was to be carried for $224,000 a year. "The company wanted $300,000," reported the Idaho City paper, "but the government couldn't see it."[69]

United States mail service in the Pacific Northwest was typical of that in frontier areas: it was considered inadequate and a matter for continuing complaint. Because of the region's rapid development, Congress provided for the appointment of an additional agent for the Pacific Coast, and Quincy A. Brooks of Portland was named Postal Agent for the State of Oregon and the territories of Idaho and Washington. Within a month after Brooks assumed his responsibilities in September, 1865, J. E. Vinton was named a special agent for Idaho and Montana territories and was dispatched up the Columbia River to supervise the mail service.[70]

The Overland Mail came into Boise during the winter "half frozen" much of the time, but it was of tremendous interest to the readers of the *Idaho Tri-Weekly Statesman.* "In the Overland Mail from the East last night came four letters and a half a dozen or so papers," noted the editor.

> Two of the little packages which more resembled chunks of ice than exchanges, fell to our lot. One of them had so much ice and dirt frozen to it that it was unrecognizable at first, but unheeding the taunts of the "devil" and two or three compositors, we thawed out the stuff, dried and carefully put it together and found we had a copy of the Daily Reese River REVEILLE, one of our most valued exchanges, from which we re-publish a synopsis of the President's Message this morning.[71]

Throughout the winter, both the Oregon and the Idaho newspapers devoted a large percentage of their columns to a crusade for better transportation and communication and improved mail facilities. In Boise, the editor of the *Idaho Tri-Weekly Statesman* wrote an editorial on "Thoroughfares," stating in part:

> . . . Half a dozen stages arrive and depart from this town daily, in different directions, and the traveling community are but partially accommodated. A fast freight line is running to the Columbia river. Hundreds upon hundreds of teams are constantly employed in hauling goods and machinery from the Columbia river to our Territory alone, and still the wants of the public are poorly provided for. Passengers pay from thirty to forty cents per mile for stage fare, and freight brings them ten to fifteen cents per pound from the Columbia river here, a distance of two hundred and forty miles. Staging and teaming is all very good but they must soon give way to more certain and expeditious modes of travel. . . .[72]

The specific proposal was the construction of a railroad from Salt Lake City through Idaho to

[68] *Daily Mountaineer*, September 4, 1865, p. 2, c. 1.

[69] *Ibid.*, October 12, 1865, p. 2, c. 1; *Idaho World*, October 28, 1865, p. 2, c. 2.

[70] *Weekly Mountaineer*, August 4, 1865, p. 1, c. 2; *Idaho World*, September 23, 1865, p. 2, c. 1.

[71] *Idaho Tri-Weekly Statesman*, December 16, 1865, p. 2, c. 1.

[72] *Ibid.*, November 16, 1865, p. 2, c. 1 and 2.

the Columbia River and Portland. The Boise editor chided the Oregonians for lagging behind California in promotional activities, suggesting the Blue Mountains were nothing in comparison with the Sierra Nevada as an obstacle to construction. He thus anticipated the construction of the Oregon Short Line by several years.

The *Owyhee Avalanche* was most concerned over the contract to carry the mails to and from that district with "celerity, certainty, and security." The editor was upset because some "rogue or fool" had submitted a bid to carry the mail from Humboldt City, Nevada, to Boise City via Owyhee once a week for $14,000. Proper stations could not be built on the road for that. Any contractor attempting to deliver at that price would lose from $50,000 to $100,000. No trip had yet been made. The editor concluded bitterly:

> The government supplies all the people with no more important service than the mail. It affects every man and woman, or should, therefore delinquent contractors and others aiding them should receive the bitterest execration of every citizen. They should expect nothing else.[73]

Hill Beachey had attempted to obtain the mail contract between Humboldt City, Nevada, and Boise City, and the Owyhee editor became a champion of Beachey's cause:

> We hope and believe he will succeed. Beachy [sic] is a man of more performance than words. There is not a more energetic man in the country than him, and if any man can, the mails will be carried promptly by him. This line will bring us within six or seven days of San Francisco, and two or three days from the telegraph at Star City, instead of fifteen to twenty from the former and six to eight from the latter, as we are now.[74]

Apparently Beachey had submitted two bids to the Post Office, one to carry the mails until June 30, 1866, the expiration date of the unfulfilled contract, and a second for the next four-year period. Senators and Congressmen in Nevada and Idaho's territorial delegate, E. D. Holbrook, were urged to support his cause, which was widely known.[75]

Hill Beachey

The *Owyhee Avalanche* was also deeply concerned about the failure of the Post Office Department to carry out the law in providing an adequate post office and service for Ruby City. Joseph Leach had carried the mail to Boise City tri-weekly without a contract for many months. When the contract had been let to another party in the fall of 1865, no attempt had been made to carry it out and Leach had just continued without compensation. William Clemmens, the postmaster, soon sent a letter to the *Owyhee Avalanche* explaining the situation. Pierce & Francis of Chico-route fame had arrived in Ruby City somewhat earlier, claiming that they had mail contracts from Boise City to Humboldt by way of Ruby City. Francis claimed to have received a subcontract to carry the mail from Boise City to Ruby City, a distance of 65 miles. Apparently the postmaster had signed certificates so Pierce & Francis could be paid by the government. The local editor, in despair, now doubted that Joseph Leach could be paid: he had been completely swindled by the Chico promoters.[76]

[73] *Owyhee Avalanche*, November 4, 1865, p. 1, c. 2.

[74] *Ibid.*, November 18, 1865, p. 2, c. 4.

[75] *Daily Mountaineer*, November 25, 1865, p. 2, c. 1.

[76] *Owyhee Avalanche*, November 18, 1865, p. 3, c. 1, November 25, 1865, p. 2, c. 1.

The residents of the Owyhee District remained disgusted with the inadequate mail deliveries in winter. The residents in the county were depositing mail matter in Ruby City at the rate of 2,000 letters a week, and often a full week passed between deliveries. The editor of the *Avalanche* urged Nevada and Idaho representatives in Washington, D.C., to press for a mail service from the termini of the Pacific Railroad and the Idaho towns.[77] The Post Office Department replied that the authorization had been given to make a contract for mail delivery in July, 1864, whereby Ruby City would receive mail but not for a price exceeding the income of the local post office and limited to $750 per annum. Ruby City was never named a point on the mail route between Humboldt City and Boise City. Brown & Coggswell of Susanville, California, had indeed contracted to deliver on the route for $14,000. Admittedly they had not done so and would receive no payments until they did. The *Owyhee Avalanche* editor stated,

> The above is plain and to the point. It settles a question or two and gives us a couple of bits of new information on the subject. Ruby City has always been and is yet out in the cold — not on any mail route, and to this day is only a special office, and parties who carry the mails to and from it are distinctly informed that the net proceeds of the office is all they can hope to receive. Talk is talk, but it takes more than $14,000 to carry a weekly mail over 300 miles of desert and mountains such as lie between Boise City and Humboldt City.[78]

VARIOUS AND CONFLICTING reports continued to circulate concerning the Chico route. The editor of the *Weekly Mountaineer*, still hostile, reported that both the Chico and the Red Bluff route had been abandoned for the season. "Our California neighbors commenced the season with any amount of blowing, and now before it is half over they abandoned the field in disgust. *Sic transit gloria mundi*," he wrote.[79] Some freighters had used the route to deliver flour and other supplies but found they could not compete because of the high costs of delivery.[80] The *Owyhee Avalanche*, ever optimistic, thought the Chico route was practical and attacked the *Mountaineer's* misrepresentation of the route's status. The *Idaho Tri-Weekly Statesman* also maintained confidence in the route; it reported that Captain Mullan would go through to Chico in six days but had hopes of reducing the time to four. "When they get fairly under way we shall be gratified to hear the latest opinion of the Oregon papers on the horned toad route."[81]

Apparently there was enough freighting business on the Chico road to threaten those favoring the Columbia River route. B. M. DuRell & Co., the most influential banking firm in both Boise and Idaho City and business ally of Ben Holladay, announced that it was establishing a "fast freight" service between Boise and Umatilla.[82] At The Dalles, the *Mountaineer* reported:

> We noticed at the wharfboat, yesterday evening, a number of express wagons, designed to be placed upon the road between Umatilla and the Boise mines. They are got up in the style of the ordinary express wagon, with the exception of being about double the size, and built proportionately strong. The proprietors calculate they can make the trip through with express freight in three days.

The Oregon newspaper revealed a plan to carry freight through at a fast rate and to carry passengers on the return. Oregonians were in agreement that the Umatilla route would be superior to the Chico route.[83]

During the fall of 1865, the route to Chico was in the news more than ever before because Idaho residents hoped that Captain Mullan, with the aid of military detachments, would at last be able to place stagecoaches on the through route three times a week. Elaborate, detailed advertisements of the stage service were published throughout Idaho, including distances and fares to various places on the route. The advertisements suggest that Wells

[77] *Ibid.*, December 23, 1865, p. 2, c. 2.

[78] *Ibid.*, December 30, 1865, p. 2, c. 2.

[79] *Weekly Mountaineer*, August 4, 1865, p. 1, c. 1.

[80] *Ibid.*, August 25, 1865, p. 3, c. 1; *Daily Mountaineer*, August 13, 1865, p. 2, c. 1.

[81] *Owyhee Avalanche*, August 19, 1865, p. 3, c. 3 and 5, p. 4, c. 1 and 2; *Idaho Tri-Weekly Statesman*, September 5, 1865, p. 2, c. 1.

[82] *Ibid.*, August 24, 1865, p. 4, c. 1, quoting the *Umatilla Advertiser*.

[83] *Daily Mountaineer*, August 24, 1865, p. 3, c. 1; *Weekly Oregonian*, August 26, 1865, p. 3, c. 1 and 2. The latter article was reprinted in the *Idaho World*, September 2, 1865, p. 4, c. 1.

Fargo & Co. was actively interested in this new route. Stage tickets could be purchased at the Wells Fargo office in Boise City from William A. Yates, agent, and in Ruby City from J. L. Browne, agent. The Idaho and California Stage Company advertised that it carried not only mails but the express of Wells Fargo & Co., and it was also reported that Wells Fargo was dispatching messengers on the route.[84]

DuRell & Co. were prepared to meet the challenge of the Chico road, real or imagined. The firm placed advertisements during September offering to buy 100 tons of hay and 50,000 pounds of oats to be delivered to stations along the route of the Boise, Idaho and Umatilla Fast Freight and Express Line. "The second wagon of the fast freight line arrived last night in scheduled time, loaded with merchandise for various parties in this and Idaho cities," the *Idaho Tri-Weekly Statesman* noted on September 16. The fast freights were bringing in merchandise from Portland in ten days, in contrast to the thirty or forty days required by ox teams, and this "fast freight" service had advantages over the stage lines that had to give preference to passengers and the mails and seldom had room for anything more than light, small parcels. The line did not terminate at Boise City but went on to Idaho City, and arrangements were being made to extend the service into Alturas and Owyhee counties. For packages under 100 pounds the charges were 15 and 20 cents. Passengers were also carried at reduced rates.[85] DuRell & Co. had reduced the time between Umatilla and Boise to five days and brought in as many as fifteen passengers on a single trip. Rumor had it that there was to be another fast freight service from Boise and Idaho City to Umatilla, and the newspapers were sure there was enough business for all.[86]

Word came through in October that the Indians had driven off a large quantity of stock and burned several stations on the Chico route so Captain Mullan would be unable to run his line of stages during the winter.[87] Oregon papers were quick to respond to the news. The *Oregonian* reported the demise of the Chico route. "DuRell & Co.'s Fast Freight Line, between Umatilla and Idaho, has 'played hob' with Chico." The *Umatilla Advertiser* noted that advocates of the Chico route had dropped off one by one until the field was left to the *Owyhee Avalanche*.[88] Within a week, the Silver City newspaper also gave up hope that the Chico route might be opened to stages. After publishing a long editorial entitled "Chico, Idaho, Stages, Mails, and Mullan," the editor concluded, "We confess to being beautifully bilked." Still there was an expression of hope. "The freight business over the route will be a big item next summer, but it amounted to comparatively nothing the past season."[89]

Apparently the Chico route was never in shape for stage traffic in 1865. The company left the impression it had a mail contract, but in reality it was carrying mails on horseback with a two-man escort as a courtesy to a limited number of individuals. When one expressman was killed, the whole line was abandoned for the season. The collapse was blamed on the Indians. However, the *Owyhee Avalanche* suggested a different reason why the stages that had left Ruby City in care of Mullan never arrived at their destination: they and the stock had been attached by the sheriff in Susanville, California.[90]

Stagecoaches on the established routes between the Boise Basin and the Columbia River towns were held up on occasion. During the third week in September six highwaymen attempted to stop the stagecoach headed for Umatilla just as it emerged from the canyon into Pleasant Valley. According to Howard Bledsoe, Wells Fargo & Co. messenger, the driver tried to ride on but the highwaymen opened fire, killing one of the lead horses. The driver and thirteen passengers abandoned the stage and headed for the next station, which

[84] *Owyhee Avalanche*, September 2, 1865, p. 2, c. 2, September 9, 1865, p. 2, c. 4; *Idaho World*, September 9, 1865, p. 2, c. 1, 3, and 5.

[85] *Idaho Tri-Weekly Statesman*, September 16, 1865, p. 2, c. 1, 3, and 4.

[86] *Ibid.*, September 19, 1865, p. 2, c. 3, and p. 3, c. 3, September 21, 1865, p. 2, c. 1, September 26, 1865, p. 2, c. 3, September 28, 1865, p. 2, c. 1.

[87] *Ibid.*, October 12, 1865, p. 2, c. 2.

[88] *Weekly Oregonian*, October 21, 1865, p. 1, c. 2.

[89] *Owyhee Avalanche*, October 28, 1865, p. 3, c. 3.

[90] McIntosh, "The Chico and Red Bluff Route," 15.

was in sight. The stage, three ladies, and one male passenger left behind were robbed of $12,000. At the station, the stagecoach from Walla Walla to Boise City pulled up and the driver helped the robbed stage into the station and on its way. The news spread far and wide. One disgruntled passenger who had remained in the coach and suffered heavy losses insisted that if the passengers, half of whom were armed with revolvers, had just remained in the stage with the treasure, the robbery would not have succeeded. It was his opinion that "two more cowardly sets, passengers and robbers, could not be found."[91]

AS THE WINTER season approached, the most important concern in Idaho Territory was freighting in enough supplies to get through the winter months—an effort that produced new rivalries. At The Dalles, the *Mountaineer* seized the opportunity to publish a long account on "Fast Freight and Stage Line" from the Columbia River to the Boise mines, explaining the financial realities of the services and urging once again the establishment of a line from The Dalles to Boise City by way of Canyon City with a branch to the Owyhee District.[92] As earlier noted, DuRell & Co. had scarcely started its fast-freight service when rumors circulated that another fast-freight line would be established between Idaho City, Boise City, and Umatilla. In October, the competing Pioneer Stage Co. announced that it would carry fast freight at the same rates during the winter rather than following the custom of raising them at that time of year: 15 cents a pound from Umatilla to Boise and 20 cents a pound to Idaho City and Owyhee on packages over one hundred pounds. For those weighing less than one hundred pounds an additional five cents was charged. Joseph Pinkham, the firm's agent, was sure the time from Umatilla to Boise City would be three days, three and one-half to Idaho City, and four to Owyhee—about half the time for delivery promised by DuRell's fast-freight wagons.[93] DuRell did not immediately attempt to meet the competition; his rates in Boise and Idaho City were five cents more per pound beginning November 1, and ten cents more into Ruby City and South Boise.[94] Instead of lowering rates, DuRell & Co. emphasized the superiority and comfort of its thorough-brace wagons. Passengers stopped at night and had a more comfortable journey by taking five days to make the trip. Families were being transported at reduced rates.[95] But before the month of November was over, DuRell reduced his rates on packages of 100 pounds to those of the Pioneer Stage Company and launched a vigorous advertising campaign. The *Idaho World* asserted that service had "become one of the great institutions of Idaho."[96]

The *Oregonian* again suggested that DuRell's Fast Freight Line had done more than anything else to kill the Chico route.

> It is the intention of the company to carry freight and passengers during the winter months, and they now have sleighs prepared for that purpose, and will be enabled to make better time in winter on the snow. The line has succeeded beyond the expectations of its projectors, and will be changed in the spring from a tri-weekly to daily service.[97]

DuRell's line received more publicity than did any other transportation service in the territory during December, 1865. The company employed twenty-one teams, some of six and some of four horses. The average distance traveled was fifty miles a day, but stations along the route where a fresh relay of horses was available were from fifteen to eighteen miles apart. Travelers took six days out of Umatilla to reach Boise, and seven to Idaho City and Owyhee. Plans for the spring of 1866 included the operation of a joint service with the Oregon Steam Navigation Company, which was constructing the steamer *Shoshone* for the Snake River trade. From the upper landing on the Snake River, DuRell planned to run

[91] *Owyhee Avalanche*, September 30, 1865, p. 1, c. 5 (Bledsoe's report to Yates); *Weekly Oregonian*, September 30, 1865, p. 3, c. 1; *Statesman*, September 29, 1865, p. 2, c. 1; *Idaho Tri-Weekly Statesman*, September 23, 1865, p. 2, c. 2 and 4; *Daily Mountaineer*, September 26, 1865, p. 2, c. 3, quoting the *Umatilla Advertiser*.

[92] *Weekly Mountaineer*, October 15, 1865, p. 2, c. 2.

[93] *Ibid.*, October 19, 1865, p. 2, c. 3.

[94] *Idaho Tri-Weekly Statesman*, October 28, 1865, p. 4, c. 2.

[95] *Ibid.*, October 10, 1865, p. 4, c. 2.

[96] *Idaho World*, October 28, 1865, p. 3, c. 4 and 5, November 11, 1865, p. 3, c. 1.

[97] *Weekly Oregonian*, November 25, 1865, p. 3, c. 2.

coaches and wagons both ways—one route to Boise and the other to Owyhee. The *Oregonian* claimed the trip from San Francisco to Boise or Owyhee could be made in eight days, for the section from Portland would only take four days. The editor concluded,

> Oregon is not a whit behind California in making an energetic effort to establish a steady, certain, and profitable trade with the mining districts which lie just beyond our borders. Aided by the Columbia and Snake rivers, we have great odds in our favor, and by pressing our advantages, we must surely succeed.[98]

To the end of the year the role of Captain Mullan and the Chico route continued to be a controversial subject among the various newspaper editors. The *Chico Courant* admitted that Captain Mullan proved a "bilk" and that Idaho residents had been cheated out of their line, but it urged patience. "Let the *Avalanche* and the people of Owyhee and Idaho hold their temper. Next spring will give them a stage line, and mail from Chico direct and continuous," wrote the California editor. "But the agitation has done some good, caused a howling in Oregon, and the reduction in the price of freight and travel to the Columbia River."[99]

Among the local stage lines, Messrs. Greathouse & Kelly were recognized as running a most effective service between Placerville and Idaho City carrying passengers, packages, and sundry newspapers. The *Idaho World* paid tribute to the firm.

> Messrs. Greathouse & Kelly have reduced the science of staging to the most unexpected perfection, when we consider the obstacles they have overcome. In this they have been assisted materially by the never changing good humor and politeness of the drivers.[100]

[98]*Ibid.*, December 16, 1865, p. 2, c. 3. This article was reprinted in the *Idaho Tri-Weekly Statesman*, December 16, 1865, p. 2, c. 3 and 4, and the *Owyhee Avalanche*, December 23, 1865, p. 2, c. 1.

[99]*Chico Courant* quoted in the *Owyhee Avalanche*, December 23, 1865, p. 4, c. 1.

[100]*Idaho World*, September 30, 1865, p. 2, c. 1.

[101]*Idaho Tri-Weekly Statesman*, December 16, 1865, p. 2, c. 1.

[102]*Owyhee Avalanche*, October 28, 1865, p. 2, c. 2.

[103]*Ibid.*, December 30, 1865, p. 2, c. 4. John Hailey states that Barns & Yates operated between Boise City and Silver City in 1865 and that Hill Beachey bought out their route. Evidence in the newspapers of Idaho indicates that Hailey's memory of the situation was not correct; Joseph Leach & Co. ran the stages between those two points and, in turn, sold to Hill Beachey. See Hailey, *History of Idaho*, 123.

To Chico!

BY STAGES.

The Idaho & California Stage Co.'s Stages

Will hereafter leave Ruby City for Chico, California, every

TUESDAY, THURSDAY AND SATURDAY MORNINGS,

CONVEYING NEVADA AND CALIFORNIA MAILS.

Also, Wells, Fargo & Co.'s Express.

THE entire route is now **stocked and fully protected** from any and all **dangers, and the Stages** will leave hereafter as above named, for **California.**

FARE, 60 Dollars.

IDAHO STAGE CO.
Per J. L. BROWNE, Agent.
Ruby City, Sept. 2, 1865. 4-tf.

Owyhee Avalanche, Sept. 16, 1865

Greathouse & Co. also ran stages between Idaho City and Boise and made a major effort to keep that route open throughout the winter. The Boise newspaper reported in mid-December:

> The Idaho stage has been running on sleighs from Idaho City to within seven miles of this place, for the last week or more, and this morning they will start from here on runners. Good time for a pleasant ride to the Basin.[101]

In spite of the cold and snow, the firm had decided to keep daily stages running.

Jos. Leach & Co. continued to run stages between Boise and Silver City. The *Avalanche* observed:

> This place has a tri-weekly mail and express, and for the tri-weekly part of it our citizens are indebted to Jos. Leach & Co., proprietors of the stage line between here and Boise City. The weekly average of letters sent from this camp is eight hundred. Six hundred leave the Post Office and two hundred go by W. F. & Co.'s Express.[102]

At the very end of 1865 word came that Hill Beachey had purchased Leach's stage line from Boise to Owyhee, probably in anticipation of obtaining a mail contract.[103]

At Walla Walla, the new excitement in September of 1865 was the mining activity in the Blackfoot District of Montana Territory. Waldron's Express, closely associated with Wells Fargo & Co., expanded its connection with the Kootenay region of British Columbia to deliver to Frenchtown, Hellgate (Missoula), and on to Blackfoot City. D. V. Waldron, whose office was with Wells Fargo in Walla Walla, promised to connect with all the Montana mining camps and stated that all letters and packages addressed through Wells Fargo & Co. would be promptly attended to. A competing Blackfoot Express, Dwight & Bacon, Proprietors, was running from Walla Walla via Lewiston to Virginia City, Helena, Ophir, and Blackfoot City.[104] The potential of the new district was noted throughout the Northwest. Seattle's *Puget Sound Gazette* announced that the new express lines had been established between Walla Walla and the Blackfoot mines and suggested:

> The country is now said to be richer than Boise was, and miners from all sections of the upper country are turning in that direction. The indications are that the Blackfoot country is the point to which the next grand rush will be made.[105]

The fall of 1865 also witnessed changes in the banking fraternity in Idaho. B. M. DuRell & Co.'s dominance was challenged by the Bank of British North America. The *Idaho World* noted on September 9,

> Mr. W. L. Sutherland, agent of the Bank of British North America, has been in town this week for the purpose of a personal examination of the prospects of the place and of the adjacent mining districts. If found favorable, a branch of the bank may be established here in the Spring. A house of that character would be of the greatest convenience to businessmen here, and an advantage to the whole country.[106]

The Bank of British North America did not wait until spring but decided to operate immediately—not in Idaho City but in Boise. DuRell & Co. made arrangements with its potential rival to draw bills of exchange on the principal cities in the eastern United States and Europe as well as Portland and San Francisco. The *Idaho Tri-Weekly Statesman* carried an elaborate joint advertisement and commented:

> This will at once afford the community an exchange that business men can well appreciate. The rate, one per cent to Portland or San Francisco, is so low that it would seem that no other exchange will be used as soon as it is thoroughly understood.[107]

THROUGHOUT THE FALL and winter months of 1865 it was business as usual for Wells Fargo & Co. and its employees. Newspaper editors continued to be favored by both agents and messengers. In Boise City, the *Idaho Tri-Weekly Statesman* regularly expressed appreciation to William A. Yates for exchanges from both Oregon and California. "We 'weather the rim' of our sombrero to Mr. Wm. A. Yates, for files of late papers. You are always up to time, Yates," the editor noted on one occasion.[108] Apparently, the Wells Fargo agent in Silver City was as well thought of there as Yates was in Boise. "J. L. Browne, Esq. of W. F. & Co., has been thrusting papers at us for some weeks—and we gobbled them up," wrote the editor of the *Owyhee Avalanche*. "J. L., you suits us and are a public blessing." In Walla Walla, the *Statesman* dwelt on the same theme.[109]

Wells Fargo & Co. continued its business of gathering the treasure from the Idaho mining camps and sending it down the Columbia River. The *Oregonian* reported in late October:

> Heavy Treasure—Messenger West, of Wells, Fargo & Co.'s Express line, arrived by the Cascades steamer on Tuesday evening, bringing eight sacks of gold dust and six sacks of crude bullion and bars, the whole amounting to nearly $175,000. He reported plenty left in the upper country, and even a larger shipment may be looked for yet this week. Last evening Mr. Holland brought more than an ordinary amount.[110]

The Boise newspaper reported that Wells Fargo & Co. was sending two armed messengers with each stage that carried a treasure shipment to Umatilla and was ready

[104] *Statesman*, September 29, 1865, p. 2, c. 5, p. 3, c. 2. The company also advertised in the *Daily Mountaineer*, October 19, 1865, p. 1, c. 2.

[105] *Puget Sound Gazette* (Seattle), October 7, 1865, p. 2, c. 2.

[106] *Idaho World*, September 9, 1865, p. 1, c. 2.

[107] *Idaho Tri-Weekly Statesman*, September 14, 1865, p. 2, c. 3, p. 3, c. 2.

[108] *Ibid.*, October 21, 1865, p. 2, c. 2.

[109] *Owyhee Avalanche*, October 28, 1865, p. 2, c. 1; *Statesman*, November 24, 1865, p. 2, c. 3.

[110] *Weekly Oregonian*, October 28, 1865, p. 3, c. 2.

for any highwaymen intent on another robbery on the route.

PREPARED FOR THEM – Wells, Fargo & Co. are running their treasure express to Umatilla with a full knowledge of the danger they incur from robbery and with abundant preparation to meet it when necessary. By every stage that carries any considerable amount of treasure, they send two or more messengers armed in the best manner that experience can suggest. It is also understood that if attacked the boys must fight. They must not come back robbed with any such excuse as being outnumbered or taken by surprise, but that is hardly necessary, for the character of the boys is such as leaves no room for doubt on that point. They will fight any body or any number of road agents that can give them a show, and come out best too. They don't have any idea of being robbed alive to say the least, and we have little fear that they will be attacked at all, though it seems pretty near time for another demonstration of the kind.[111]

Ironically, Wells Fargo & Co. never hesitated to advertise the size of its treasure shipments through public displays. The *Statesman* editor in Walla Walla commented,

at Wells, Fargo & Co.'s office, on Sunday last, our attention was directed to an immense mass of bullion the aggregate weight of which was three thousand pounds. The whole glittering pile was brought down by Saturday's stage, and was the largest amount ever received in one day,... Passengers who came down by the stage state that such was the weight of treasure that they were unable to make the usual time.[112]

In Owyhee, the citizens tried to keep their spirits high during the dull times of winter by raising $900 to purchase a large silver brick to present to Governor Lyon of Idaho. The local paper noted, "Parties desirous of a peep at the brick can be accommodated at Wells, Fargo & Co.'s office."[113]

In November, 1865, Wells Fargo & Co. extended its express service from Boise City to Rocky Bar, where the firm had previously experienced difficulty in maintaining connection with its office. The *Idaho Tri-Weekly Statesman* reported the details:

WELLS, FARGO & CO., have extended their express from this place to Rocky Bar, the messenger, Charley Barnes, leaving Boise City every Friday morning and returning Wednesday following. We are glad to learn the Company have awarded Mr. Barnes the contract for carrying the express between the two points, as the route this winter will undoubtedly require a man with indomitable energy and pluck. Those of our citizens who remember the regularity with which he made his trips to Owyhee last winter and the difficulties he had to contend with, will join us in saying that Charley is the man for the place.[114]

Before the month was out, the paper reported, "Charley Barnes, the fast expressman, employed by Wells, Fargo & Co., arrived at 2 o'clock P.M. yesterday, in two days from Rocky Bar."[115] This new service by Wells Fargo's express was reported elsewhere in the Pacific Northwest as well.[116]

During 1865, Wells Fargo & Co. had continued to deliver express and transport treasure on the stage lines between the mining communities of the Boise Basin and to the towns along the Columbia River in care of messengers who now were armed for purposes of security. The treasure drift down the Columbia River into Portland continued ever larger. The company's express business to the outlying settlements in the Boise Basin, carried by local stage organizations, had led to the establishment of additional express offices. Wells Fargo had assumed responsibility for the route from The Dalles to Canyon City when the stage company, carrying its express, had collapsed financially. The company had expressed interest in projected routes from Owyhee to California and anticipated sending its express and messengers on any route that appeared practical. It had also sponsored Waldron's pony express service out of Walla Walla to the Kootenay District of British Columbia and through Montana Territory to the Blackfoot Mining District. The route between the Boise Basin communities to a new office in Rocky Bar in the South Boise District was also sustained. Wells Fargo's network of service grew wider as it continued to respond to both need and opportunity.

[111] *Idaho Tri-Weekly Statesman*, October 31, 1865, p. 2, c. 1.

[112] *Statesman*, quoted in the *Puget Sound Gazette*, November 24, 1865, p. 3, c. 1.

[113] *Owyhee Avalanche*, December 9, 1865, p. 2, c. 1.

[114] *Idaho Tri-Weekly Statesman*, November 16, 1865, p. 2, c. 2.

[115] *Ibid.*, November 30, 1865, p. 2, c. 2.

[116] *Daily Mountaineer*, November 26, 1865, p. 2, c. 3.

While the railroads brought enormous change to the West, the town created when the lines from east and west were joined in 1868 was no metropolis. This photograph shows Promontory City, Utah, in 1869. Courtesy of Special Collections and Archives, Utah State University.

TO THE "GRAND CONSOLIDATION" OF 1866

AS MIGHT BE expected, maintaining communication and transportation facilities in spite of adverse weather conditions was a major concern of the citizens of Idaho Territory in the mid-winter months of 1865-66. Ben Holladay's Overland Stage Company brought the mail into Boise from Salt Lake City in uncertain fashion. Once the mail arrived, the Boise postmaster was very deliberate (if not slow) in having it forwarded on to Idaho City or the Owhyee country, prompting complaints from the local newspaper editors.[1] Winter conditions had forced the abandonment of the Thomas road over the Blue Mountains and all travel was going by way of the Meacham road into Umatilla, thus wiping out most communication with Portland. Not only was the Columbia River frozen solid and the routes into Idaho blocked by snow and cold, but communication among the Idaho communities in the Boise Basin was also disrupted. Snow slides on the route between Boise and Idaho City were so large that the stages could not go around or over them and crews of men had to be dispatched to dig a passage through. Toward the end of January, road conditions were bad enough that B. M. DuRell & Co. announced that the Fast Freight Line from Boise to Idaho City would have to be temporarily discontinued. Stagecoach service was also disrupted on the land route along the banks of the Columbia River.[2]

Wells Fargo & Co. succeeded in keeping some channels of communication open in spite of the severe weather. The company's messenger, Howard Bledsoe, arrived in Boise City on January 17, 1866, bringing the western newspapers and express. He had been seven days coming from Walla Walla.[3] There was also unusual interest in the South Boise Express on the route to Rocky Bar: there was no authorized mail service and Wells Fargo was employing expressmen to deliver both mails and express. On one occasion Charley Barnes, the indomitable expressman, arrived in Boise from Rocky Bar after enduring eleven days of hardship and suffering. When he left Rocky Bar the snow was five feet deep and the trail unbroken. Four days later it was reported,

[1] *Idaho World* (Idaho City), January 6, 1866, p. 2, c. 5, January 13, 1866, p. 2, c. 4, January 20, 1866, p. 2, c. 1.

[2] *Idaho Tri-Weekly Statesman* (Boise), January 6, 1866, p. 2, c. 1, January 20, 1866, p. 2, c. 2, January 23, 1866, p. 2, c. 2, January 25, 1866, p. 2, c. 3, January 27, 1866, p. 2, c. 4; *Daily Mountaineer* (The Dalles, Oregon), January 26, 1866, p. 2, c. 2.

[3] *Idaho Tri-Weekly Statesman*, January 18, 1866, p. 2, c. 2.

Charley Barnes will attempt Rocky Bar again, tomorrow morning. He will go in the Overland Stage to Junction House, and there resort to snow shoes. He was practicing his muscles on a new pair about twelve feet long, yesterday, and looked much like a genuine Norwegian. There is, probably, no chance at all to get a horse through the snow. Such is winter travel in the mountains of Idaho where the winds drift a track full in thirty minutes after it is made.[4]

The *Idaho World* of Idaho City was more interested in direct communication with Rocky Bar than in routes to Boise. The Idaho legislature had adopted a memorial requesting mail service on this forty-five-mile route rather than having the mail carried one hundred miles out of the way. The newspaper editor noted the valiant effort of the South Boise Express, but it had succeeded in establishing communication between Boise and Rocky Bar only three times since the first of the year. Messrs. Macy & Goodrich inaugurated a direct service from Idaho City and proposed to make the trip through in sixteen hours, carrying letters for one dollar and packages at three dollars a pound. On January 27, 1866, the Idaho City newspaper announced:

Mr. Macy, the regular messenger, will leave the Poujade House this evening at nine o'clock, for Rocky Bar direct. No Norwegian in Idaho can beat Mr. Macy's time on snowshoes, and no Express can execute orders or carry letters and packages with any more promptness or fidelity than the company of which he is a member. They are quite independent, however, and don't care a fig whether anybody patronizes them or not. Anybody who can "keep-up" will be piloted over the route, free.[5]

As the winter progressed, Wells Fargo & Co. continued its express and treasure delivery along the Columbia River and into Idaho.

During the suspension of navigation, four expresses from below, all of which have been brought through under circumstances of great hardship and considerable danger, attest at once the energy and liberality of Wells, Fargo & Co.'s management of affairs up the Columbia,

the editor of The Dalles *Weekly Mountaineer* observed January 5, 1866. "Upon the arrival of the express from above, messengers will at once be sent to Portland with the letter mail." Major L. L. Blake, the company messenger, had traveled by steamer to the Cascades and had made the rest of the journey on foot, with the mail carried on the backs of two Indians who accompanied him.

Wells Fargo also kept the treasure moving.

Wells, Fargo & Co. yesterday sent by the *Idaho* twelve hundred pounds of treasure, of which seven hundred and fifty were gold dust and gold coin, and over four hundred and fifty pounds in silver bricks, of the aggregate value of $225,000,

reported The Dalles newspaper, whose editor regularly paid tribute to Wells Fargo.

Since the freeze-up we have been so frequently under obligation to Wells, Fargo & Co. that an ordinary newspaper expression of thanks does not cover the case. It is to the enterprise of the express company, and its agent here, Mr. Buchanan, that the community are indebted for communication with the outside world for the last month.[6]

In January, 1866, Wells Fargo & Co. moved into a new office in Boise, prompting the local editor to comment:

NEW QUARTERS—Agent Yates, of Wells, Fargo & Co. has got himself snugly located in his new and commodious quarters in May & Brown's new brick building, at the corner of Main and Sixth streets. It affords us pleasure to see the agents and messengers of the express in a comfortable building for if any class of men deserve it they do. They have the whole width of the building, twenty-five feet, running back far enough to make a convenient office, counting-room and sleeping apartments. The office and the building, when completed, will be an ornament to the city.[7]

Scarcely had Wells Fargo vacated their old office next door to the Stage House when the Territorial Treasurer moved in.[8]

Wells Fargo continued to advertise its services in the Idaho press, including the *Idaho World*.[9]

[4] *Ibid.*, January 6, 1866, p. 2, c. 1.

[5] *Idaho World*, January 6, 1866, p. 2, c. 1, p. 3, c. 1, January 13, 1866, p. 3, c. 1, January 20, 1866, p. 3, c. 2, January 27, 1866, p. 3, c. 1.

[6] *Weekly Mountaineer* (The Dalles, Oregon), January 5, 1866, p. 2, c. 1, p. 4, c. 1, January 12, 1866, p. 1, c. 6, p. 2, c. 6.

[7] *Idaho Tri-Weekly Statesman*, January 30, 1866, p. 2, c. 1.

[8] *Ibid.*, p. 2, c. 1.

[9] *Idaho World*, February 3, 1866, p. 1, c. 5.

WELLS. FARGO & CO.

NEW YORK AND CALIFORNIA

Express and Exchange Company!

WELLS, FARGO & CO. having recently established Offices at Boise City, Ruby City, and Rocky Bar, are prepared to forward Freight, Packages and Letters from those point to all parts of the world; also, Collections and Commissions attended to. [44tf]

When the ice began to melt in the Columbia River in late February, bridges and ferries were taken out and the lesser streams were at flood stage. Nevertheless, the Wells Fargo messenger, Howard Bledsoe, was able to get through. Where the roads were impassable for vehicles he had ridden horseback.[10] On March 1, 1866, the *Idaho Tri-Weekly Statesman* announced:

> The Columbia River is opened at last, and navigation is resumed. The steamer *Tenino* made the first trip on the upper river, and her passengers came up on the last stage. All accounts agree in stating that there is a big rush of travel coming from below, some of it for Blackfoot [Montana] and some for this territory. Let 'em come.[11]

The *Walla Walla Statesman* confirmed that the boats of the Oregon Steam Navigation Company were making tri-weekly trips to Wallula.[12]

RESIDENTS OF the Owyhee District were more isolated than most in Idaho Territory during the winter. To improve the situation, B. M. DuRell & Co. extended its Fast Freight Line there after January 15, 1866.[13] Meanwhile, DuRell's fast freight continued to make regular trips between Boise City and Umatilla. Passengers were carried for $25, and reduced rates were offered to those wanting to go only as far as Boise Ferry, Baker City, Union Town, La Grande, or Crawford's (at the foot of the Blue Mountains). In addition to DuRell & Co.'s service, Thomas & Co. continued to operate between the Columbia River and Boise, carrying the mails. The stages came through from Umatilla in five and a half days; the freight took nine.[14] Early in February, DuRell's fast freight began operating into Owyhee as promised, and in Boise the managing agent of the line announced that the company was poised and waiting for spring.[15]

The *Owyhee Avalanche* urged DuRell to establish a fast freight on any of the lines running to the Sacramento River in competition with the delivery system on the Columbia. The editor argued that fast freight which was run from the eastern terminus of the Central Pacific Railroad or a base in Chico or Red Bluff could deliver goods into the Owyhee District as quickly as by way of Umatilla. The land route could be traveled year round, unlike the Columbia River route, and the nine times that goods had to be unloaded and loaded on the latter route could also be avoided.[16] In May, DuRell & Co. responded, announcing dramatic changes in both the nature and route of service for passengers, express, and "fast freight" by using a combination land-and-water route. Arrangements had been made with the Oregon Steam Navigation Company to place the steamer *Shoshone* on the Snake River, operating between Olds Ferry and Owyhee Ferry. From Umatilla, the freight wagons arrived at Olds Ferry, ninety miles west of Boise, and were taken up the river to the Owyhee Ferry, only thirty-three miles from Boise and somewhat closer to the Owyhee towns. This arrangement was expected to reduce the time between Umatilla and Boise, or Ruby City, to four and a half or five days. However, John Hailey revealed that it cost more to load and re-load and haul the last thirty-three miles into Boise City than it did to haul straight through the ninety-mile distance from Olds Ferry over a far superior land route. There was an additional charge for the steamer service, and experience proved that no time was saved. Thus, the experiment with the *Shoshone* ended in failure.[17]

AT THE END of June there was an unexpected announcement: "DuRell's Fast Freight Line has been sold to Greathouse & Co. We hear that $31,000 was paid." Hill Beachey was to assume responsibility for a daily delivery of freight from Boise City to the Owyhee Ferry on the Snake River and to Ruby City. The

[10] *Idaho Tri-Weekly Statesman*, February 15, 1866, p. 2, c. 2.

[11] *Ibid.*, March 1, 1866, p. 2, c. 2.

[12] *Statesman* (Walla Walla), March 2, 1866, p. 2, c. 3.

[13] *Owyhee Avalanche*, January 13, 1866, p. 3, c. 1.

[14] *Idaho Tri-Weekly Statesman*, January 27, 1866, p. 2, c. 4, February 6, 1866, p. 2, c. 2.

[15] *Owyhee Avalanche*, February 10, 1866, p. 2, c. 2; *Idaho Tri-Weekly Statesman*, February 13, 1866, p. 2, c. 1.

[16] *Owyhee Avalanche*, March 7, 1866, p. 3, c. 2.

[17] *Idaho World*, May 5, 1866, p. 3, c. 1, June 2, 1866, p. 3, c. 1, June 16, 1866, p. 2, c. 5, p. 3, c. 1, June 2, 1866, p. 2, c. 2; *Idaho Tri-Weekly Statesman*, March 27, 1866, p. 1, c. 2 and 3; John Hailey, *The History of Idaho* (Boise: Syms-York Company, 1910), 123-124.

Downtown Boise in 1866, as seen from a building across Main Street from Wells Fargo's new office.

section from Idaho City to Umatilla was to run via the Ruckell & Thomas road over the Blue Mountains.[18] Confusion prevailed as to just who controlled this route between the Boise Basin and the Columbia River. DuRell apparently sold to a partnership of Hailey, Greathouse, and Kelly; by July, 1866, the service was being operated by John Hailey & Co. Hailey advertised that his Pioneer Line of Concord coaches was carrying both the United States mail and Wells Fargo's express from Umatilla directly to Boise, Idaho, Centerville, Placerville, and Pioneer cities and connecting with the *Shoshone* at Olds Ferry en route to Owyhee, Ruby, and Silver cities.[19]

Within two months the Oregon Steam Navigation Company expressed dissatisfaction with the service of Greathouse and Hailey. "In their greed for gain, [they] have reduced the line from a daily to a tri-weekly," reported the *Weekly Mountaineer*, "and are feeding their miserable stock on grass alone, consuming four days from Umatilla to Boise City—overloading their mud wagons with passengers and freight, greatly to the discomfort of passengers and damage of the route." Both the *Mountaineer* and the *Weekly Oregonian* announced the organization of a more effective opposition service supported by the steamship company.[20] The Boise newspaper revealed the nature of the opposition when Wells Fargo advertised the establishment of a "Fast Freight" service all the way from Portland to all the major communities in Idaho Territory.

NOTICE
On and after August 1, 1866
THE PIONEER STAGE COMPANY
WILL DISCONTINUE CARRYING FREIGHT
Wells, Fargo & Co.
Having made arrangements with them for the transportation of all Freight going over their route.

WELLS, FARGO & CO.'S
FAST FREIGHT
LINE
GREAT REDUCTION
ON
FREIGHT TO IDAHO!
THROUGH IN SIX DAYS TO
BOISE CITY

FROM AND AFTER AUGUST 1ST, 1866, until further notice, our rates for FAST FREIGHT will be as follows:

From Portland to Boise City .... 25 cts. per lb.
" " to Idaho City .... 30 " per lb.
" " to Ruby City .... 35 " per lb.
" " to Rocky Bar .... 40 " per lb.

Portland, July 30th, 1866

WELLS, FARGO & CO.

The Boise paper said,

[18] *Idaho World*, June 20, 1866, p. 3, c. 1; *Idaho Tri-Weekly Statesman*, June 28, 1866, p. 3, c. 1; *Weekly Oregonian* (Portland), July 7, 1866, p. 3, c. 1.

[19] *Daily Oregon Herald* (Portland), July 14, 1866, p. 2, c. 6.

[20] *Weekly Oregonian*, August 18, 1866, p. 3, c. 1; *Weekly Mountaineer*, August 17, 1866, p. 2, c. 1.

The public will take note of the new arrangement in the Fast Freight business between Portland and all places in Idaho Territory. The stage line gives up entirely the carrying of freight except for Wells, Fargo & Co. and that company, whose messengers and agents are scattered all along the route, have taken entire charge of that business. The well recognized principle that a classification of labor leads to the best results is adopted by these companies in the change, with sure satisfaction to all parties concerned.[21]

In noting the change, the *Idaho World* commented, "The price charged for the transportation of freight has been greatly reduced to this Territory."[22]

IN THE Owyhee District, the *Owyhee Avalanche* remained concerned about an outlet to the southwest into Nevada and California.

We have good reason to believe that our place will soon be connected with Virginia, Nevada by a daily mail—and a liberal contract to carry it. Senator [William M.] Stewart, of Nevada, has taken the matter in hand and his efforts are uniformly successes. He can hardly do his own state or Idaho a greater favor than by securing this service.

The Virginia City (Nevada) *Union* reported in January that Beachey was still seeking to open the route between the Owyhee District and Star City to operate a tri-weekly line of stages in the spring. He had again petitioned the Post Office Department for a mail contract. Then came the disappointing news:

Rejected—Hill Beachey's proposal to the P. O. Department to carry the mail from Boise City via Ruby to Humboldt City, Nevada, up till July 1, 1866, has been rejected; and the mails ordered sent via Salt Lake City,

the *Avalanche* announced. "This is quite handy, only about a thousand miles out of the way. Generally we like to have things go as far as possible—but this matter pleases us too well."[23]

The newspaper editor was no more pleased with the service of Wells Fargo than with that of the Post Office Department. "W. F. & Co. . . . Notwithstanding the unexcelled character of this Company, for dispatch and responsibility, they have for the past two months substantially failed to furnish Owyhee with mail or express matter," he complained on February 10.

This is from no inherent lack of vigor or disposition on the part of the company but solely because they have chosen to adhere to a route lined with obstacles next to unsurmountable most of the year. The United States mail comes via Salt Lake with a sort of irregular certainty, but the express via Portland has ceased to be expected. If the Company wish to conduct business in Idaho, they must establish an overland route to connect with one passing through Nevada, or go direct to Chico. It would be much better to dispatch all their Express matter via Salt Lake. It has been fully two months since San Francisco dates have been received by Express. The Company are culpable and the public should so view them until they correct the matter in question. Although ostensibly connected with the outer world by one of the most efficient Express Lines, at present it is simply a mockery and injury.[24]

Part of the problem was that Leach & Co. had announced at the beginning of the year that they would no longer carry the mails between Boise and Ruby City without compensation. As a result, mail deliveries during the winter had been by express. Upon the rejection by the Post Office Department of his proposal to carry the mail, Beachey made an arrangement with the postmaster in Boise City, subject to departmental approval, to carry the mails between the two towns on a tri-weekly basis—knowing that the chances of compensation were slim. Throughout February, the service was maintained on schedule even though a portion of the route had to be traversed on sleighs. There was continuing difficulty with the Indians.[25]

A Washington dispatch of early April announced that mail contracts had been let from Susanville, California, and from Humboldt, Nevada, both going to Boise City. The first had gone to L. T. Williamson for $35,000 and the latter to Albert R. Leckery for $29,000. The *Owyhee Avalanche* was aghast, suggesting that Louis McLane of the Pioneer Stage Company was using Leckery (presumably a relative) as a front. It was suggested that the service could not be

[21] *Idaho Tri-Weekly Statesman*, August 9, 1866, p. 2, c. 1 and 3.

[22] *Idaho World*, August 18, 1866, p. 2, c. 5, p. 3, c. 1.

[23] *Owyhee Avalanche*, January 20, 1866, p. 2, c. 4, p. 3, c. 1, p. 4, c. 1, quoting the Virginia City, Nevada, *Union*.

[24] *Ibid.*, February 10, 1866, p. 3, c. 2.

[25] *Idaho Tri-Weekly Statesman*, February 6, 1866, p. 3, c. 2, February 8, 1866, p. 2, c. 1, February 13, 1866, p. 2, c. 1, February 15, 1866, p. 2, c. 4.

performed for the money and that a practical alternative was to have the two lines converge near the Sink of Queen's River and from that junction run jointly into Boise. Meanwhile, Beachey's proposal had been ignored. With a note of desperation, the editor cried out, "Dependent and helpless Owyhee! . . . How long, O Lord, about *how* long—that's the question."[26]

The next month the mail route designated "Humboldt City to Boise via Owyhee" was abolished. Congress established a new route from Virginia City, Nevada, to Boise via Unionville, Star City, Glen Dun, and Ruby. Proposals were invited by the Post Office Department for weekly, tri-weekly, and daily service.

BEACHEY'S FORTUNES at long last took a turn for the better. In March, 1866, he had written to Charles Crocker of the Central Pacific's "Big Four," proposing the establishment of a stage line to meet the railroad and run thence to the mining camps of the Humboldt and Owyhee districts. The proposal had appeal because of the continuing struggle between the Central Pacific-California Steam Navigation Company interests and the Oregon Steam Navigation Company. Crocker wrote to Beachey endorsing the proposal and revealing the construction plans and timetable fo the railroad.

> We shall have the railroad running to Dutch Flat in May; to Crystal Lake, within fifteen miles of the Summit, in August, and to the Summit, if not to the Truckee river this year. . . . During the year 1867 we shall get the road running east as far as the Big Bend of the Truckee, if not farther. We hope to lay the track at the rate of two hundred miles a year when we are once over.

Crocker encouraged Beachey to establish the stage line, offered financial support, and guaranteed that the rate for freight to the railroad would be competitive and that he had obtained the promises of military protection for the route. Crocker wrote:

> If you persevere in maintaining your stage route from Star City it will be one of the best paying routes in the country. Our Company are offering the most liberal inducements to get the freight going this way, and when the freight once gets going passenger travel will soon follow. Anything in reason we can do to promote this trade we are willing to do. . . . You can assure the merchants of Ruby City and vicinity that this is the shortest and cheapest route for their goods.

Later in the month Crocker wrote a long letter to J. L. Browne, Wells Fargo agent in Owyhee, elaborating on the proposal. He was convinced that as the railroad construction progressed, the Chico-Red Bluff route would diminish in importance; that Wells Fargo would likely put on a line of stages from the terminal to deliver express over the Humboldt route; and that freight and express rates would be steadily reduced as construction progressed.[27]

Late in June, Hill Beachey was finally informed that he would receive no pay for carrying the mails between Boise City and Owyhee, just as had been the case with Joe Leach & Co. before him. The standard reason given was that the mails for Boise were to go by way of Salt Lake City. On June 30, 1866, news arrived that the contract for the daily mail service from Virginia City, Nevada, via the Humboldt route to Boise City for four years from September 1 had been given to Jesse D. Carr, formerly of Monterey, California.[28] The Nevada delegation in Congress had labored long and hard to get the mail route established from Idaho to Virginia City by way of the Humboldt District. Congressman D. R. Ashley notified the Owyhee editor that when the bids were opened Carr had the lowest: $75,000 a year to deliver the mail three times a week. The congressman who knew Carr had found him an active and efficient contractor.[29]

Beachey nevertheless remained active in Idaho, staging throughout the summer months. Not only was he negotiating for participation in the contract Carr held, but he also continued to operate his stages between Silver City and Boise. Carr traveled to Sacramento, then traversed the route via Star City and arrived

[26] *Owyhee Avalanche*, April 7, 1866, p. 3, c. 2.

[27] *Ibid.*, p. 4, c. 2, May 26, 1866, p. 2, c. 1. These developments are summarized in Victor Goodwin, "William C. (Hill) Beachey: Nevada-California-Idaho Stagecoach King," *Nevada Historical Society Quarterly* (Spring, 1967), 10:5-46.

[28] *Idaho World*, June 20, 1866, p. 4, c. 3.

[29] *Owyhee Avalanche*, July 7, 1866, p. 1, c. 2.

Ben Holladay

in Ruby City after six and a half days. Here he revealed that Hill Beachey was part owner of the line, would be its general manager, and had been awarded a $4,000 contract to carry the mail between Ruby City and Boise on the stage line he had earlier purchased from Barnes & Yates.[30]

The route used by Beachey and Carr followed the immigrant trail from Virginia City along the Carson River to Ragtown and then to settlements at Stillwater, Antelope Valley, Unionville, and Star City, and thence northward to Idaho. At Virginia City, the line met the stagecoaches of the Pioneer Stage Company, which was carrying passengers from there to Lake's Crossing, the future site of Reno, and thence across the Sierra to the railhead of the Central Pacific. In August, 1866, Beachey put on a pony express to handle the mail between Silver City/Ruby City and Star City until stagecoach service could be put on the line. Some authorities have suggested that "Pony Bob" Haslam rode on this route.[31]

Beachey was having his "usual luck" on the route from Silver City to Star City. He wrote Carr that the Indians were on the rampage as they had been the previous June. One man had been killed at Summit Station in eastern Oregon and trouble was brewing on the Quinn River below Willow Springs and Camp McDermitt. Beachey had asked for the services of fifty soldiers but none had been dispatched to his aid. In spite of difficulties, Beachey put his stages on the road by September 1, 1866, and continued to run them on time. Soon he bought out Carr. On September 7, 1866, the Railroad Stage Line was organized with Beachey, George and Henry Greathouse, John Hailey, and the Boise stage man, Sam Kelly, as incorporators.[32]

THROUGH TO
SAN FRANCISCO IN FIVE DAYS!
BY THE
RAILROAD
STAGE LINE!
FOR SACRAMENTO, VIA HUMBOLDT &
Virginia, Nev.,
CONNECTING WITH THE
PACIFIC R. R. AT CISCO!
93 miles This Side of Sacramento,
CROSSING MOST OF THE SIERRA NEVADA
BY RAILROAD!
STAGES LEAVE RUBY CITY, I. T.,
Every Other Day!
For further particulars—inquire at the Office of the Idaho Hotel.
HILL BEACHEY
Gen'l Sup't.[33]

Sept. 22, '66

IN ADDITION to its concern over the lack of mail service, the *Owyhee Avalanche* lamented the absence of a bank in the district and urged at least one of the California banks to establish a branch in Ruby City or Silver City. The *Idaho Tri-Weekly Statesman* announced on April 10, 1866, that Owyhee was going to get its long-sought banking and assay house. The firm was Messrs. King, Webb & Co., which had favorable connections in Portland, San Francisco, and New York. King had for several years been assayer in the San Francisco mint, was a partner in the well-known firm of Tracy & King in Portland, and had later worked as an assayer for Wells Fargo. Webb had been connected with B. M. DuRell of Boise. Two weeks later the *Avalanche* reported that Webb

[30] *Ibid.*, July 28, 1866, p. 3, c. 2, August 4, 1866, p. 3, c. 1.

[31] Goodwin, "Beachey," 28-29.

[32] *Owyhee Avalanche*, September 8, 1866, p. 2, c. 1; Goodwin, "Beachey," 29.

[33] *Owyhee Avalanche*, September 29, 1866, p. 2, c. 3.

& King had started the construction of a building in Silver City and that they expected to be ready to open in the early part of June.[34]

Simultaneously, Wells Fargo sponsored the competing firm of Thomas Cole, Jr., & Co. in Ruby City.

> THOMAS COLE, JR. & CO.
> BANKERS,
> . . AND . . .
> Agents of Wells, Fargo & Co.
> Ruby City, Idaho
>
> DRAW SIGHT EXCHANGE ON SAN Francisco, available in all the principal towns of Oregon, Nevada and California. Sell Wells, Fargo & Co.'s Exchange on New York, available throughout the Eastern States, Montana, Salt Lake City and the Canadas. Certificate & Special Deposits received.
>
> Purchase Bullion and Gold Dust.
> GOLD COIN, LEGAL TENDERS and REVENUE
> Stamps constantly for sale.
>
> Refer to—Louis McLane . . . . San Francisco
> Alsop & Co. . . . . "
> Henry S. Babcock, Manager British and
> California Banking Co. . . . . "
> June 7, '66

The *Avalanche* commented,

> Banking House—The attention of the public is directed to the card of Thos. Cole & Co., Bankers. The reliability of the House is unquestionable. Their business connection with the firm of Wells, Fargo & Co., gives them excellent facilities for Banking. We hail this institution as a powerful aid to burst up the illegitimate dust traffic.[35]

Wells Fargo had apparently decided that the Owyhee District had a future as a mining and transportation center. It was announced in Ruby City in July that Wells Fargo as well as the Cole bank would move to the rapidly growing nearby community of Silver City. The company was reported to "have a very commodious and well located building that is now undergoing the finishing strokes."[36]

THE *Mountaineer* continued its campaign to improve mail facilities through The Dalles during the winter months. A special session of the Oregon Legislature had passed a resolution requesting the states' senators and representatives to work for the establishment of a mail service from The Dalles via Canyon City to Boise City.[37] Somewhat more rapidly than expected, the Post Office called for bids for a service on the route, including proposals for daily, tri-weekly, semi-weekly, and weekly service. The *Mountaineer* reported that everyone was taken by surprise; time did not allow for careful consideration by contracts. The editor held out hope for a tri-weekly service if a minimal bid, allowing only for a modest profit, were submitted. The *Idaho Tri-Weekly Statesman* in Boise announced that it favored the Canyon City route over that from Walla Walla or Umatilla.[38]

The route had its problems. At the end of March a serious accident was reported when the stage, in attempting to cross the South Fork of the John Day River, overturned and the Wells Fargo treasure box was lost. But at the end of April Wells Fargo had a bit of good luck. The messenger from The Dalles arrived in Canyon City with the treasure box. It had been found about a mile downstream. Approximately $3,000 in treasure and letter express was recovered.[39]

Quincy A. Brooks, the postal agent in Portland, received a telegram from Washington in early April telling him that the postal route to Canyon City had been established and that the contract for carrying the mails had been awarded to Messrs. Robbins, Wheeler & Weaver beginning July 1. No mention was made of the long-sought route beyond Canyon City to Boise. Soon it was announced that the Canyon City Stage was five days overdue. On April 12, the Wells Fargo express messenger arrived at The Dalles, having left the stage at Muddy, where it was delayed because of the want of horses—presumably stolen by Indians. Then came the blow.

[34] *Ibid.*, January 20, 1866, p. 3, c. 1; *Idaho Tri-Weekly Statesman*, April 10, 1866, p. 2, c. 4; *Owyhee Avalanche*, April 28, 1866, p. 3, c. 1.

[35] *Ibid.*, June 9, 1866, p. 2, c. 2 and 4, p. 3, c. 3; *Idaho World*, June 20, 1866, p. 3, c. 1.

[36] *Owyhee Avalanche*, July 30, 1866, p. 2, c. 2, August 4, 1866, p. 3, c. 2.

[37] *Daily Mountaineer*, February 2, 1866, p. 2, c. 2 and 3, February 10, 1866, p. 3, c. 1.

[38] *Weekly Mountaineer*, February 9, 1866, p. 3, c. 2; *Daily Mountaineer*, February 13, 1866, p. 2, c. 1, February 14, 1866, p. 2, c. 2, February 15, 1866, p. 3, c. 1, March 9, 1866, p. 2, c. 1.

[39] *Ibid.*, March 20, 1866, p. 2, c. 1, April 29, 1866, p. 2, c. 2.

> Owing to the Indian hostilities between the Dalles and Canyon City, Wells, Fargo & Co. refused to carry treasure over the route. The letter express left here yesterday with a guard of three men. A sad state of affairs, and one that calls for immediate action on the part of the military authorities,

the *Mountaineer* suggested.[40] Nevertheless, preparations for the mail service continued, "Messrs. Robbins, Weaver & Co. have opened their stage agency in the room lately used by Jo. Teal as a broker's office."[41] In the interim, the Dalles and Canyon City Stage Company continued to operate and advertised that it was carrying both the United States mails and Wells Fargo's express in Concord coaches.[42] Great hopes were held for the route once the mail contract began July 1. "This is the first link of the Great Overland Mail Line, which will before long pass over this route to Boise, and thence east by the Overland Line to the Atlantic States," The Dalles editor proclaimed.[43]

THE MOST active mining rush in the spring of 1866 was to the Blackfoot mines of Montana. The *Oregonian* published reports that San Francisco merchants were convinced that the best route to Montana was by way of Oregon, via Portland and the Columbia River. Financial support was available for the improvements of a road from the most feasible point on the Columbia into Montana. The Walla Walla *Statesman* reported that San Francisco merchants had endorsed the Mullan Road and urged its re-opening.[44]

Messrs. Edgar, Buchanan & Waldron announced the establishment of the Blackfoot Express to run from Walla Walla to Helena, Montana, in April. When S. A. Buchanan prepared to leave The Dalles to inaugurate the Blackfoot Express with his partners, the *Mountaineer* announced,

> Mr. B. has been a clerk in Wells, Fargo & Co.'s office in this city for some time past, and has by his courteous and gentlemanly conduct made many friends in the Dalles, who will regret his departure.... We recommend Sam. to the people of the upper Columbia as a gentleman, who is well worthy of their confidence.[45]

The *Oregonian* published a report that Messrs. Edgar, Waldron & Buchanan's plans for the Blackfoot Express were fully matured and they were making regular trips by late April.[46]

Wells Fargo & Co. also had a vital interest in this new enterprise, as the following advertisement indicates:

> D. V. WALDRON A. D. EDGAR SAM R. BUCHANAN
> WALDRON'S BLACKFOOT EXPRESS.
> MESSRS. WALDRON, BUCHANAN & EDGAR, (lately in the employ of Wells, Fargo & Co.) have established an
> EXPRESS TO BLACKFOOT CITY,
> HELENA, DEER LODGE, VIRGINIA CITY, and all the Mining Camps in Montana Territory. Connecting at Walla Walla with
> Wells, Fargo & Co.'s Express
> The Blackfoot Express will leave Walla Walla tri-monthly.
> Ship Treasure at lowest rates, purchase Goods of every description, execute Commissions of all kinds and make Collections.
> All letters and packages sent through Wells, Fargo & Co. will be promptly forwarded.
> WALDRON & CO.[47]

Soon a controversy raged over the best route to Montana. The Portland capitalists who owned the Oregon Steam Navigation Company encouraged travelers to use a route by way of Pend 'Oreille rather than by Coeur d'Alene and the Mullan Road. Those who did so regretted it, according to the Walla Walla *Statesman*, which referred to the more northern route as "humbug."[48]

By August, the Blackfoot Express was well established. In addition to the usual letter and newspaper express, the messenger on occasion carried as much as $75,000 in treasure. He revealed that extensive improvements were being made in Helena, where many of the merchants were building fireproof stores of stone, some four and five stories high. Boats

[40] *Ibid.*, April 11, 1866, p. 3, c. 1, April 12, 1866, p. 2, c. 1, April 14, 1866, p. 2, c. 2.

[41] *Ibid.*, April 19, 1866, p. 2, c. 1.

[42] *Ibid.*, May 26, 1866, p. 2, c. 3.

[43] *Weekly Mountaineer*, June 29, 1866, p. 3, c. 1.

[44] *Daily Mountaineer*, March 23, 1866, p. 4, c. 1, quoting the *Oregonian; Statesman*, March 9, 1866, p. 2, c. 1, March 16, 1866, p. 2, c. 1.

[45] *Daily Mountaineer*, April 17, 1866, p. 2, c. 1.

[46] *Weekly Oregonian*, April 28, 1866, p. 3, c. 1.

[47] *Statesman*, June 22, 1866, p. 3, c. 4.

[48] *Ibid.*, June 8, 1866, p. 2, c. 1.

loaded down with passengers were leaving Fort Benton.[49]

COMPETITION IN the stage and freighting business between the Columbia River and Boise Basin was fierce during the 1866 season. DuRell & Co.'s coaches were still carrying passengers from Idaho City to Umatilla for twenty-five dollars. From Boise to Umatilla the fare was twenty dollars; from Boise City to Idaho City, five dollars each way. The *Idaho Tri-Weekly Statesman* commented,

> It will be noticed by their card in another column that the proprietors of the Fast Freight Line have reduced the fare on all their routes to very low figures. Opposition makes cheap travelling. A year ago fare from here to Umatilla was sixty dollars.[50]

Wells Fargo's fast freight service had largely been responsible for this reduction.

F. F. Marx had written from Washington, D.C., that he had the mail contract from Boise City to Rocky Bar. He planned to leave Boise City every Monday morning and Idaho City on Tuesday morning and return the latter part of the week. Messrs. Kelly & Greathouse had a sub-contract to carry the mail between Boise City and Idaho City, and C. L. Goodrich from Idaho City to Rocky Bar. The contract did not start until June 1, but Marx had decided to institute the service immediately.[51]

Wells Fargo & Co. employees were busier than ever all over the Northwest during the spring and summer. Every newspaper in eastern Oregon and Washington Territory and throughout Idaho Territory paid regular tribute to the agents and messengers of the company. Scores of notices mentioned the service and favors of agents Yates in Boise, Browne in Owyhee, and Buchanan at The Dalles. The same was true of messengers on the stage routes and on the steamships that plied the waters of the Columbia River: Bledsoe, Holland, West, Cann, and Page.

OREGON NEWSPAPERS reported in April: "The Calfornians have not yet learned enough to cause them to desist in their efforts to transport freight overland from the Sacramento river to the Idaho mines."[52] The Chico route was far from abandoned. Telegraphic dispatches to Idaho via San Francisco revealed that Captain John Mullan had now organized a joint stock company with New York and Baltimore capital of $300,000 to open up a stage and mail route from Boise to Chico. The San Francisco *Bulletin* expressed hope that Mullan's "Chico Project" would be as successful as his construction of the Mullan Road from the headwaters of the Missouri River to the Columbia.[53] The *Mountaineer* reported that the citizens of Chico had recently held a meeting to make final arrangements concerning the transportation of freight from that point to Idaho, and an agent of the California Steam Navigation Company announced that the company would reduce the price of freight transportation on the Sacramento River to Chico to such an extent as to be satisfactory.[54]

In California, Mullan and his associates were busily making preparations to resume service on the Chico-Ruby City route. John Bidwell, Chico's representative in Congress, and E. D. Holbrook, Idaho's territorial delegate, had succeeded in getting the mail contract from Susanville to Boise City that had been let to L. T. Williamson, one of Mullan's backers in San Francisco, authorized. Then Bidwell managed to shift the western terminus of mail from Susanville to Chico rather than Oroville.[55] According to the Sacramento *Union*, the mail contract on the road between Susanville and Boise, originally let to Williamson, was taken over by Mullan and was to go into effect on July 1, to continue for four years.[56]

[49]*Ibid.*, August 10, 1866, p. 3, c. 1; *Weekly Oregonian*, August 18, 1866, p. 3, c. 1.

[50]*Idaho Tri-Weekly Statesman*, May 26, 1866, p. 2, c. 1 and 4, p. 3, c. 2.

[51]*Idaho World*, May 12, 1866, p. 3, c. 1.

[52]*Daily Mountaineer*, April 4, 1866, p. 2, c. 2, quoting the *Oregonian*, which had picked up the news item in the Sacramento *Union*.

[53]*Idaho World*, April 14, 1866, p. 1, c. 3, quoting from the San Francisco *Bulletin*.

[54]*Daily Mountaineer*, April 25, 1866, p. 2, c. 1.

[55]Clarence F. McIntosh, "The Chico and Red Bluff Route: Stage Lines from Southern Idaho to the Sacramento Valley, 1865-1867," *Idaho Yesterdays* (Fall, 1962), 6/3:18-19. McIntosh's summary is based upon a careful survey of the *Chico Weekly Courant*.

[56]Quoted in *Statesman*, July 13, 1866, p. 4, c. 2.

Stages began operation on the section of the road between Chico and Susanville about June 20, 1866, making tri-weekly trips. At midnight on July 1, the first regular coach left Chico for Idaho. It arrived three days and five hours later in Ruby City. The passenger fare was sixty dollars.[57] On July 7, 1866, the *Owyhee Avalanche,* under the heading "New Stage Line—Mails—Fast Time," announced that the

> Chico and Idaho Stage Co. have got into successful operation. Nothing but Indian raids will prevent the permanent success of the line. The route is stocked and stations selected and men fitting them up and cutting hay.[58]

It was also announced on July 7:

> The Chico and Idaho Stages will leave and arrive here every other day, connecting with Hill Beachey's line [to Boise]. The first stage for California will leave today—probably this evening. Fare $60. The coaches are excellent and time not exceeding three days.[59]

The California and Idaho Stage Line instituted operations with concern over possible Indian attack. In less than two weeks the *Idaho Tri-Weekly Statesman* printed an ominous report: "The Owyhee stage came in yesterday in good time, but brought no news from the Indian hunters. The Chico stage has been due two days and not heard from."[60]

Meanwhile, Thomas Cole had gone to California in August, returned over the Chico road, and pronounced it "the best natural route he ever saw—and its pass over the Sierras superior to any other traveled."[61] The Chico *Courant* reported:

> Two treasure boxes and a half dozen letter bags, for Wells, Fargo & Co.'s Express from Chico to Idaho, were brought up from San Francisco by Mr. Cole, the agent in Ruby City, and taken through on the Idaho Stage which left Wednesday night. Bullion will soon begin to arrive in heavy doses.[62]

[57]McIntosh, "The Chico and Red Bluff Route," 19.

[58]*Owyhee Avalanche,* July 7, 1866, p. 2, c. 2.

[59]*Ibid.,* p. 3, c. 1.

[60]*Idaho Tri-Weekly Statesman,* July 17, 1866, p. 4, c. 1.

[61]*Owyhee Avalanche,* August 25, 1866, p. 2, c. 3.

[62]*Idaho World,* September 1, 1866, p. 2, c. 3, quoting the *Chico Weekly Courant.*

[63]*Owyhee Avalanche,* August 4, 1866, p. 3, c. 2; *Idaho Tri-Weekly Statesman,* August 22, 1866, p. 2, c. 1.

CALIFORNIA AND IDAHO

STAGE & FAST FREIGHT COMPANY.

THE CALIFORNIA AND IDAHO STAGE Line leaves Oroville and Chico for Ruby, Silver and Boise Cities (Idaho)

EVERY OTHER DAY

ON ARRIVAL OF SACRAMENTO MAILS,

MAKING THE TRIP IN FOUR DAYS,

Carrying U. S. Mails and Wells, Fargo & Co's Express. Returning, leaves Ruby, Silver and Boise Cities every other day for California, connecting at Oroville, the railroad terminus for Sacramento.

This Line runs via Big Meadows, Susanville, Granite Creek, Black Rock, Fort McGarry, (Summit Lake) Pueblo, Camp C. F. Smith, (White Horse) and Camp Lyon At Big Meadows it connects each way, DAILY, with Stage Line to Indian Valley, without delay to passengers.

FARE FROM

Chico to Ruby or Silver City,.................$60
Oroville to Ruby or Silver City.................. 62
Marysville to Ruby or Silver City,.............. 64
Sacramento to Ruby or Silver City,............. 68
Sanfrancisco to Ruby or Silver City,............ 73
Silver or Ruby to Boise City,..................... 18
Oroville to Susanville or Indian Valley....... 12
Chico to Susanville or Indian Valley,.......... 10

Passengers allowed thirty pounds baggage.—Extra Baggage or Freight from Chico to Ruby or Silver Silver City, *Thirty Cents per Pound;* to Boise City, *Ten Cents Additional*

Chico Office..............John T. Shaaff, Agent:
Oroville Office..........Lowry Brothers, "
San Francisco Office.....Stephen Duncan,
No. 206 Bush st., opposite Cosmopolitan Hotel,.............................. "
Susanville,...............W. H. D. Haven, "
Marysville Office,........Lowry Brothers, "
Sacramento Office,...........C. J. Shaw, "
Silver and Ruby,.........Chas. N. Mullan, "
Boise City,....................Hill Beechy, "

To whom Apply in Person or by Letter for Further Information.

In July, Stages leave Chico on even dates; in August, on odd dates; in September on even dates of the month, etc. [Sept. 1, 1866n45tf

Wells Fargo & Co. were already using this route and had dispatched over a hundred letters by the stage as early as August 4. "Passengers speak well of the route and pronounce it favorable to any other road in operation in California," the *Avalanche* reported. "As per a published order of Wells, Fargo & Co., hereafter all mail matter and express packages will come over the route," noted the Boise *Statesman.*[63]

The California and Idaho Stage and Fast Freight Company advertisements emphasized that it carried the United States mails and Wells Fargo express. The editor of the *Idaho World* explained,

The stages over the Chico road for Silver City are now making regular trips through in four days, carrying Wells, Fargo & Co.'s Express and fast freight. It leaves every day. Passage from Ruby City to Chico $60—each passenger being allowed thirty pounds of baggage.[64]

Within the week, news arrived in Idaho that

the Idaho Stage [to Chico] met with a couple of highwaymen . . . who relieved the passengers of about $18,000 and opened the Wells, Fargo & Co.'s box, but found nothing. [The holdup] occurred at the summit, fifty miles from Chico.[65]

Other reports claimed the loss amounted to only $1,200 and the robbers had been caught in Oroville.[66]

On November 17, 1866, the *Avalanche* announced:

Chico Stage makes its last trip to-morrow—particulars set forth in posters. Will continue to run stages as far as Summit Lake through the winter, from which point the mails will be carried to Ruby on horseback. Through staging will be resumed in early Spring, when due notice will be given. Fare to Chico to-day and to-morrow, $50.[67]

BEN HOLLADAY'S operations were much in the news during the summer of 1866. Both the *Oregon State Journal* in Eugene and the *Weekly Mountaineer* reprinted an article from the *Fort Kearny* (Nebraska) *Herald* entitled "Ho! For the New Route," the essence of which was that Holladay's Overland Mail & Express Company had purchased seven new stagecoaches and that he was heading west in July to stock his routes.[68] Holladay planned a dual service: in addition to carrying the mails under government contract, he planned to deliver express and treasure as a private venture. Separate advertisements for each service appeared in the western newspapers. The editor of the *Idaho Tri-Weekly Statesman* commented,

The Holladay Overland Mail and Express Company having put messengers on their line to Salt Lake City, Montana and Blackfoot and the Eastern States, will hereafter send letters and express packages, gold dust, &c. once a week to those places, at the very lowest rates, commencing Monday next. Letters closed in their envelopes will be forwarded every stage and promptly delivered at all points along their line. Messengers will also be put on at the same time between Idaho City and Boise City. Their envelopes can be had at their post offices in either of the last mentioned places.[69]

In far-away Seattle, the *Puget Sound Gazette* reprinted an account from the *Springfield* (Massachusetts) *Republican* reporting that Ben Holladay had consolidated his interests with the "Butterfield Opposition" in the Great Plains and was aggressively moving into the Montana-Idaho region from a base in Salt Lake City, expanding his stage and mail service to include express.[70] He apparently had in mind challenging the successful operations of Wells Fargo in the Northwest.

In August, Holladay extended the Overland Express line into Owyhee with offices at DuRell & Moore's store in Ruby City. The *Owyhee Avalanche* announced:

Will carry letters, packages, treasure, and other express freights to all points east of Boise City—Montana, Utah, and all States and principal cities east of the Rocky Mts. Letters 10 cts—treasure from 4 to 5 per ct.

Holladay immediately placed an advertisement in the local newspaper to the effect that he had promptly moved to Silver City and had an office with King, Webb & Co., Bankers.

The banking situation became very competitive in Owyhee. In addition to Thomas Cole, Jr., & Co., supported by Wells Fargo, and King, Webb & Co., allied with Ben Holladay, a third bank, Paxton & Thornburgh, entered the field. The editor of the *Avalanche*—newly moved to Silver City—announced:

[64] *Idaho World*, September 1, 1866, p. 2, c. 5, p. 3, c. 1.

[65] *Idaho Tri-Weekly Statesman*, September 8, 1866, p. 1, c. 4.

[66] *Owyhee Avalanche*, September 8, 1866, p. 2, c. 1 (this item was reprinted in the *Statesman*, September 21, 1866).

[67] *Ibid.*, November 17, 1866, p. 1, c. 3.

[68] *Weekly Mountaineer*, July 13, 1866, p. 4, c. 2; *Oregon State Journal* (Eugene), June 30, 1866, p. 1, c. 3.

[69] *Idaho Tri-Weekly Statesman*, July 21, 1866, p. 3, c. 3, July 24, 1866, p. 2, c. 4.

[70] *Puget Sound Gazette* (Seattle, Washington), July 23, 1866, p. 4, c. 1, quoting from the *Springfield* (Massachusetts) *Republican*.

Messrs. Paxton & Thornburgh have opened a Banking House in Silver. This firm is well and favorably known all over the Pacific States and Territories. They are prepared to do everything they advertise with dispatch and reliability. Also are Agents for the Imperial Insurance Company.[71]

Ben Holladay's prominent role in Idaho continued into the fall. The Union Pacific Railroad had been completed as far as Manhattan, Kansas, making two days' less staging to the east, and the Holladay Overland Mail and Express Company by making connections could carry bullion, treasure, letters, and express packages to New York City in twenty days for less than 5 per cent tariff. The *Idaho World* reminded readers of this service and the fact that letters by express left every day; treasure, accompanied by a messenger, every six days.[72]

THE NEWSPAPERS in Idaho Territory, eastern Oregon, and Washington Territory continued in the fall to express dissatisfaction with the region's transportation services, particularly that of the Oregon Steam Navigation Company. The *Idaho Tri-Weekly Statesman* concentrated on the freighting situation. Before the summer the Oregon route had monopolized the business. The Sacramento route had now come into competition with it, but freight was lying around at both ends of this route. Competition among freighters to and from the Boise Basin and the Columbia River had been so fierce in the summer months that the price of freight had been reduced below cost, while during the winter teams were scarce and the rates so high no one could afford them. The editor called upon the Oregon Steam Navigation Company to lower its rates on freight between Portland and Umatilla while still leaving a profit for all. The Californians had done so on the Sacramento River. More important, a Teamsters' Association should be organized comparable to the California Teamsters' Association to fix rates and services.[73]

Meanwhile, the steamers of the Oregon Steam Navigation Company made daily trips from Celilo to Wallula. Stages connected with the boats at the latter place and left for Walla Walla every afternoon at 4 P.M. The steamship company attended to its business. R. R. Thompson, accompanied by a partner in the Portland banking firm of Ladd & Tilton, made a tour of the Idaho communities to see for himself what changes and improvements were needed in the management of the business of the company. In reporting their departure on the western stage, the *Idaho Tri-Weekly Statesman* suggested: "Their visit will undoubtedly prove of advantage to the Company."[74]

The *Mountaineer* complained about inadequacy of the stage lines from the Columbia River into Idaho since the competing lines had all been consolidated. As usual, the editor had suggestions. A daily line of stages was needed, as was a tri-weekly freight service rather than the tri-weekly stage service that had been introduced since the consolidation. An opposition line was needed from The Dalles via Canyon City to Boise, with a branch going to Owyhee.[75]

There were changes in the ownership of the local stage lines during the autumn. At the end of September, Ed Pinkham, who for a long time had been the agent of Greathouse & Co. in Idaho City, purchased the stage lines from there to Placerville, Centerville, and Pioneer. He planned to place some lighter covered stages on the road for use in the fall, and several sleighs had been ordered for winter use.[76] As winter approached, the residents of both Idaho City and Boise City were concerned over the lack of a daily mail service between the two communities. "A daily mail is much wanted between this city and Boise City," wrote the editor of the *Idaho World.* "The stages run daily, and the Express dispatches letters and packages daily. The mail ought not to lag." "For a long time Greathouse & Co.

[71]*Owyhee Avalanche,* August 4, 1866, p. 3, c. 1, August 11, 1866, p. 2, c. 2 and 3.

[72]*Idaho World,* September 1, 1866, p. 3, c. 1.

[73]*Idaho Tri-Weekly Statesman,* September 6, 1866, p. 2, c. 1 and 2.

[74]*Statesman,* September 7, 1866, p. 3, c. 1; *Idaho Tri-Weekly Statesman,* September 8, 1866, p. 4, c. 1.

[75]*Weekly Mountaineer,* September 7, 1866, p. 2, c. 2.

[76]*Idaho World,* September 29, 1866, p. 3, c. 1, October 20, 1866, p. 3, c. 1.

have gratuitiously furnished a daily mail communication between this and Boise City, as their contract provides only for a tri-weekly service," the *World* reported on December 15, 1866. "They have got tired of doing extra service without pay, and who can blame them? Our people are grateful to them for past favors. It now rests with the Department to give us a daily mail between here and Boise City."[77]

The *Idaho Tri-Weekly Statesman* reprinted an item from the *Idaho Times*, revealing that the residents of Idaho City had made a proposition to Messrs. Greathouse & Co. asking them to continue to carry the mail daily when their stages ran—in exchange for a petition to the Post Office Department asking for an increase in the company's pay to that for daily service. "This is as it should be, and we hope to see the petition generally signed; also, that our Boise City neighbors will take enough interest and go and do likewise," suggested the Idaho City paper. In response, the *Idaho Tri-Weekly Statesman* noted, "Since the above was written we are informed that the daily service has been resumed by Haley, Greathouse & Co."[78]

The big news of October was the order of the Postmaster General to establish a *daily* mail service from Salt Lake City all the way to The Dalles, via Walla Walla.[79] The *Weekly Mountaineer* reprinted a long account from the San Francisco *Bulletin* giving Oregon's Senator John Nesmith the credit for the establishment of the service. The editor, however, resumed his crusade to have the mail delivered from Salt Lake City, via Boise City and Canyon City into The Dalles, rather than via Walla Walla.

> The mail route just established from Salt Lake City to this point will do more than any one thing to bring about the desired results which we have mentioned. The line would be more self-sustaining if it came via Boise City, Owyhee and Canyon City, because it would take so much of the way travel; but we are thankful for any changes that will place Oregon independent of California.[80]

The new daily line was placed in the charge of Ben Holladay. The *Avalanche* reported:

> We have just been shown a letter from the agent of Holladay's Stage and Express Line, at Boise City, stating that orders have been received from headquarters immediately to stock that route to the Dalles as a daily line. Holladay has the mail contract to that point and it is now a fixed fact that his line of stages will be extended to the Columbia River.[81]

The news was hailed in the Oregon newspapers. The *Oregon State Journal* remarked:

> The *Oregonian* has information to the effect that the mail from Salt Lake to the Dalles is to be increased to six times per week. It is said that the new arrangement will go into operation as soon as additional stock can be procured and distributed along the line—probably within a month. This will give us our daily mail direct instead of meandering through Nevada and California as at present.[82]

Although Ben Holladay had the contract for the new daily mail service, he sublet the section from Boise to The Dalles to G. F. Thomas & Co. On October 19, 1866, the *Weekly Mountaineer* stated: "We are informed that Mr. Thomas is now on the road making the necessary disposition of the stock, so that in a week or so we may expect the first overland coach to leave the Dalles."[83]

Hill Beachey's Railroad Stage Line was in full operation by October. The western terminus was at Hunter's Station, a crossing on the Truckee River a few miles east of the Nevada-California line. The connection with the Pioneer Stage Line was at this point rather than at Virginia City, Nevada, as it had been previously. Beachey made arrangements with the Pioneer Stage Line to carry the mails between Hunter's Station and Virginia City. As a result, the difficult stretch of road into Virginia City, used by the earlier line established by Beachey and Carr, could be

[77] *Ibid.*, November 3, 1866, p. 3, c. 1, November 17, 1866, p. 2, c. 1, December 15, 1866, p. 3, c. 1.

[78] *Idaho Tri-Weekly Statesman*, December 20, 1866, p. 2, c. 3.

[79] *Idaho World*, October 13, 1866, p. 2, c. 1.

[80] *Weekly Mountaineer*, October 19, 1866, p. 1, c. 3, p. 2, c. 1, p. 3, c. 1.

[81] *Owyhee Avalanche*, October 6, 1866, p. 2, c. 2. This item was reprinted in the *Idaho World*, October 13, 1866, p. 1, c. 3, and in the *Weekly Mountaineer*, October 26, 1866, p. 4, c. 1.

[82] *Oregon State Journal*, October 20, 1866, p. 2, c. 1, October 27, 1866, p. 3, c. 1.

[83] *Weekly Mountaineer*, October 19, 1866, p. 2, c. 1.

KING, WEBB & CO.

abandoned.[84] Idaho passengers could now travel directly to San Francisco without detouring by way of Virginia City. The *Avalanche* explained:

Through passengers by this line to California need not go to Virginia, and will reach San Francisco in four and one-half days.... Hill Beachey has accomplished what few stage men ever have. He started out alone, made his arrangements, stocked his line of four hundred miles through a wild, Indian-infested country in a few weeks, and has never missed a trip nor arrived an hour behind his time since he started in September. The line is a necessity and we are pleased to inform the public a fixture.[85]

According to a recent scholar, the Railroad Stage Line ran from Hunter's Station via the California Trail along the Humboldt River to Junction House, now Oreana. At this point, to avoid springtime flooding of the river bottoms between Oreana and present Winnemucca, the stage line and wagon road swung eastward through Limerick Canyon and over the Humboldt Range to Unionville, Star City, and Dun Glen. From Star City the route led northward to the Humboldt again at Mill City and from there proceeded upstream along the Humboldt to old French Bridge, renamed Winnemucca on February 1, 1866. Out of Winnemucca the road led northward to Willow Point Station in Paradise Valley on the Little Humboldt River, thence over Paradise Hill Pass to Quinn River, thence to Rattlesnake Creek on the Owyhee drainage, and, after crossing the Owyhee, up Jordan Valley to Reynolds Creek and thence to Silver City. Highway 95 from Winnemucca to Boise roughly parallels this route.[86]

The *Idaho Tri-Weekly Statesman* published an exceptionally early advertisement for the Central Pacific Railroad in December, 1866, revealing the business connection between the railroad and Hill Beachey's stage line.

CENTRAL
Pacific Railroad
OPEN TO CISCO,
93 Miles from Sacramento
FOR FREIGHT & PASSENGERS,

TRAINS LEAVE SACRAMENTO DAILY, Sundays excepted, connecting at CISCO with the stages of the Pioneer Stage Co. for

Virginia City, Austin
And all parts of NEVADA

Also, connect with the Overland Mail Stages for

SALT LAKE CITY,
UTAH AND MONTANA.

The stages of the Pioneer Stage Co. connect at HUNTER'S, on Truckee river, with

Hill Beachey's Line,

To Ruby and Silver Cities, Owyhee: also Boise City, Idaho City, Placerville, Centerville, and all parts of Idaho.

This extension of the
Central Pacific R. R.

In connection with the new Wagon Road now open via Humboldt river, will enable passengers between Idaho Territory, Owyhee and California, to make a trip in FOUR DAYS, being much less time than by another route, and one-half the time formerly consumed via the Columbia river; also at much less risk and expense.

Arrangements for transporting freight have been made to guarantee SPEED, PROMPTNESS and ECONOMY, avoiding delays and damage.

The past season the bulk of Merchandise of Owyhee district has taken this route with satisfaction to shippers. The Railroad is progressing rapidly, constantly shortening the conveyance by teams and reducing the rate of transportation. Merchants and shippers are requested to try this route. Shippers are assured that freight will receive DISPATCH and CAREFUL HANDLING.

Information of the routes cheerfully given by our Agents.

A. G. RICHARDSON,
Gen'l Freight and Passenger Ag't

LELAND STANFORD,
Pres't C.P.R.R. Co.

Office of the Company: San Francisco, corner of Front and California streets, rooms 5 and 6, up stairs.[87]

[84]Goodwin, "Beachey," 29.

[85]*Owyhee Avalanche*, October 27, 1866, p. 2, c. 3.

[86]Goodwin, "Beachey," 29-30.

[87]*Idaho Tri-Weekly Statesman*, December 18, 1866, p. 2, c. 3.

In December, 1866, Hill Beachey received a jolt when the Post Office Department announced that it would receive bids for the delivery of mail over the Railroad Stage route on a once-weekly basis rather than the previous tri-weekly basis. The *Avalanche* at first thought the advertisement a mistake. Then the editor recalled a communication requesting the endorsement of the Chico route for a daily mail service or else the stage company would "fail." Congressman John Bidwell was accused of using his influence to save John Mullan's Chico and Idaho Stage Company by prevailing upon the Post Office to weaken the C.P.-Hill Beachey route and build up the Chico-Red Bluff route. Both the Idaho and Nevada legislatures memorialized Congress to restore the tri-weekly service on Beachey's line. The editor concluded,

> It is a matter of business—business necessities—that make us favor the Humboldt route. The Railroad Stage Line on this route has carried the mails with such promptness as to elicit unqualified public approbation. To have the service reduced to a worthless condition is grossly wrong, and one that no honest man knowingly would favor.[88]

The public outcry was so great, coupled with the Central Pacific's political influence in Washington, that nothing further was heard of the Post Office's attempt. By the end of 1866, it was clear that Beachey's Railroad Stage Line had defeated its rival out of Chico.

MAJOR CHANGES were taking place in Wells Fargo at this time and they were not overlooked by the Idaho press. "Louis McLane, for years the Chief Superintendent of Wells, Fargo & Co.'s Express and Banking House on this coast has gone to New York to assume the Presidency of the Company," noted the *Idaho World*. "John J. Valentine, traveling superintendent of Wells, Fargo & Co. has been paying his respects to Owyhee this week," reported the *Avalanche*. "Taking a superficial view of him, we should say that he is a jolly soul—one that is 'fat, sleek, and sleeps well o'nights,' and gives prompt attention to business at all times."[89]

News of the "Grand Consolidation" of the mail, express, and stage companies reached Boise on November 13, 1866, prompting two announcements in the *Idaho Tri-Weekly Statesman.*

> Consolidated.—A telegram from Salt Lake to San Francisco on the 3d inst. says: A consolidated has been effected between Holladay's overland mail and express company and the Overland Mail Company, the Pioneer stage company, Wells, Fargo & Co. and the American Express Company, under Holladay's charter, with a capital of $10,000,000. It is understood that Ben Holladay secures a million and a half in cash, and a half million in stocks for his Overland Stage Line, and remains a director of the company. Louis McLane has been elected President.

A slightly different version read:

> Great Consolidation of Mail, Express and Stage Companies.—We are informed that in addition to the consolidation of the Holladay Overland Mail and Express Co., and the Pioneer Stage Co., with Wells, Fargo & Co., that the United States Express Co. and the American Express Co., of the Atlantic side, are also included in the new arrangement, which dates from the first of the present month.[90]

Four days later, the *Idaho World* announced the consolidation and reported that business would be conducted under the name of Wells Fargo & Co. A week later, the *Owyhee Avalanche* also learned of the change and suggested: "This consolidation will make an institution of unusual strength and consequently more safe." News of the consolidation also was published in the *Oregon City Enterprise* of December 1.[91]

The significance of the development was recognized by the *Idaho World* in an article entitled "Wells, Fargo & Co."

> This substantial and established Banking and Express Company has lately undergone an almost complete reorganization. . . . they own every mail and express line overland west of the Mississippi, save the comparatively small area still run by Adams' Express Company west of that river and south of the State of Missouri. The new

[88] *Owyhee Avalanche*, December 29, 1866, p. 2, c. 2 and c. 3.

[89] *Idaho World*, October 13, 1866, p. 2, c. 3; *Owyhee Avalanche*, October 27, 1866, p. 2, c. 3.

[90] *Idaho Tri-Weekly Statesman*, November 13, 1866, p. 4, c. 2.

[91] *Idaho World*, November 17, 1866, p. 2, c. 1; *Owyhee Avalanche*, November 24, 1866, p. 3, c. 1; *Oregon City Enterprise*, December 1, 1866, p. 3, c. 1.

Company have sole charge and control of all the stages and express lines between the Mississippi river and the Pacific Coast. They own over 4,000 miles of stage roads, and have control of several railroads, in express and mail matters. Louis McLane, long the Chief Superintendent of the old Company in San Francisco, is President of the new Company, and is stationed in New York City. As he is intimately conversant with all the resources, wealth, prospects, and interests of the whole Pacific coast, his services in his new post will add materially to the benefit of each Pacific State and Territory.[92]

Wells, Fargo & Co.'s basic services to the communities of the Pacific Northwest appeared to be unaffected by the "grand consolidation" for the remainder of 1866. In Idaho City, the *World* published the usual acknowledgments:

We are indebted to Messrs. Paige and Foster, Messengers for Wells, Fargo & Co. between the Dalles and Portland, to Cann, Messenger from the Dalles to Umatilla, and to the Road Messengers hither, for regular files of the Portland papers in advance of the mails. Also to the Agents of Wells, Fargo & Co. in Boise City and here for favors in the same line.

In December, the editor again expressed thanks.

In these days, when the mails fail so frequently, the kindly favors of Wells, Fargo & Co.'s Agents here, and Messengers along the route to Oregon—French, Loup, Shephard, Cann, Paige, Holland, Foster and Jones—by whom we are pretty regularly supplied with the Portland dailies, are most opportune and kindly appreciated. Good gentlemen, all, we thank you.[93]

One change was made shortly after the "grand consolidation." Wells Fargo & Co., which had delivered express over The Dalles-Canyon City line for many months, discontinued the business. With the competition from Holladay removed, and Wells Fargo undertaking the delivery of express and mails throughout the Northwest, the express service on the Canyon City Stage Line was no longer essential. Under the heading, "Sold Out," the *Weekly Mountaineer* announced: "We understand that Wells, Fargo & Co. have sold the express route from here to Canyon City, to Mr. A. W. Buchanan, who will continue the business. Buck is a thorough express man and no doubt will make it pay."[94]

At Portland, the Columbia River steamers arrived almost daily with treasure in the care of Wells Fargo messengers. On November 3, 1866, the *Weekly Oregonian* noted five shipments the previous week running anywhere from $16,000 to $80,000. Each issue of the newspaper for the rest of November reported arrival of dust and bullion worth from $12,000 to $60,000. December brought shipments of $50,000.[95] The final issue of the year reported,

The messenger of Wells, Fargo & Co. brought last evening from the North, $80,000 in treasure. Although the season is so far advanced that travel from the mines is generally supposed to have ceased, we still see miners arriving with their golden store. Last evening's boat from the Dalles brought quite a number of returning gold seekers who seem to have been well rewarded for their toil.[96]

By the end of January, 1867, the *Idaho Tri-Weekly Statesman* had published a series of advertisements explaining the nature of and participants in the consolidation and the new role and network of Wells Fargo. The company operated an Overland Stage and Express Line carrying the mails between the Atlantic and the Pacific, daily, including branch lines to towns in Montana, Colorado, and Utah territories as well as Idaho, Oregon, and Washington. Idaho residents could travel eastward to Omaha and Leavenworth or westward to Sacramento. Fares from Boise, payable in greenbacks, were announced:

From Boise City		to	Helena, M. T.,	$185
"	"	"	Virginia City, M. T.,	160
"	"	"	Bear River,	78
"	"	"	Salt Lake, U. T.,	120
"	"	"	Denver City, Col.,	271
"	"	"	Omaha, Nebraska,	305
"	"	"	Sacramento, Cal.,	318

Messengers were aboard every stagecoach when treasure was transported, and shipments

[92] *Idaho World*, December 8, 1866, p. 2, c. 1.

[93] *Ibid.*, November 17, 1866, p. 3, c. 1, December 8, 1866, p. 3, c. 1.

[94] *Weekly Mountaineer*, December 21, 1866, p. 3, c. 1.

[95] *Weekly Oregonian*, November 3, 1866, p. 3, c. 1, November 10, 1866, p. 3, c. 1, November 17, 1866, p. 3, c. 1, November 24, 1866, p. 3, c. 1, December 8, 1866, p. 3, c. 3.

[96] *Ibid.*, December 29, 1866, p. 3, c. 2.

"Off to the Mines," from Marvels of the New West *(1887)*.

of coin and gold dust were insured at the following rates:

From Boise City to Virginia, M. T.,		4c., coin.
" " "	Salt Lake City,	2 " "
" " "	Omaha or Leavenworth cities,	5 " "
	Tariff on Gold Bars	
From Boise to Leavenworth or Omaha,		4½c.
From Salt Lake City to Omaha or Leavenworth City,		3c.
On Coin or Dust,		3"
On Gold Bars,		2"

Charges for packages and freight were also advertised:

PACKAGES AND FREIGHT:

Our Charges, when 'WAY-BILLED,' will be as follows:

A letter parcel, 'no value,' to Montana or S. L. City	$1.00
" " " Omaha or Leavenworth City,	1.50
Boxes or Cases of Merchandise to Helena or Virginia City, per pound,	75c coin.
Boxes or cases of merchandise, to Salt Lake City, per pound,	50c coin.
From Salt Lake to Omaha or Leavenworth City, per pound,	1.25 cur.

All packages and merchandise were to be carefully protected from the weather by an oilcloth covering inside the shipment case. Letters mailed in Boise would be transported in locked leather bags all the way to their destination.

Wells Fargo continued its fast freight business from Umatilla into Boise, Idaho City, and Ruby City. During the winter, packages weighing thirty pounds or more were carried from Umatilla to Boise for twenty-five cents a pound, to Idaho City for thirty-five cents a pound, and to Ruby for thirty-seven cents a pound. Shipments from Portland cost three cents more per pound. Additional advertisements reminded the public that the company gave special attention to collections and to the forwarding of treasure to all parts of the United States and Europe, carefully insured. Commissions and purchase of goods in both Portland and San Francisco would also receive prompt attention.[97]

Wells Fargo & Co. undertook the responsibility for the delivery of passengers, express, mail, and freight at the most difficult time of the year. Along with all staging outfits, the company had problems with the road conditions in the winter months. "The roads are everywhere terrible," reported the *Idaho Tri-Weekly Statesman.* "The sleighing is good over the Blue Mountains, but the mud is deep all the way from here to there. The road is no better. To Idaho it is snow and mud. The stage has a new batch of snow to break through at almost every trip."[98]

No matter what the condition of the weather and the roads, mail service was a primary concern of residents in the towns along the Columbia River, and in March, 1867, at least one editor reminded his readers that the responsibility was now in the hands of Wells Fargo.[99] In Walla Walla, the *Statesman* came to the defense of the company when residents between there and The Dalles complained about the mails, noting that the mail arrived daily with the stages which were arriving and departing every other day. The Oregon Steam Navigation Company was bringing the mails

[97] *Idaho Tri-Weekly Statesman,* January 31, 1867, p. 2, c. 4, 5.

[98] *Ibid.,* February 6, 1867, p. 2, c. 2.

[99] *Weekly Mountaineer,* March 23, 1867, p. 2, c. 6.

thrice weekly. Wells Fargo was reported to be procuring eight Concord coaches in San Francisco to put on the route between The Dalles and Walla Walla. The journalist suggested: "All that is required is a little patience, and in anticipation of any enterprise, which will give us better mail facilities, and the benefits thereof arising, our people can afford to bear a little while longer."[100] In Portland, the *Weekly Oregonian* complained that the mail for that city was still sent from Salt Lake to Sacramento and northward rather than through Idaho and down the Columbia River. However, the Overland Mail that had once come from the east via St. Louis was now moving through Chicago and Omaha, and Wells Fargo was congratulated by other western newspapers for keeping the mails moving away from the railroad terminus as rapidly as possible.[101]

The shipments of treasure by stagecoach from the Owyhee District and by steamers down the Columbia River continued to be a lucrative business. Wells Fargo's agent in Owyhee reported the following amount of bullion shipped from the company's office in 1866.

Bullion	$660,667.49
Gold Dust	90,216.06
Gold Coin	26,144.05
Legal Tender (coin value)	28,902.74
Total	$805,930.34[102]

The flow of treasure continued in the early months of 1867. By March, each steamboat arriving in Portland carried at least $20,000; the total for the month received by Wells Fargo in the Portland office totaled $122,000. The next month's total was $170,000.[103] At The Dalles, Thomas H. Cann, Wells Fargo messenger, often brought down as much as $40,000 on the steamers. From mid-May to mid-June, the total amount handled was $297,920, slightly less than the amount for the corresponding period in 1866.[104]

[100]*Statesman*, January 25, 1867, p. 2, c. 4.

[101]*Weekly Oregonian*, January 26, 1867, p. 2, c. 2, March 23, 1867, p. 1, c. 2; *Idaho World*, March 30, 1867, p. 2, c. 2, quoting the Denver *Rocky Mountain News*.

[102]*Owyhee Avalanche*, January 26, 1867, p. 3, c. 1.

[103]*Weekly Oregonian*, March 2, 1867, p. 3, c. 2, March 30, 1867, p. 3, c. 2, April 6, 1867, p. 3, c. 1 and 3, April 13, 1867, p. 3, c. 1, April 27, 1867, p. 3, c. 3, May 4, 1867, p. 3, c. 2 and 3, May 11, 1867, p. 3, c. 3, May 25, 1867, p. 3, c. 1, June 1, 1867, p. 3, c. 3, June 8, 1867, p. 3, c. 4, June 15, 1867, p. 3, c. 2 and 3.

[104]*Weekly Mountaineer*, June 8, 1867, p. 3, c. 1, June 22, 1867, p. 2, c. 1 and 2.

An early panoramic view of Idaho City, below, showing the terrain around the Boise Basin.

THE YEAR OF GREATEST ACTIVITY

WELLS FARGO & Co.'s responsibility and effectiveness in providing Overland Mail service was a major source of concern throughout Idaho Territory, as elsewhere in the West, in the spring of 1867. Much of the criticism originated with the editor of the Salt Lake *Vedette*, a newspaper generally critical of the mail service and notoriously hostile to Wells Fargo. The editor of the *Owyhee Avalanche*, thoroughly frustrated with the irregular mails to Silver City, republished every criticism of the service that came out of Utah.

The failure of the mails had been traced to New York City, where the postmaster complained that the lack of sacks with locks compelled him to send valuable mails in standard unlocked sacks. Passengers reported that mail was promiscuously scattered from the Missouri River to Fort Laramie because the worn-out sacks tore readily. Accepting such reports without question, the Owyhee editor asserted: "Such conduct is in every way inexcusable and should be published to the powers that be by every means possible. It is an outrage of the grossest nature." The next week, when the newspaper received only a fraction of the anticipated mail, he stormed:

> There must be a bushel of papers and many letters back belonging to this concern that we know of, and presume that thousands of people in and west of the Rocky Mountains can complain in the same manner—and never be comforted, either. But such is life in the mountains.[1]

In Idaho City, the *World* wrote in much the same vein, repeating reports published in the *Vedette* that no mails had arrived in Salt Lake for several weeks and no newspapers from the east had been forwarded in stagecoaches for ten days. Moreover, the company had refused to book passengers from Boise to Salt Lake City.[2] In response to this latter assertion, the *Idaho Tri-Weekly Statesman* stated:

> We can assure our readers that it is untrue in every particular. Wells, Fargo & Co. are now and always have been taking all passengers that are offered, and they put them through to Salt Lake in four days—sometimes less, sometimes, a few hours more.

The passenger service had been disrupted only for three or four days while the company was constructing a bridge over a different section of the road.[3]

Late in May, the Boise paper republished a letter written by four passengers on the Wells Fargo stage between Denver and Salt Lake and published in the *Vedette*. They asserted that on one occasion three bags of mail had been picked up by overland travelers and brought into a home station after having fallen from the coach unseen by the driver. The correspondents were also unhappy because they had been transported in lumber wagons without seats or springs rather than by a

[1]*Owyhee Avalanche*, April 6, 1867, p. 3, c. 4, April 13, 1867, p. 2, c. 2.

[2]*Idaho World* (Idaho City), May 4, 1867, p. 2, c. 2.

[3]*Idaho Tri-Weekly Statesman* (Boise), May 7, 1867, p. 2, c. 3.

The Dalles, Oregon, a major shipping junction, as photographed by Carlton Watkins in 1867. Used by permission of the Oregon Historical Society.

stagecoach. Following this communication, a long editorial statement expressed disappointment in Wells Fargo's effectiveness in handling the Overland Mail.

When the Overland mail line was in the hands of Ben Holladay it was conducted in a most negligent and careless manner. The destruction of mail bags was notoriously of common occurrence. Nobody expected anything better of him, and there was no hope to escape from the evil while his contract lasted. But the well known character of Wells, Fargo & Co. for promptness and integrity in all their business transactions, promised something better. Their name created a feeling of confidence in the public in the Overland mail line which was never before experienced....

The editor admitted that he had no complaint about Wells Fargo's service in the Boise Basin.

Now it is only fair to say that there has been a great improvement in the management of the line since it came into the hands of W. F. & Co., so far as we have had opportunity to observe from this end of the line, a fact which gives no small satisfaction to the public, but we don't like to hear of such things away out in the plains. A great many things happen to stages and mails which people will grumble and call for the press to notice, without thinking that going through snow and mud and over swollen streams is attended with difficulties. That amounts to nothing, but when there is good evidence of wanton carelessness, we don't think it is any one's duty to overlook it. The Overland mail is a public service of immense importance to all the West.... We don't like to hear of mail bags being "shucked" into mud-holes to drive teams on, nor of their being shook off along the road.[4]

The *Idaho World* launched an investigation of the situation to determine if the agents, drivers or other employees of Wells Fargo were responsible or if the fault was the responsibility of the postmasters along the route. Informants claimed to have seen two or three large piles of printed mail matter along the overland route. At the last crossing of the Platte River there was a large pile of printed matter; one of the sacks was torn open, exposed to the elements and the mercy of all who passed by. Many of the abandoned items were addressed to the newspapers and residents of Idaho. However, the informant added that he was certain the pile of mail had been left there by Holladay's drivers and that Wells Fargo was not responsible for its deposit.[5]

OVERLAND MAIL—This institution is under full control of Wells, Fargo & Co., a Company which bears a national reputation for promptness in express matters, and its reputation has probably saved it from merited criticism in carrying the mails,

asserted the *Avalanche* as it rejoined the anti-Wells Fargo crusade. The editor insisted that the company gave less priority to mail delivery than to express and claimed that not one tenth of the overland newspaper mail had reached its destination in the previous five months and much of the letter mail was known to be lost or delayed. If conditions did not improve, delivery

[4] *Ibid.*, May 28, 1867, p. 2, c. 1.

[5] *Idaho World*, June 1, 1867, p. 2, c. 2.

of the mails by steamer would be preferred. The Indians might be bad and the roads worse; but, the editor concluded in a note of bitterness, "government would do well to note carefully whether the Indians are so troublesome as to prevent the *regular* carriage of the Company's express matter."[6]

As a portion of the responsibility for the failure of the mails to be delivered was attributed to the Indian disturbances on the Great Plains, the Owyhee editor observed: "The sentiment seems gaining a hold upon the Press and public that extermination must take precedence of the blanket and bead and ammunition policy of the Government." He launched a tirade against the "red devils" and "savages" and called for a war of annihilation.

Put all the available troops on the war path and so punish and kill off the Indians to insure the safety of travelers, station-keepers and mails before attempting to start up again.... Passengers should go by Steamer to the States and mails be sent that way until there is a large number of Indians killed on the Plains.[7]

By the end of June, Boise newspaper appeared to be more satisfied with Wells Fargo's service, routinely noting changes in the schedule of the stagecoaches as they steadily attempted to shorten the time of travel.[8] In contrast, the *Avalanche* continued to follow the critical stance adopted by the *Vedette.* The Silver City editor proclaimed that the Overland Mail had become wholly unreliable as a means of communication: "The most reckless and wilfully negligent conduct of Holladay is now rendered creditable compared to that of Wells, Fargo & Co." Critics of the company insisted the stages regularly ran full of passengers, often "dead-head" senators and representatives and noted travelers, carrying express and freight while neglecting the mail—and particularly the newspaper exchanges. The press was called upon to expose the "swindling company."[9]

There were complaints as well about the mail service on the Overland Route between Boise and Umatilla, most often that from the west. The fault was laid at the door of the post office and not Wells Fargo & Co.; the reason was again the shortage of mailbags. The ineffective and now defunct route to Chico was said to have caused the problem: the postmaster in Boise had continued to send the mail by that route long after it had ceased arriving and the bags were invariably lost. Locks were also in short supply, and on alternate days the mailbags were forwarded tied only with a string. Regulations provided that the through mail should be secured with a brass lock that could not be opened at the waystations. As the locks were not always available, the through mail and way mail were being forwarded together in bags under an iron lock—the usual custom for the way mail—so that they might be opened at all the way stations.[10]

Wells Fargo & Co. had unquestionably experienced difficulty in assuming responsibility for the Overland Mail during the winter months. Confusion resulting from the takeover from Ben Holladay in late 1866 had extended into the spring, but by mid-June the *Idaho World* reported a significant improvement in the route and service of the Overland Mail between the Boise Basin and the Columbia River communities. The stages were running regularly from The Dalles to Salt Lake City via Boise,[11] and Wells Fargo had at last caught up with the backlog of mail that had existed when the firm assumed responsibility for the overland mail service.

The company announced a reduction in freight rates on packages over fifty pounds between Boise and Umatilla on June 1, 1867, that cut a third off the earlier winter rates. "We have no doubt that it is a sensible plan for the company; it is certainly gratifying to the public," the Boise *Statesman* commented. The *Daily Oregon Herald* of Portland and the Umatilla *Columbia Press* advertised Wells Fargo's continuing fast freight service. As the summer season opened Wells Fargo also took the opportunity to advertise its long-standing

[6]*Owyhee Avalanche,* June 1, 1867, p. 4, c. 2.

[7]*Ibid.,* June 15, 1867, p. 2, c. 3.

[8]*Idaho Tri-Weekly Statesman,* June 25, 1867, p. 2, c. 3.

[9]*Owyhee Avalanche,* June 29, 1867, p. 1, c. 2, p. 2, c. 3.

[10]*Idaho Tri-Weekly Statesman,* May 4, 1867, p. 2, c. 1.

[11]*Idaho World,* June 12, 1867, p. 2, c. 1.

services as collection agents and forwarders of insured treasure.[12]

FOLLOWING A FIRE in Idaho City in May, 1867, Wells Fargo offices were temporarily located in a brick building that had been previously occupied by a printing concern. The company moved into a new office in July. The *World* revealed,

> Wells, Fargo & Co.'s office in this city was removed on Monday from the quarters temporarily occupied since the fire, to the new and commodious office built and fitted up, expressly for the Company, on the site of the old Poujade House, corner of Main and Commercial streets. The office is eligibly located for the convenience of merchants and miners equally, it is roomy, well adapted, and in every respect a credit to the city.[13]

Wells Fargo's personnel continued to be recognized repeatedly by the various newspapers in eastern Oregon and Washington Territory as well as Idaho Territory for their trustworthiness and service. The *Weekly Mountaineer* at The Dalles commented,

> Mr. Thomas Cann, Messenger of Wells, Fargo & Co. has been in their employ five years this week, running from this city to the upper country, during which time he has brought down over twenty millions of treasure, and has never lost a package or parcel entrusted to his keeping. This is the kind of gentlemen that find employment [with] W. F. & Co. on this coast, and as a rule they are the best business men and the most reliable, we have in our communities.[14]

The company often offered its services without charge to foster worthy causes. An exceptional amount of publicity was given to the company's role in handling funds that were raised in Idaho communities for the Southern Relief Fund, after disastrous floods in the southeastern United States. A ball in Boise had raised $286.27 that was immediately deposited with Wells Fargo to forward to Thomas C. Shelby, the treasurer of the fund for the West Coast, in San Francisco. An additional $486.75 was raised in Idaho City; Wells Fargo immediately published a receipt for the funds and forwarded it gratis in the form of a gold bar to San Francisco.[15]

By midsummer, Wells Fargo's operations were in full swing in Idaho Territory and throughout the Pacific Northwest. Between Portland and Umatilla the company utilized the steamships of the Oregon Steam Navigation Company. The company's express was being carried on the Pioneer Stage Line between Umatilla and Idaho City and all intermediate towns in Idaho, according to the advertisements of John Hailey & Co.[16] Actually, Hailey's Pioneer Line ran only from the Columbia River to Boise; the route between Boise and Idaho City and between Boise and Silver City was controlled by Hailey, Greathouse & Co., with Henry Greathouse largely responsible for the Boise-Idaho City service and Samuel Kelly for the Boise-Silver City route. From Boise to Salt Lake there was the Overland mail and stage service via Helena; from Silver City to the railhead of the Central Pacific en route to San Francisco both express and treasure were delivered by Hill Beachey's stage line. Within the Boise Basin, Wells Fargo's express traveled on Pinkham's line of stages, which radiated out of Idaho City to all the smaller communities.

A most important development in transportation was Wells Fargo's decision in July, 1867, to send passengers from Boise to Benton City, Montana Territory, for $210 as long as the Indian disturbances continued on the Great Plains. At Benton steamer passage to go down the Missouri River to Omaha and St. Louis could be obtained. The stage trip could be completed within seven days, the steamer passage would take from nine to fifteen days. Fare on the river ranged from thirty to sixty dollars and travelers could stop at any point on the Missouri River that they desired.[17]

AT THE BEGINNING of 1867, Idaho citizens had launched a campaign to establish daily mail service on Hill Beachey's line rather than the tri-weekly that had been authorized by the

[12] *Daily Oregon Herald* (Portland), July 4, 1867, p. 1, c. 7; *The Columbia Press* (Umatilla), July 20, 1867, p. 3, c. 5; *Idaho Tri-Weekly Statesman*, June 1, 1867, p. 2, c. 4.

[13] *Idaho World*, May 18, 1867, p. 3, c. 1, July 17, 1867, p. 3, c. 1.

[14] *Weekly Mountaineer* (The Dalles, Oregon), July 13, 1867, p. 3, c. 1.

[15] *Idaho Tri-Weekly Statesman*, May 21, 1867, p. 2, c. 1; *Idaho World*, June 1, 1867, p. 2, c. 1, June 8, 1867, p. 2, c. 4.

[16] *Daily Oregon Herald* (Portland), July 4, 1867, p. 1, c. 7; *Weekly Oregon Herald* (Portland), August 31, 1867, p. 8, c. 4; *Idaho Tri-Weekly Statesman*, July 2, 1867, p. 3, c. 3.

[17] *Idaho Tri-Weekly Statesman*, July 6, 1867, p. 2, c. 4.

A panoramic view of part of Silver City. The largest structure is the Idaho Hotel; the one to its right probably housed Hill Beachey's offices.

federal government. A memorial to Congress was adopted by the territorial legislature asking for such a service from Boise via the Owyhee towns and the post offices in the Humboldt Mining District on to Hunter's Station on the Truckee. A petition with the same request had been circulated in Owyhee. The Central Pacific Railroad and the Pioneer Stage Company, running from the rail terminus into Virginia City, Nevada, were using their powerful influence to increase the service.[18] Advertisements of the railroad clearly emphasized the essential relationship between rail and stage operations:

This extension of the Central Pacific R.R. in connection with the New Wagon Road Now Open via Humboldt River, will enable Passengers between the Territory of Idaho, Owyhee and California, to MAKE THE TRIP IN FOUR DAYS being much less time than by any other route, and one-half the time formerly consumed via the Columbia River; also at Much Less Risk and Expense.

The railroad corporation also emphasized speed, promptness, and economy in handling freight.

The past season the bulk of Merchandise of Owyhee district has taken this route with satisfaction to shippers. The Railroad is progressing rapidly, constantly shortening the conveyance by teams and reducing the rate of transportation. Shippers are assured that Freight will receive DISPATCH and CAREFUL HANDLING.[19]

Not every traveler was impressed with this route. One San Franciscan who had just made the journey described the trip for the San Francisco *Times* as both perilous and uncomfortable. Soldiers did not provide adequate protection, and sensitive citizens would be amused at the huts called "stations" that were "built of sod and gravel with one side occupied by the horses and other used by the station keeper." In spite of the inconvenience, this traveler insisted that the route of Hill Beachey was far superior to the Chico route or the roundabout way by Umatilla and down the Columbia River.[20]

In February, 1867, Hill Beachey and his agent Jo. Coombs were on the stage route distributing new stagecoaches, checking stations and personnel. Beachey also had his stable and stage equipment moved from Ruby City to Silver City and re-erected in connection with the Idaho Hotel on Jordan Street, a much more convenient arrangement for the rapidly growing town.[21] Toward the end of the month, Idaho newspapers reported that Beachey had purchased the interest of his partners in the Railroad Stage Line and was now the sole proprietor. The *Avalanche* offered hearty congratulations to Beachey upon his success and future prospects and paid tribute to his division agents, his "right bowers"—John Early, Charley Combs, and Charley Barnes. In reporting the news, the *Idaho World* commented,

Beachey has sold his line from Boise City to Silver City to Hailey, Greathouse & Kelley, who also own the routes from Boise City to Idaho City, and from Idaho City to Umatilla. Beachey's route to San Francisco is the favorite with Idahoans because it is the safest, shortest, and best in every respect.[22]

[18] *Owyhee Avalanche*, January 5, 1867, p. 3, c. 2.

[19] *Ibid.*, p. 4, c. 2.

[20] *Idaho World*, January 18, 1867, p. 1, c. 1 and 2, quoting the San Francisco *Times*.

[21] *Owyhee Avalanche*, February 16, 1867, p. 2, c. 4, p. 3, c. 2.

[22] *Ibid.*, February 23, 1867, p. 2, c. 2; *Idaho World*, March 2, 1867, p. 2, c. 2.

Years later, John Hailey recalled that the line from Boise City to Silver City was taken over by his partners as part payment for their interest in the route from Owyhee to the railroad.[23] Immediately following the change in proprietorship, Hill Beachey launched an advertising campaign for the new arrangement. His goal was to shorten the time of the journey to three days.[24]

In Idaho City, the interest quite naturally was on the stage lines radiating out of that community.

> Haley [sic], Greathouse & Co. are again running a daily line of stages—sleighs, we ought to say—between here and Boise City, and very generously carrying the mails each day, although their contract is only tri-weekly. Pinkham's line between this city and Centerville, Placerville, and Pioneer City, also runs daily, and thus accomodates all who wish to travel to or from either place.[25]

The Boise *Statesman* called the public's attention to the fact that the Railroad Stage Line would be in bitter competition with the Oregon Steam Navigation Company and the stage lines from Umatilla to Boise during the summer season. The editor was convinced that the returning miners would patronize the Humboldt route because the railroad would be constructed to within two hundred miles of Boise. He concluded:

> We tell you, gentlemen of the O.S.N. Co., and business men of Portland and along the Columbia, that the entire business of Idaho is slipping through your fingers. When we can reach the railroad with two hundred miles of staging, and from that point be within ten or twelve hours of San Francisco, we will have no further use for you. You will miss more of it this year than you did last, and after that it will vanish altogether, though the business itself will be all the while augmenting. Start the Columbia and Salt Lake railroad and that will end the difficulty and become to Oregon and Portland what the Central is to San Francisco and California. Can't you see it?[26]

The *Oregonian* meanwhile contrasted the advantages of building a north-south rail line between San Francisco and Portland with that proposed to run across Idaho to Salt Lake City, insisting the former was more important. The *Statesman* answered: "The Columbia and Salt lake branch is practicable. There is a disposition on the part of the Union Pacific to build it. Help the cause along. Enlist your delegation in Congress in the matter."[27]

In contrast to Hill Beachey's success, the Chico route was being publicized throughout the Pacific Northwest as a scandal. The *Weekly Mountaineer* at The Dalles reviewed the controversy between the Chico *Courant* and the Idaho newspapers concerning the collapse of the mail service in a humorous vein. The *Oregonian* noted the delight of the Columbia River towns when the Idaho newspapers admitted that the Chico route had been a failure and ridiculed the undertaking by General John Bidwell and Captain John Mullan. The *Avalanche* contrasted the speed with which the mails arrived over Beachey's line with the latest uncertainty over the Chico route. Finally, in disgust, the *Avalanche* editor commented,

> Chico Mail—Last issue we announced the non-arrival of said institution for over ten days. It has not yet arrived, and we never heard any one thing so universally execrated in Idaho. . . . The Chico route, good enough in itself, has ever been in the hands of Philistines. Whether the people have a Sampson [sic] at Washington with sufficient jaw-bone to slay them, we can't say. Not wishing any damage to public property, yet should a pillar in the Capital be induced to slop over on some of those villainous contractors, we'd say—amen. Red tape is painfully slow—but the Chico mail never does come on time.

The *Idaho World* denounced "The Chico Swindle," documenting the failure of the Idaho Stage Company to deliver the mails and urging the cancellation of the contract if it could not be transferred to the Humboldt Line of Hill Beachey.[28]

The Railroad Stage Line continued to operate most effectively during the spring of

[23] John Hailey, *The History of Idaho* (Boise: Syms-York Co., 1910), 124.

[24] *Idaho Tri-Weekly Statesman*, February 28, 1867, p. 2, c. 2. An identical advertisement was run in the *Idaho World*, March 16, 1867, p. 2, c. 5. See also *Owyhee Avalanche*, March 30, 1867, p. 4, c. 3.

[25] *Idaho World*, March 23, 1867, p. 3, c. 1.

[26] *Idaho Tri-Weekly Statesman*, March 16, 1867, p. 2, c. 2.

[27] *Ibid.*, March 30, 1867, p. 2, c. 1, March 26, 1867, p. 2, c. 1, and extra edition. The discussion of the comparative advantages of the routes to the Pacific was temporarily terminated by news that the Indians had attacked the stage between Silver City and Boise, with three men killed, the stage rifled, and the mailbags cut open and letters scattered.

[28] *Weekly Mountaineer*, January 4, 1867, p. 4, c. 3, February 8, 1867, p. 1, c. 5; *Weekly Oregonian*, January 19, 1867, p. 3, c. 2; *Owyhee Avalanche*, January 19, 1867, p. 3, c. 2, January 26, 1867, p. 3, c. 3, February 9, 1867, p. 3, c. 2, February 16, 1867, p. 2, c. 4, March 30, 1867, p. 2, c. 2.

1867. Concord coaches had been added to the fleet of "mud wagons" on the route, more horses had been purchased, more drivers and hostlers hired, and more stations built. Hunter's Station was crowded with applicants for seats in April, with business sufficient for a daily line. Business was so brisk that the fare was raised from $60 to $75. Just as things were going very well on the Hill Beachey line, the Indians once again attacked the Summit Springs station and drove off all the stock in the area. A party of twenty-four Indians had driven off sixteen of the stage horses and five more belonging to two teamsters. Pursuit ended in failure, and two days later the same party drove off seventeen horses and mules from Broughton's Ranch, on Flat Creek twenty miles below Camp McDermitt.[29]

Uncertainty over the mail contract continued. In April, the Post Office Department in Washington informed the Ruby City postmaster that the mail contract formerly let to the Mullan group had been discontinued from Chico to Boise City and a new contract for a weekly delivery between Chico and Ruby had been awarded to another Chico resident by the name of F. P. Benjamin. Soon word was received that the property of the California and Idaho Stage Company was being auctioned off in Chico. Under the heading "Flickered Out," the *World* announced: "The Chico and Idaho Stage Company has at last become defunct, and all the stock, effects, etc. sold at auction. It was a great humbug in its day, with Capt. Mullan and Gen. Bidwell as its chief humbuggers." Finally, toward the end of May, the Post Office Department announced another change in the mail service between California and Idaho. The contracts on the Chico route had at last all been cancelled, and the mails were to go via the Central Pacific Railroad to Hunter's Station. As a final word on the subject, the *Avalanche* reported in September that F. P. Benjamin, who had undertaken the mail contract on the Chico route, had failed to perform the service. Now that the rivalry between the Chico and the Humboldt route had been settled and the latter was clearly the more important route, the editor issued a plea for those towns on the old route that were without mail service.[30]

EXTENSIVE CHANGES IN the ownership and operation of stagecoach lines for the delivery of passengers, express, and mails occurred in Idaho Territory during August, 1867. The integrated stage lines running from Silver City to Idaho City and Boise and on to Walla Walla and Umatilla were broken up. The *Avalanche* put it this way: "The stage firm of Hailey, Greathouse & Co., has been dissolved—the same individuals separately running the same route as before. Samuel Kelly has the line from Silver City to Boise City; Henry Greathouse, the one from Boise City to Idaho City; and John Hailey, the one from Boise City to Walla Walla and Umatilla."[31] Some months earlier an "Opposition Stage Line" had been organized to operate between Idaho City and Boise by Lute Lindsey, Billy Hise (a careful and popular stage driver), and McClintock & Stewart. The dominance of Henry Greathouse was being challenged. The editor of the *Idaho World* was steady in his praise of the new partnership throughout the early summer; by mid-June the partners in the Opposition Line had been so successful that they were considering extending their service to Silver City in the Owyhee District and Sam Kelly had a potential rival. In Boise City, the *Statesman* appeared unimpressed by the development of competition on the road to Idaho City. At the end of the month, the *World* again demonstrated its support:

Every trip up and down, between this place and Boise City, the Opposition Line of Lindsey & Stewart gets nearly all the patronage and goes full. We are glad to see this, for they are accomodating owners, their driver is careful, skillful, and obliging, and they make better time, with better stock,

[29]Victor Goodwin, "William C. (Hill) Beachey: Nevada-California-Idaho Stagecoach King," *Nevada Historical Quarterly* (Spring, 1967), 10:31; *Owyhee Avalanche*, April 13, 1867, p. 3, c. 3, April 27, 1867, p. 3, c. 3, May 4, 1867, p. 2, c. 1, May 25, 1867, p. 3, c. 2, June 15, 1867, p. 2, c. 1, June 29, 1867, p. 2, c. 2; *Idaho World*, May 29, 1867, p. 2, c. 1, June 19, 1867, p. 2, c. 1; *Owyhee Avalanche*, April 18, 1867, p. 3, c. 1.

[30]*Owyhee Avalanche*, April 20, 1867, p. 3, c. 2, April 27, 1867, p. 2, c. 2; *Idaho World*, May 4, 1867, p. 2, c. 1; *Weekly Mountaineer*, May 18, 1867, p. 2, c. 5.

[31]*Idaho World*, August 7, 1867, p. 3, c. 1; *Owyhee Avalanche*, August 10, 1867, p. 3, c. 3; Hailey, *History of Idaho*, 124.

than the only monopoly line. Patronize the local line, owned and run by our citizens.[32]

On August 1, 1867, Hill Beachey announced that he would inaugurate a daily service on the Railroad Stage Line and that he had the contract for carrying the mails. In addition, Jesse D. Carr had been awarded a contract to carry the mail between Silver City and Boise, and he had sublet the contract to Beachey. The stage and mail service between Silver City and Boise was daily; from Silver City to Hunter's Station the mail service was also daily, but it was carried on alternate days by pony since the stages ran only every other day.[33]

Late in July, Wells Fargo had put passengers on Beachey's stages and planned to deliver treasure on that route from Boise, Idaho City, and Silver City. Within the first two weeks, $200,000 in treasure was transported by the company over the route, $55,000 of it from Owyhee.[34] John Hailey's Pioneer Stage Company attempted to meet the competition by announcing a new tariff price from all the principal towns in Idaho through to Umatilla, Portland, and San Francisco. The fare from Boise to Umatilla was only $40, to Portland $51.50, to San Francisco steerage, $65, cabin, $80. From Idaho City to Silver City the rates were only $7 to $8 additional. The time from Boise to Umatilla was reduced to two and a half days and from Idaho City and Silver City to three and a half.[35] In response, Hill Beachey posted advertising posters throughout Idaho Territory, Nevada, and California offering tickets for passage from Silver City to Hunter's Station for $50, to Sacramento for $70, and to San Francisco for $75. The time for the through trip was to be less than five days. The *Weekly Oregonian* insisted that the stagecoach journey was much harder than the longer water route by steamer. Time was the key factor. The editor suggested: "Could the time by way of the Columbia, be shortened to eight or even ten days, and the fare reduced to about the same figures, there could be little doubt that most persons would prefer to make the journey this way."[36]

Wells Fargo agents and messengers continued to operate on both the Humboldt and Columbia River routes, handling mails, express, and treasure. The *Owyhee Avalanche* emphasized that the company was transporting gold over the Humboldt route. For the week ending August 16, 1867, for example, the amount shipped was $32,000. Wells Fargo kept a close watch on the changing transportation patterns. The *Idaho World* reported,

> Mr. Woodward, General Traveling Superintendent for Wells, Fargo & Co. came by stage last evening, having travelled all the way from San Francisco by the Central Railroad and Hill Beachey stage route. He informs us that the road all the way to Owyhee is clear of Indians.[37]

The struggle between Hill Beachey's Stage Line and the Hailey interests for Idaho transportation patronage resulted in the elimination of small opposition lines operating in the territory. By the end of August, Henry Greathouse had so improved the service on his line that nothing further was heard of the "Opposition Line" between Boise and Idaho City operated by Lindsey & Stewart. A similar "Opposition Line" had been operated between Boise and Silver City by Jake Brinkerhoff in midsummer, but his interests were purchased and Samuel Kelly soon found himself again without competition. By way of contrast Ed Pinkham, who had close business connections with John Hailey, was not adversely affected by the changing ownership of the Idaho stage lines and continued to operate his Boise Stage Lines. "Ed Pinkham is now running two lines daily from this place," reported the *World*. "He runs his splendid new wagons and fine teams, . . . Pinkham is a tip top stageman, and labors hard to please the public." Month after month, Pinkham continued to carry both the

[32] *Idaho World*, May 25, 1867, p. 3, c. 1, June 1, 1867, p. 3, c. 1, June 12, 1867, p. 3, c. 1, June 15, 1867, p. 3, c. 1, June 26, 1867, p. 3, c. 1; *Idaho Tri-Weekly Statesman*, June 20, 1867, p. 2, c. 2.

[33] *Idaho Tri-Weekly Statesman*, July 25, 1867, p. 1, c. 5; *Owyhee Avalanche*, August 10, 1867, p. 2, c. 2.

[34] *Owyhee Avalanche*, July 20, 1867, p. 3, c. 2, August 10, 1867, p. 3, c. 2 (reprinted in the *Idaho World*, August 14, 1867, p. 4, c. 1).

[35] *Idaho Tri-Weekly Statesman*, July 25, 1867, p. 2, c. 1. A similar advertisement appeared in the *Idaho World*, August 10, 1867, p. 2, c. 4.

[36] *Weekly Oregonian*, August 17, 1867, p. 3, c. 3.

[37] *Owyhee Avalanche*, August 17, 1867, p. 2, c. 2; *Idaho World*, August 10, 1867, p. 3, c. 1, August 17, 1867, p. 1, c. 4, August 21, 1867, p. 3, c. 1.

United States mails and Wells Fargo & Co.'s express.[38]

Wells Fargo was dependent upon Hailey's Pioneer Line to deliver the mails on the overland route, under contract, and its express messengers continued to distribute newspaper exchanges on the route.[39] Moreover, Wells Fargo also continued to make treasure shipments down the Columbia. In July, these shipments ranged from $10,000 to $30,000. Throughout the month of August the steamers arrived in Portland two or three times each week, and on each was a small shipment of treasure. The pattern continued through September, with receipts (usually recorded twice each week) amounting to $12,000, $25,000, $10,000, $20,000, $35,000, and $10,000.[40] On September 28, 1867, the *Columbia Press* of Umatilla commented: "We understand it is the intention of Wells, Fargo & Co. to again ship all their treasure by the Columbia River route, instead of dividing their shipments with the Hill Beachey line." An increase in shipments was noted in early October. The *Daily Oregon Herald* reported: "Heap of Treasure: The Cascades brought down yesterday to Wells, Fargo & Co., $41,000 in treasure from Idaho and eastern Oregon. This is a larger amount than the average of late."[41] And throughout November, the treasure in care of Wells Fargo arriving in Portland amounted to anywhere from $15,000 to $52,000. The *Columbia Press* of Umatilla revealed,

> H. C. Paige, Wells, Fargo & Co. Agent at Umatilla furnished a statement of the treasure which came from Idaho and below for the eleven months ending Nov. 30th, which exhibits a total of 6,406 pounds of dust, valued at $1,444,350, and 958 pounds of bullion, valued at $76,640—a grand total of $1,520,990. This be it observed, is the amount which was sent through Wells, Fargo & Co., and by that route. Doubtless, as much more [was] sent by private hands and through other parties, and an equal amount was likewise dispatched over Hill Beachey's Owyhee and Central Railroad route. The figures show a very handsome gold shipment from Idaho for the year just closing. It will be greater next year, we predict.[42]

The suggestion that Wells Fargo would use the Columbia River route exclusively in delivering treasure proved inaccurate. The company took $83,000 from Silver City over the Hill Beachey-Central Pacific Line during the month of September and shipped gold and silver bullion worth $70,000 over the route in November. "This is quite a nice little sum, and is exclusive of large amounts carried away by private parties," the *Avalanche* observed. At the end of the year the Silver City newspaper stated:

> Wells, Fargo & Co.'s shipment of bullion from this place to San Francisco during the present month, December, amounts to $105,000, all the product of Owyhee, being an increase of $35,000 over that of last month and nearly twelve times as much as was shipped from here in December '66, which was only $9,386. The figures speak for themselves.[43]

In October, 1867, Hill Beachey learned that the Indians had once again attacked his stages. This time it was at the Cottonwood Station about fifteen miles from Silver City; one of the horses was killed, but fortunately neither driver nor passengers were injured.[44] But early in November the editor of the Boise newspaper declared that, all things considered, Beachey's route was superior for Idaho travelers to that down the Columbia via Portland into San Francisco. The only justification for taking the latter route, in his opinion, was business to attend to in Oregon. Moreover, Beachey's route was in every way better than that from Portland up the Willamette Valley to California.[45]

Early in December, Beachey purchased the stage line between Silver City and Boise from Sam Kelly. "Hill Beachey now has control of the entire stage route from Hunter's into Boise

[38] *Idaho Tri-Weekly Statesman*, July 2, 1867, p. 2, c. 2; *Idaho World*, July 3, 1867, p. 3, c. 1, July 10, 1867, p. 3, c. 1, July 20, 1867, p. 4, c. 4, August 21, 1867, p. 2, c. 2, August 24, 1867, p. 3, c. 1; *Owyhee Avalanche*, July 20, 1867, p. 2, c. 3, August 10, 1867, p. 3, c. 3.

[39] *Idaho World*, September 11, 1867, p. 3, c. 1, September 18, 1867, p. 2, c. 3, September 25, 1867, p. 2, c. 3, p. 4, c. 1.

[40] *Weekly Oregonian*, issues from July 6 through September 28, 1867.

[41] *The Columbia Press*, September 28, 1867, p. 3, c. 1; *Daily Oregon Herald*, October 13, 1867, p. 3, c. 1.

[42] *The Weekly Oregonian*, November 2, 1867, p. 3, c. 3 and 4, November 16, 1867, p. 3, c. 1, November 23, 1867, p. 3, c. 3, November 30, 1867, p. 3, c. 3; *The Columbia Press*, quoted in the *Idaho World*, December 18, 1867, p. 2, c. 1.

[43] *Owyhee Avalanche*, November 30, 1867, p. 3, c. 2, December 28, 1867, p. 3, c. 2.

[44] *Owyhee Avalanche*, October 26, 1867, p. 3, c. 1. See also *Idaho Tri-Weekly Statesman*, October 29, 1867, p. 1, c. 5; *Weekly Mountaineer*, November 2, 1867, p. 2, c. 4.

[45] *Idaho Tri-Weekly Statesman*, November 2, 1867, p. 2, c. 2.

City. This is as it should be—Boise City is the proper termination of the Railroad Stage Line," the *Avalanche* commented.

The change will result favorably in a pecuniary point of view for Beachey; and, without detracting from the merits of the former proprietors of the Boise Stage, the public can now rest assured the mails will be carried with the utmost regularity and dispatch.[46]

The *Idaho World* added a comment: "Next Spring he intends to run his stages over the road in the quickest possible time, so that passengers can make the trip between Idaho City and San Francisco in five days certainly, and perhaps in four days. Beachey can do it, and he will."[47] There was not too much activity on the Boise-Silver City road in midwinter. "The Owyhee stage now makes a change from wheels to runner on the hill about two miles from Babington's," the *Idaho Tri-Weekly Statesman* reported. "Mr. Wm. Hise, the driver, says the sleighing from there to Silver is first rate."[48]

WORD OF WELLS Fargo & Co.'s decision to withdraw its express services on the route from The Dalles to Canyon City at the end of 1866 reached Walla Walla in January of 1867. The Washington *Statesman* reported:

Wells, Fargo & Co. have discontinued the express route heretofore established between Dalles and Canyon City. The reason for this I am unable to explain, as the route was always a paying one. A. W. Buchanan, Esq., agent of Wells, Fargo & Co., at the Dalles, is now running a weekly express to Canyon City.[49]

The editor apparently overlooked the fact that Wells Fargo had undertaken to deliver the daily overland mails to The Dalles and that the mail and express service would be carried on the same stagecoaches. The management of the company undoubtedly hesitated to over-extend its services.

[46] *Owyhee Avalanche*, December 7, 1867, p. 2, c. 2.

[47] *Idaho World*, December 11, 1867, p. 2, c. 1.

[48] *Idaho Tri-Weekly Statesman*, December 7, 1867, p. 3, c. 1.

[49] *The Statesman*, January 11, 1867, p. 2, c. 5.

Wells Fargo's headquarters in Idaho City, as shown in Elliott's 1884 History of Idaho Territory.

Mail service continued to be foremost in the minds of both residents and journalists along the Columbia River. The Postmaster General had advertised proposals to carry the United States mail once a week from Boise City to Canyon City, a distance listed as 220 miles. The *Mountaineer* suggested that the distance was only 176 miles and that efforts should be made to increase the service to daily. Editors elsewhere disagreed as to the best type of service needed. At Umatilla, the newspaper editor was concerned that the Omaha mail was being delivered by a stage route twelve miles away when the same service could be performed by a existing steamboat whose terminus was The Dalles. The *Mountaineer* ridiculed the suggestion.

> Certainly the service should be performed by steamboats, and it should be left optional with the Navigation Company to carry the mails whenever they please to do so. The idea of carrying a daily mail on steamboats making tri-weekly trips is ridiculous. Has our neighbor forgotten that navigation on the Columbia above The Dalles is generally closed for about three months in the year?[50]

But on March 1 the Oregon Steam Navigation Company instituted daily service from Portland all the way to Wallula. From Walla Walla a daily mail service was available both to Portland and to Salt Lake via Boise. The editor of the *Statesman* observed: "There is one thing certain, whatever other causes of complaint we may have, certainly we have no reason to complain of a lack of mail facilities."[51]

The *Oregonian* reported on April 13, 1867, that an important change was to be made in the Overland Mail in eastern Oregon. A private dispatch from Senator Henry W. Corbett of Oregon stated that the mails were to go direct from Umatilla to La Grande, instead of making the circuit by Walla Walla.[52] The proposed change in the route became known in Idaho a week later, and the Boise editor was pleased.

> We claim the privilege to share in the satisfaction to accrue from the new arrangement. It has for three years been one of the mysteries of the circumlocution why through mails should be required to be carried around by Walla Walla while the stages have always been making the trip to Umatilla in one day less time. The change will be quite acceptable to the southern portion of Idaho.[53]

In addition to shortening the route, stagecoach service between The Dalles and Umatilla was changed in June from a tri-weekly to a daily service. Stages were to leave each end of the line every morning at three o'clock, going through the same day.[54] Thus Wells Fargo's daily overland mail service could be delivered by stagecoaches on land or down the Columbia River from Umatilla by steamers. Wells Fargo messengers reported that the land route between The Dalles and Umatilla was being improved and the distance shortened by forty miles. Stages were to run regularly from The Dalles to Salt Lake City via Boise.[55]

The Dalles and Umatilla Stage Line, W. M. Ward, Proprietor, had advertised as early as April 20, 1867, that its stages were carrying the overland United States mail, arriving at Twelve-Mile House on the Umatilla River the same day, and connecting with John Hailey & Co.'s Pioneer Line for Walla Walla, Boise, and Idaho cities and Owyhee. The fare was nine dollars, significantly less than passage by steamer. Soon the citizens of Umatilla built an improved road to Twelve-Mile House, and the two stage lines made connections there.[56]

Good news circulated in The Dalles concerning an additional mail service to Boise.

> It was rumored on the street last evening that Messrs. Robbins & Weaver were awarded a contract for carrying the U. S. Mail from here to Boise, via Canyon City, three times a week, commencing on the 1st day of July. We hope there may be some truth in it,

the editor of the *Weekly Mountaineer* observed.[57] A correspondent from The Dalles wrote to the Walla Walla *Statesman:*

> For years it has been the ambition of our citizens to have The Dalles connected with the mining districts by means of a stage line. Several projects have been set on foot at various times, looking to this result; but owing to Indian troubles, and constant outside opposition, the enterprise

[50] *Weekly Mountaineer*, January 4, 1867, p. 2, c. 2.
[51] *The Statesman*, March 1, 1867, p. 3, c. 1.
[52] *Weekly Oregonian*, April 13, 1867, p. 1, c. 2.
[53] *Idaho Tri-Weekly Statesman*, April 18, 1867, p. 3, c. 1.
[54] *Weekly Oregonian*, June 8, 1867, p. 2, c. 2.
[55] *Idaho World*, June 12, 1867, p. 2, c. 1.
[56] *Weekly Mountaineer*, April 20, 1867, p. 2, c. 2, April 27, 1867, p. 3, c. 2 and 3.
[57] *Ibid.*, April 13, 1867, p. 2, c. 6.

was never carried into practical operation. But at last our ambition is to be gratified. Robbins & Weaver intend to run a tri-weekly stage line to the Boise Basin, via Canyon City, as soon as the necessary arrangements can be perfected.[58]

Meanwhile, Buchanan & Co. continued to operate an express service between The Dalles and Canyon City. Messengers reported that the Indians were still stealing stock from the farmers in John Day Valley.[59] The snows of winter were melting in April, with streams flooded and some bridges carried away.

On June 1, 1867, C. M. Lockwood & Co. advertised a new Dalles and Canyon City Passenger and Fast Freight Stage Line that would carry both the United States mail and Buchanan & Co.'s express. Plans called for a Concord coach to leave once a week and make the trip to Canyon City in four days. Passage was $30 and freight was to be carried for twenty-five cents a pound.[60] Then, in mid-June, news arrived that the mail contract between The Dalles and Boise City had gone not to Robbins & Weaver but to the Dalles and Umatilla Stage Company and would be delivered by way of Walla Walla rather than by Canyon City. Moreover, the Oregon Steam Navigation Company has at last yielded to the universal cry for a reduction in fare. Passage from The Dalles to Wallula was expected to be reduced to six dollars.[61]

For a month or six weeks the Dalles and Umatilla Stage Line continued to carry the Overland Mail, Wells Fargo's letter express, and passengers for a fare of seven dollars.[62] Early in July,

Madam Rumor says that the Umatilla & Dalles Stage Company have discontinued their line. If the story proves to be correct, great will be the regret of the traveling public. The Company has been very popular; prices have been reduced, and travelers have expressed themselves much pleased with the line. I [the editor of the Walla Walla *Statesman*] sincerely trust the report may be groundless.[63]

The route to Canyon City, with a hoped-for extension to Boise City, continued in the news at The Dalles. Messrs. Moore & Robbins placed a second stage line on the Canyon City road in July. The Walla Walla editor suggested: "The fact that there is one good stage line running to Canyon City already, argues that the staging business is profitable. If the two companies were to unite, and extend their line to Boise City, a great deal of good would result."[64] It was reported in September that the stages from Canyon City were carrying over two hundred pounds of gold dust, and the 180 miles' distance between The Dalles and Canyon City was being made in twenty-nine hours on occasion. However, the Indians were getting troublesome again. In fact, highwaymen disguised as Indians were attacking freighters on the route until they were captured.[65]

In September, another change was made in the mail deliveries between The Dalles and Canyon City when Ad Edgar & Co. advertised that it had the mail contract with the United States government. Weekly stages would carry not only the mails but fast freight and passengers.[66] For the remainder of the year the two stages—C. M. Lockwood's still carrying Buchanan & Co.'s Express and Ad Edgar's the United States mail—continued to operate regularly. The road remained in good condition through November, a considerable amount of gold dust was being carried, and the Indians were quiet. By December, rains had begun to fall, there was occasional snow, and the roads were said to be in horrible condition.[67] Meanwhile, the determined citizens of The Dalles had circulated a petition asking Congress to establish a tri-weekly mail service to Boise by way of Canyon City. In a long editorial, the *Mountaineer* urged that the proposed road beyond Canyon City be run up the main valley of the John Day River to the Toll House at the foot of the Blue Mountains, a level distance of twenty-five miles. Beyond the mountains on the east side, twenty-five miles' distance, the Malheur River was reached by a steeper grade than that on the west side

[58] *The Statesman*, April 26, 1867, p. 2, c. 2.

[59] *Weekly Mountaineer*, April 27, 1867, p. 3, c. 2.

[60] *Ibid.*, June 8, 1867, p. 3, c. 4.

[61] *The Statesman*, June 14, 1867, p. 2, c. 4.

[62] *Daily Oregon Herald*, July 4, 1867, p. 1, c. 7.

[63] *The Statesman*, July 5, 1867, p. 2, c. 4.

[64] *Ibid.*

[65] *Idaho World*, September 4, 1867, p. 4, c. 1, September 7, 1867, p. 4, c. 1; *The Statesman*, September 6, 1867, p. 3, c. 1.

[66] *Weekly Mountaineer*, September 6, 1867, p. 3, c. 1.

[67] *Ibid.*, November 23, 1867, p. 2, c. 1, December 14, 1867, p. 2, c. 2.

of the mountains. From there to where the proposed road left Willow Creek to newly discovered mining deposits was another fifteen miles. Then it was fifty miles to the Boise Ferry on the Snake River and another fifty miles to Boise. The entire distance from The Dalles to Boise was three hundred sixty miles, the route from Canyon City exactly half that distance. Travel on the route could, according to reports, save a day's travel time. By the end of the year there was a new provider: General Hazard Stevens (son of General I. I. Stevens) had purchased the weekly mail service between The Dalles and Canyon City.[68]

During the summer of 1867, while Wells Fargo's express business and treasure shipments were flourishing in the Pacific Northwest, criticism mounted in many of the western states about the company's handling of the mail contract and about the general service on the overland route. Residents of both Idaho Territory and Oregon learned about the criticism largely by their newspapers, which reprinted items published elsewhere. According to the *Idaho World*:

> The Vedette tells of Wells, Fargo & Co.'s stages coming in regularly to Salt Lake City from the East with passengers and Express, all right; but without the U. S. mail, which they contract to carry. It seems there are now about 200 sacks and bags of letter and newspaper mail between Denver and Salt Lake City, which have been left by Wells, Fargo & Co.'s stages, in order to bring through their own Express and passengers. This gross wrong needs remedy.[69]

The *Owyhee Avalanche* reprinted another tirade from the *Vedette:*

> On Monday evening the Eastern Stage came in [to Salt Lake City] in fine style, with smoking hay horses prancing wildly. It unloaded twenty-two boxes and packages of express matter in front of Wells, Fargo & Co.'s office, consisting of light Summer goods for some of the merchants here, *but not one pound of mail matter did it bring*; although 190 sacks of mails are strewn on the route between here and Denver. As an Express Company, Wells, Fargo & Co. do well, in promptly delivering express matter; but as mail carriers, it is a miserable failure, an injury to the public and a horrid nuisance; and the contract should be given to some enterprising, honest company.[70]

The *Avalanche* launched an attack of its own, largely based on information coming from Utah. Residents in the Salt Lake Valley had telegraphed the New York *Tribune*, complaining about the failure of its newspapers to be delivered by the Overland Mail without the payment of letter postage and urging support in getting that provision in the federal legislation repealed. Wells Fargo was bitterly assailed in the meantime for refusing to deliver papers without adequate postage.[71]

The *Idaho World* continued to complain about the "Postal Swindle" that required letter postage for newspapers but apparently felt the Congress and Post Office Department rather than Wells Fargo were the source of trouble. The law required that newspapers be sent by the shortest route; at the same time, postmasters were to give preference to those routes over which the lowest postage for papers was charged. Postmasters were accused of sending school books and newspapers to Idaho City on the overland route, where letter postage had to be paid, rather than by the ocean route. The editor of the *World* suggested that postmasters were in league with Wells Fargo to deliberately increase the profits of the mail contractors. Upon inquiry, the Postmaster General, through his assistant, insisted that western postmasters were instructed when possible to transmit all books and papers by routes on which special rates were approved. The Idaho City editor urged: "Parties interested ought to see that the Postmasters generally on the coast observe the law as expounded by the Postmaster General. It is especially important to newspaper publishers, news agents and book sellers."[72]

In response to the complaints originating in Utah Territory concerning the failure of the New York *Tribune* to arrive in the overland mail, that newspaper published a long article complaining about the way in which Wells Fargo was handling the service and the responsibility of the federal government—

[68] *Ibid.*, December 28, 1867, p. 2, c. 2.

[69] *Idaho World*, July 17, 1867, p. 1, c. 3, quoting the *Vedette*.

[70] *Owyhee Avalanche*, July 27, 1867, p. 1, c. 3. *The Oregon City Enterprise* reprinted this article and others criticizing Wells Fargo & Co. in its issue of August 10, 1867, p. 2, c. 1 and 6.

[71] *Ibid.*, August 10, 1867, p. 2, c. 2.

[72] *Idaho World*, August 24, 1867, p. 2, c. 2.

which was paying $750,000 a year for the transportation of the mails between the railroad termini.

The contract for this service is held by the express freighting firm of Wells, Fargo & Co. There is a manifest impropriety in allowing any express company to take a contract for carrying the United States mails, ... because there must always be more or less competition between such private companies and the Postoffice; but a recent act of Congress has aggravated the mischief by providing that books, pamphlets, newspapers, and all mailable matter except letters, shall be charged, when sent by overland mail, the full letter postage.... Letter postage is 96 cents per pound; the express charge is $1 per pound, Wells, Fargo & Co., under the laws respecting common carriers are liable for loss and damage, while the postoffice is not.

The result of this system might easily be predicted. We are assured that only a fraction of the mail bags sent west by this route ever reach their destination, while Wells, Fargo & Co. seldom fail to deliver their own packages promptly.... If the company can transport private packages with speed and safety, it is an insult to common sense to tell us that they cannot do the same for the mails.

They have now got into their hands the transportation of nearly all transient printed matter and more than half the letters between California and Utah. Business men are glad to pay the regular postage and three times as much in express charges additional, because there is no reasonable expectation of their correspondence being safely delivered otherwise.[73]

The *Rocky Mountain News* of Denver had for some time been explaining to its readers the reason for Wells Fargo's difficulties in delivering the mails. The editor finally exploded in anger at the New York paper, claiming it had no right to complain because it had protested the efforts of the government to bring the Indians of the Plains under control so the overland mail could be promptly delivered.[74] Also tiring of all the criticism, the *Idaho Tri-Weekly Statesman* came to the defense of Wells Fargo:

There is a decided improvement in relation to mail service on the overland line. The old stock of last January, February and March mails seem to have run out, and the eastern mail is now coming through with all the regularity and dispatch that can be desired. In fact a mail from New York in fifteen days is so much better and different from all past experience that we feel very good about it....

[73]The articles from the *Tribune* were widely reprinted in the West. As late as December 14, 1867, this account appeared in *The Weekly Oregonian*, p. 3, c. 5.

[74]*Rocky Mountain News* (Denver, Colorado), October 16, 1867, p. 1, c. 4.

[75]*Idaho Tri-Weekly Statesman*, September 17, 1867, p. 2, c. 2.

The editor admitted that there was indeed cause for complaint, but not against the directors of Wells Fargo.

During the spring and part of the summer the line did not have adequate protection. We may never know how much the agents and drivers along the line presumed upon that state of affairs to leave the mails along the road. That may have been done when it could not be avoided, but not with the consent of the managers and directors of the company.... If Wells, Fargo & Co. did take a hand at gouging the public funds in an indirect way by performing insufficient mail service, they did no more than three-fourths of the men in the United States do directly when they get an opportunity. But that has not been Wells, Fargo & Co.'s style of doing business, and we don't believe it has the sanction of the company now.

In his opinion, there was no justification for the complaints about the way the service was being conducted in Idaho Territory.

No stage line could be run more promptly than that between this city and Salt Lake. Whenever for any reason a coach is two hours over due another is dispatched to meet it, so that the schedule time adopted by the company shall be fulfilled, though the mail schedule might admit of a longer delay. The agents and drivers are men whom the public here know to be honorable, and who take a pride in sustaining the character heretofore enjoyed by the company.[75]

Under the title of "Wells, Fargo & Co. Again," the Boise editor reported that a larger part of the problem with the back mails had come about because of the severe disruption of the Smoky Hill route in Kansas by Indians and the decision of General William T. Sherman to order all coaches off the route immediately. Wells Fargo was in the position of trying to operate on the Platte River route and gather up the abandoned mails on the Smoky Hill simultaneously. The *Statesman* explained:

We can now, having awaited until the facts came out, better judge of the grand hue and cry against Wells, Fargo & Co. about the mail service on the plains. The whole western country has been in a rage at not receiving the regular mail. ... We learn from reliable authority that the old mails which we have of late been receiving were those that were left in the precipitate retreat from the Smoky Hill route when Gen. Sherman first came west.... We also are credibly informed that when Indian difficulties commenced in the spring and serious trouble became apparent, Louis McLane, the president of the company, proposed to the postoffice department for a sum in addition to the contract price to hire men and protect the route himself and carry the mails through in schedule time. There is no doubt in the mind of any business man on this coast that it would have been done if the proposition had been accepted.[76]

Just as there was disagreement among the newspaper editors in Idaho Territory over the reliability of the mail service, over where the responsibility lay, and over the effectiveness of Wells Fargo in performing the service, there were also differences of opinion in Utah Territory—the source of much of the controversy. In contrast to the extreme hostility of the *Vedette*, the *Telegraph* began to display greater understanding of Wells Fargo's problems in handling the overland mail.

The company had hardly taken possession of the line and put it in proper order, when the trouble on the railroads began. Frequently there would be no mail to carry for a week, and then it would come into them by the car load. Under these circumstances no regularity could be expected. Then the Indian war began which only rendered difficulties worse. Whenever the road was impassable the mails would accumulate. A delay of three or four days would cause the accumulation of more mail sacks than could be transported for ten days.[77]

The same division of opinion among the newspapers existed in Montana Territory, where the Helena *Herald* led the attack upon Wells Fargo and the Virginia City papers—led by the *Montana Post*—defended the company and explained that the problems with the mail service were beyond its control.[78]

Newspaper complaints and controversy finally induced the Postmaster General to dispatch a special agent, General John W. Clampitt, to investigate the mail service on the overland route. The *Rocky Mountain News* welcomed this decision, repeating its view that the blame rested with the government.[79] When Clampitt arrived in Denver in October, 1867, he was accompanied by Colonel James J. Tracy, the general agent of Wells Fargo & Co. The two men remained in Denver for a few days before proceeding on to Salt Lake City, where the postal agent planned to spend the winter. The *Vedette* announced his arrival, and soon the Idaho newspapers announced that he would pay an official visit to that territory and to Montana.[80] The postal agent made no public comment about the mail service; but in later life he reminisced about his inspection trip and the tremendous respect he had gained for James J. Tracy, who became his lifelong friend.[81]

While all the debate concerning the mails raged, Wells Fargo went about the business for which it was established—delivering express, freight, and treasure, selling drafts, or sight exchange, on the eastern states and Europe. In December the company announced "Winter Arrangements," including its Fast Freight Line from Portland into the major communities in eastern Oregon and Idaho.[82]

PROGRESS IN CONSTRUCTION and operation on the transcontinental railroad in 1868 was a prime concern of all stagecoach operators in the American West, including Wells Fargo & Co. The year opened with a severe snowstorm in the Sierra Nevada that blocked the trains of the Central Pacific Railroad. The Union Pacific was also having its troubles in the east. "The Cheyenne Argus complains of a delay in freight on the Pacific Railroad," noted the *Idaho Tri-Weekly Statesman* in Boise. "If the road cannot do business on the first five hundred miles of road built, what will be the result when the track shall be laid through?"[83] Idaho residents, as usual, read about winter storms occuring in all directions. The weather was causing annoying problems to most of the local stage lines. The stage leaving Boise for Silver City had to turn back on occasion, unable to cross the Snake River because of floating ice. In contrast, service on John Hailey's line between Boise and Umatilla

[76] *Ibid.*, September 19, 1867, p. 2, c. 2.

[77] *Oregon City Enterprise*, September 21, 1867, p. 2, c. 2, summarized the explanation in the Salt Lake *Telegraph*, as did many other western newspapers.

[78] W. Turrentine Jackson, *Wells Fargo Stagecoaching in Montana Territory* (Helena: Montana Historical Society Press, 1979), 20-22.

[79] *Rocky Mountain News*, September 4, 1867, p. 1, c. 4.

[80] W. Turrentine Jackson, *Wells, Fargo & Co. in Colorado Territory* (Denver: Colorado Historical Society, 1982); *Idaho World*, October 30, 1867, p. 2, c. 1.

[81] John W. Clampitt, *Echoes from the Rocky Mountains* (Chicago: Belford, Clarke & Co., 1889), 170-171.

[82] *Idaho Tri-Weekly Statesman*, September 12, 1867, p. 3, c. 3, December 21, 1867, p. 2, c. 4; *The Enterprise* (Oregon City), December 21, 1867, p. 2, c. 7.

[83] *Idaho Tri-Weekly Statesman*, January 4, 1868, p. 2, c. 1.

proved to be exceptionally good during early January. The weather was comparatively warm, the water in the Columbia was reported high, and there was no prospect of a freeze-up.[84]

Then on January 11, 1868, the closing of the Columbia River by ice necessitated a series of changes in both express and mail services. S. E. Briggs, Wells Fargo agent in Portland, explained the necessary adjustments to the *Oregonian.*

Mr. Briggs informs us that, in consequence of the closing of navigation of the upper Columbia, no express matter can be sent in that direction for the time being. On the arrival of the next ocean steamer, however, he will dispatch a messenger overland with letters and treasure only.

A messenger was expected to leave The Dalles headed for Portland in time to connect with the ocean steamer. These messengers had to travel by trail with a mule and could not carry over one hundred pounds. As long as the river remained closed, the express would only be carried on a weekly basis.[85] Wells Fargo messengers arriving in Boise reported that the Columbia River was not completely frozen over between Umatilla and The Dalles, but there was so much ice the steamboats could not navigate. The temperature at Umatilla was 17 degrees below zero. The route from the Columbia River into the Boise Basin was now open only because sleighs were in use.[86]

Under these conditions, the Idaho newspapers and Wells Fargo & Co. looked in other directions to maintain communication. The *Statesman* suggested that it was fortunate that "the southern route to San Francisco" was again open to travel and transportation of the mails.[87] The Wells Fargo messenger arrived in Silver City and reported that the stage road over the Sierra was in splendid condition; as proof he brought with him the "heaps of mail that accumulated" during the late storm. Hill Beachey's stages were operating with the regularity of clockwork, delivering the San Francisco mails in seven days.[88]

Meanwhile, the communities along the Columbia River struggled with the problems created by the frozen river. Steamers attempting to force their way through the ice were often stuck. Wells Fargo & Co.'s valiant and reliable messenger, T. H. Cann, managed to reach Portland from The Dalles over the land route in company of A. W. Blakely of the Oregon Steam Navigation Company. The *Oregonian* told of their heroic effort:

Mr. Cann represents the trail as, in places totally impractical, on account of snow and ice.... The snow had filled the cut so as to obliterate all traces of the trail; the snow was frozen over with a solid crust, and the only possible way to follow the trail was to dig away the snow and ice. This of course could not be done by the messengers as it would require too much time. In places where no other course was possible, they dug out the trail with axes and picks but in many places, they made no attempt to follow it preferring to cut their way through the underbrush and logs of the bottom lands and swamps of the mountain's base. Thus, for a considerable portion of the way, they literally cut their way through; and considering the distance—one hundred and fourteen miles—the accomplishment of the trip in three and a half days, exhibits a degree of enterprise, activity and endurance seldom found. Mr. Cann says that after carrying the express for ten or twelve years and having never failed on a single trip, he had not on this occasion the least idea of failure.[89]

The *Idaho World* also told of Cann's exploits, explaining that only letters were being taken through on the route because it was impossible to forward treasure on the way down or to carry packages either way. Checks for treasure were being transmitted so that business difficulties would not be experienced.[90] When messengers returned from Portland to The Dalles, the *Mountaineer* published an extra edition. Cann reported that the return trip was much easier and he hoped to make the next trip in two and a half days.[91]

Hill Beachey's Railroad Stage Line operated without difficulty during the period that the Columbia River was frozen. The stage between Boise and Hunter's arrived and departed regularly, bringing the mails and newspaper exchanges into both Silver City and Boise.

[84] *Ibid.*, January 9, 1867, p. 2, c. 1, p. 3, c. 1; *Idaho World*, January 4, 1868, p. 2, c. 2 and 5, January 8, 1867, p. 3, c. 1.

[85] *Weekly Oregonian*, January 11, 1867, p. 3, c. 3.

[86] *Idaho Tri-Weekly Statesman*, January 14, 1868, p. 2, c. 1, reprinted in the *Owyhee Avalanche*, January 18, 1868, p. 2, c. 3.

[87] *Ibid.*, p. 3, c. 3.

[88] *Owyhee Avalanche*, January 18, 1868, p. 3, c. 3.

[89] *Weekly Oregonian*, January 18, 1868, p. 3, c. 1.

[90] *Idaho World*, February 1, 1868, p. 2, c. 3.

[91] *Weekly Mountaineer*, February 25, 1868, p. 1, c. 2.

Stages left Idaho loaded with passengers every other day.[92] On occasion weather conditions in the Sierra Nevada continued to create temporary delays in passenger and mail service—as in mid-January, when a snow slide between Cisco and Crystal Lake detained the railroad cars for twenty-four hours.[93]

Wells Fargo was sending on Hill Beachey's line not only its express to California but also the silver bullion produced in the Owyhee District, the latter in charge of a messenger. During the month of January a ton and a half of bullion, valued at $150,000, had been shipped.[94] While the Columbia River remained frozen, the Boise *Statesman* confirmed the success of the Railroad Stage Line as a winter route.

> The sleighing is now first rate on the Humboldt route all the way to Hunter's. From Hunter's to Cisco the road is open and good. The usual time is made by Wells, Fargo & Co.'s stages, but the railroad experiences much difficulty from snow for twenty miles beyond Cisco. The track is kept open at enormous expense. It is estimated that it will cost as much to clear the track this winter as to have enclosed twenty miles of it with sheds.[95]

Competitive service continued during the winter. Hill Beachey established a stage office on Montgomery Street in San Francisco opposite Wells Fargo; placed Sam Kelly in charge; and began selling through tickets to the mining communities of Idaho at a reduced rate. Louis Lobenstein, who had for some time been Beachey's agent in Silver City, had decided to enter business for himself; he was replaced by Cornelius Kane, formerly of Hunter's Station.[96] Treasure shipments

[92] *Owyhee Avalanche*, January 25, 1868, p. 3, c. 1; *Idaho Tri-Weekly Statesman*, January 23, 1868, p. 3, c. 1.

[93] *Idaho Tri-Weekly Statesman*, January 28, 1868, p. 3, c. 2.

[94] *Ibid.*, February 1, 1868, p. 3, c. 3, reprinted in the *Idaho World*, February 5, 1868, p. 3, c. 1.

[95] *Ibid.*, February 8, 1868, p. 3, c. 1.

[96] *Owyhee Avalanche*, February 15, 1868, p. 3, c. 3.

The Wells Fargo office in Silver City moved to the Granite Block in time to be nearly hidden by heaps of snow.

continued. A typical weekly shipment in February was $52,000. On March 3, the largest shipment made at one time from Silver City, $58,000, was noted, and the total for the month was $147,000.[97]

As usual, complaints about the breakdown of the mail service during the winter months were heard throughout the West. Somewhat surprisingly, there was little complaint about Wells Fargo & Co.'s responsibility for the Overland Mail between Salt Lake City and Umatilla. The *Idaho Tri-Weekly Statesman* assured the postmasters to the west of Boise that Wells Fargo had failed to bring in the mail from the east on only one occasion all winter. The problem with the mails, the editor suggested, was along the Columbia River and not in Idaho.[98]

The Idaho City editor, far from satisfied, launched a crusade to improve the delivery of the mails. In January, 1868, the blame was placed at the door of Quincy A. Brooks, the special agent of the Post Office Department in the Northwest, who had notified the department in May, 1866, that he had made arrangements with Greathouse & Co. to carry the mails on a daily basis between Boise, Idaho City, Pioneerville, Centerville, and Placerville without additional cost to the government—an extra service that could have cost as much as $7,000 a year. Brooks went on:

> This arrangement, . . . places the U. S. Mail service on an equal footing with Wells, Fargo & Co.'s Express in Idaho Territory and Eastern Oregon. The result is a great increase of business on the part of the Government, with a corresponding decrease in the business of Wells, Fargo & Co.'s Express Company here. The people are delighted with these increased mail facilities, and well they may be.

The infuriated Idaho City editor denounced Brooks for "gross and culpable misrepresentation and duplicity in the matter." In his eagerness to show the department how superzealous he was in securing the maximum amount of mail service for a minimum amount of money, the agent had deceived both the department and the contractor—having assured the latter that undertaking the service on a voluntary basis would result in a more lucrative contract for a daily service. Brooks had on several occasions visited in Boise but had never traveled the thirty-five additional miles to Idaho City, location of the largest post office yielding the highest revenue in the Territory. Brooks was considered treacherous, contemptible, and vile.[99]

A month later, the *Idaho World* renewed its attack upon Brooks, suggesting that he was "so manifestly corrupt and so utterly incompetent in the discharge of his official duties" that he was a "disgrace to the position he holds." New charges were made because Brooks had ordered that the paper mail not be carried between Portland and The Dalles, much to the disadvantage of the inland newspapers. The Oregon Steam Navigation Company had the contract to carry the mail on a daily basis between those communities, but the contract was not enforced. The distance between Umatilla and The Dalles was approximately the same as that between The Dalles and Portland; when the Columbia River was frozen, John Hailey, who had responsibility for the mail deliveries between Boise City and The Dalles, ran stages or sleighs over the route on a daily basis carrying papers as well as letter mail over the route. He had not missed a trip all season. The steamship company, described as a "wealthy monopoly," had prevailed upon Brooks to permit the delivery of the mails over the land route on only a weekly basis. Wells Fargo & Co. filled the void by sending a messenger over the route at least twice a week. The comparison between the service of the government and that of private enterprise was made clear.

> They [Wells Fargo] have not failed to keep up the connection so far, and only for this the Idaho people would be almost entirely cut off from communication with Oregon, below the Dalles, for the winter. The fact that Wells, Fargo & Co. do run the route proves that it can be traveled, and that the mails can be transported over it.[100]

Throughout the winter, the editor of the *World* fumed over the situation, pointing out

[97] *Ibid.*, February 22, 1868, p. 3, c. 2, March 28, 1868, p. 3, c. 3; *Idaho World*, March 11, 1868, p. 3, c. 1.

[98] *Idaho Tri-Weekly Statesman*, February 1, 1868, p. 2, c. 3.

[99] *Idaho World*, January 8, 1868, p. 2, c. 1 and 2.

[100] *Ibid.*, February 12, 1868, p. 2, c. 1.

that T. H. Cann could carry two hundred pounds of treasure over the route but that the United States mails had prohibited newspapers. Despairing of doing anything about the mails, the *Idaho World*, by the end of February, turned to praising Wells Fargo & Co. for keeping Idaho City in touch with events in Oregon. "Wells, Fargo & Co.'s Agents and Messengers along the route from Oregon and the Columbia River, have again during the week supplied us with the last newspapers from below, and we thank them."[101]

The newspapers in Portland and The Dalles confirmed the effectiveness of Wells Fargo's service between the two communities, reporting on the trials and tribulations of the messengers on each trip and expressing appreciation for the delivery of newspaper exchanges. At The Dalles, the *Mountaineer* released extras upon the arrival of Cann and of John Shepard, another Wells Fargo messenger, publishing the latest news from the Pacific Coast.[102] Both the *Avalanche* and the *Statesman* released news items from Portland furnished by Wells Fargo and kept readers informed about what was transpiring along the Columbia.[103]

Finally, on February 27, 1868, the news circulated that the ice in the Columbia River was beginning to break up at Umatilla. However, the river was not yet open to navigation because of the blocks of ice gorging the stream.[104] Meanwhile, the *Oregonian* took issue with the *Idaho World* and other inland newspapers that had attacked Postal Agent Brooks. The Portland paper held that he had no authority to force the hands of the Oregon Steam Navigation Company because the company took the position that the closing of the Columbia River by ice each year was "an act of God." The editor thought the quarrel, if any, was with the Post Office Department for the terms of the contract that had been signed, providing for the delivery of mail by steamboats and no other way. Arrangements for carrying any mail by land had been made by the postal agent on his own authority, in the hope that the Post Office Department would approve of his deducting the cost from the contract price alloted to the steamship company.[105] The Idaho City editor was unreconciled; by mid-March, when the river was open, he compared the mail and express services, noting that the mails brought in Portland newspapers for the end of January when Wells Fargo was delivering those of the first week of March. "The difference in the two channels of communication readers will see," he concluded.[106]

THE BANKING BUSINESS continued to expand in Idaho Territory during the winter and early spring of 1868. The most important development of the previous year had been the organization in May of the First National Bank of Idaho in Boise City, with an authorized capital of $500,000 and $100,000 paid up. B. M. DuRell, a well-known merchant, was president.[107] The First National Bank of Idaho established close business ties with Ladd & Tilton, Bankers, in Portland.[108] Upon his return from the east, DuRell conferred with the editors of the Portland newspapers and stated: "The bank will assist the merchants in bringing dust down to its proper price, and after a year or so setting it aside altogether as a medium of trade."[109] In Idaho City, DuRell's representatives soon displayed $5 notes of the First National Bank, and the local editor reported: "We learn that the Bank is in most successful operation, and that [DuRell] has more business offered than the Bank can accommodate, five to one. The notes go off like hot cakes to hungry boarders on a cold

[101] *Ibid.*, February 15, 1868, p. 2, c. 1, February 19, 1868, p. 2, c. 3, February 22, 1868, p. 2, c. 2, February 26, 1868, p. 3, c. 1.

[102] *Weekly Oregonian*, February 15, 1867, p. 3, c. 2, February 22, 1868, p. 3, c. 2; *Weekly Mountaineer*, February 1, 1868, p. 2, c. 1 and 6, February 15, 1868, p. 1, c. 2, p. 2, c. 5, February 27, 1868, p. 2, c. 2.

[103] *Owyhee Avalanche*, February 29, 1868, p. 2, c. 4; *Idaho Tri-Weekly Statesman*, February 8, 1868, p. 2, c. 1, February 15, 1868, p. 3, c. 1, February 20, 1868, p. 3, c. 1, February 27, 1868, p. 3, c. 1 and 2.

[104] *Idaho Tri-Weekly Statesman*, March 5, 1868, p. 3, c. 1 (the *Owyhee Avalanche* reprinted the news on March 7, 1868, p. 2, c. 4); *Weekly Oregonian*, March 7, 1868, p. 3, c. 3.

[105] *Ibid.*, February 29, 1868, p. 3, c. 3.

[106] *Idaho World*, March 14, 1868, p. 2, c. 1.

[107] *Idaho Tri-Weekly Statesman*, May 2, 1867, p. 2, c. 4; *Idaho World*, May 11, 1867, p. 2, c. 5, p. 3, c. 1.

[108] *Weekly Oregonian*, June 1, 1867, p. 3, c. 2; *Idaho World*, June 1, 1867, p. 1, c. 5, quoting the *Portland Herald*, May 23, 1867.

[109] *Idaho World*, June 8, 1867, p. 3, c. 1, June 12, 1867, p. 3, c. 1.

morning."[110] By the end of June, the Boise *Statesman* reported, "Mr. DuRell has got the rooms nearly finished up in good style. We are assured that the business of the bank is full equal to expectation, which we are glad to hear."[111] The next month the First National Bank of Idaho had leased the brick building on the corner of Montgomery and Commercial streets in Idaho City, lately occupied by Wells Fargo, and announced an expansion of the banking business that including the buying and selling of gold dust, gold coin, and greenbacks.[112] A third branch of the bank was established in Silver City, and the *Idaho World* asserted: "Whatever our Democratic prejudices are against banking institutions it is not to be denied that this bank has filled a want in the various phases of financial transactions in the community, and of exchange requirements abroad."[113]

Even so, by October rumors began to circulate that the bank was bankrupt, apparently started by reports in the Walla Walla *Statesman.*[114] Although the reports were denied in Boise, both the *Oregonian* and the *Mountaineer* had more to say on the subject:

> Idaho Bank Suspension—An item in the Oregonian furnishes a clue to the reported failure of the First National Bank of Idaho. The Idaho Bank had overdrawn on the Bank of California to the amount of $15,000, and the draft being thrown out, gave rise to the report. Subsequent satisfactory arrangements were made, and the business of the bank is now going on as usual. The result, however, is that the notes of the Idaho Bank are in bad odor, and people generally are unwilling to receive them.[115]

Idaho bankers integrated their operations with financial institutions in both Portland and California. For example, the California Building and Savings Banks advertised the "Regulations" concerning the receipt of deposits in San Francisco in January, 1868.[116] Wells Fargo was represented in the Owyhee District by Thos. Cole, Jr., & Co. After getting established in Silver City, the banking firm also established a new bank in Boise. In January, the *Avalanche* reported:

> Thos. Cole & Co. enterprising bankers of this place, have made arrangements and will soon start a general banking business in Boise City. Mr. Cole, the chief business member of the firm, has been doing a successful business here during the last few months. A large portion of the bullion shipped below by Wells, Fargo & Co. over the Railroad Stage Line, is bought by him, for which he pays in coin or greenbacks here, or else gives checks on Wells, Fargo & Co. in San Francisco and various other places, as suits the convenience of the customers.[117]

The banking business in Idaho remained competitive and somewhat speculative. Apparently the First National Bank was forced to close down its business in Idaho City for a time; the *World* reported in February: "To Reopen—DuRell & Co.'s Banking House in this city will be re-opened March 1st, and a large and complete Assay office will be put up adjoining the bank building."[118]

By THE SPRING of 1868, the combination steamer and stagecoach service through Idaho Territory was in excellent operating condition. The delegates from Oregon to the Democratic National Convention announced plans in April to go overland. The Oregon Steam Navigation Co. promised to carry them from Portland to Umatilla in twenty-four hours; John Hailey would land them in Boise in forty-two hours from Umatilla; and Wells Fargo's Overland stages were expected to put them on the Union Pacific Railroad cars five days from Boise City. Thence the train trip to New York, via Chicago, could be made in four days, with the entire trip across the continent completed in twelve days.[119]

Proposals for new stage and express routes and rumors about new mail contracts filled the pages of the Northwestern newspapers. During the winter another strong effort had been made to have a tri-weekly mail ordered between The Dalles and Boise via Canyon City. The *Mountaineer* reported that Wells Fargo

[110] *Weekly Oregonian*, June 29, 1867, p. 3, c. 3.

[111] *Idaho Tri-Weekly Statesman*, June 29, 1867, p. 3, c. 3.

[112] *Idaho World*, July 20, 1867, p. 2, c. 4, p. 3, c. 1 and 2, July 24, 1867, p. 2, c. 4, July 31, 1867, p. 3, c. 1.

[113] *Ibid.*, October 2, 1867, p. 1, c. 4.

[114] *Ibid.*, October 30, 1867, p. 2, c. 2.

[115] *Weekly Mountaineer*, November 9, 1867, p. 2, c. 6.

[116] *Idaho World*, January 11, 1868, p. 2, c. 4.

[117] *Owyhee Avalanche*, January 25, 1868, p. 3, c. 2.

[118] *Idaho World*, February 19, 1868, p. 3, c. 1.

[119] *Ibid.*, April 15, 1868, p. 2, c. 1.

was making strenuous efforts to obtain the mail contract on the route. "Should they succeed," the editor suggested, "we will get our mail matter next summer from New York in less than fifteen days, and our San Francisco letters in about seven."[120]

Wells Fargo & Co. had worked out a schedule to shorten the time from Boise City to Salt Lake to three days and the entire journey to the terminus of the Union Pacific Railroad to seven days by mid-May. The company also reduced fares on the overland route from $305 to $236, legal tender, from Boise to the Missouri River, and fares were also reduced to all intermediate points. Passengers could go to Salt Lake for $100, to Virginia City for $140, and to Helena for $160. As the railroad progressed westward and the roads from Idaho to Salt Lake City improved, additional reductions in fares were anticipated.[121] Many considered travel by stage a pleasant experience. One person arriving in Silver City all the way from Omaha wrote the local newspaper about his experiences and observed about Wells Fargo's stages:

> The "grub" at the stations is . . . better than I was led to expect from those who very likely for want of something sensible to say, disparage the meals. At this season of the year eggs and milk are found on nearly every table and often juicy venison or antelope steak. At some of the stations pies made with fresh canned fruit and fresh peach sauce were a part of the spread. Notwithstanding an occasional old granny of a passenger kicks up a row with an employee of the Company, I will say it without fear of truthful contradition, that taken as a whole the drivers and stationkeepers make every just exertion for the comfort of the passengers. They nor the managers of the Company can prevent storms and other like incidents.[122]

Wells, Fargo & Co. continued regular shipments of treasure from the Owyhee District via the Railroad Stage Line. Inclement weather in March had undermined the road between the mines and the mill, resulting in a monthly shipment of only $80,000. In May the amount increased to $120,580 and in June to $153,965.[123] When shipments for July dropped to $142,000, the editor of the *Avalanche* said optimistically: "Henceforth the bullion shipments will be much greater, and before the end of the year we expect the figures will reach at least half a million per month." This did not come to pass. Thos. Cole, Jr., & Co. continued to forward for Wells Fargo & Co. approximately $40,000 on each of Beachey's stages that departed during September.[124] During the last half of 1868, Wells Fargo, operating through Thos. Cole, was extensively involved in banking operations in Idaho Territory. J. S. Smith, agent for the express company in Silver City, was also the manager for Thos. Cole and performed the usual banking transactions: providing exchange upon the cities of the Pacific Coast and the East and issuing checks on all the Idaho communities in addition to buying gold dust and coin and receiving deposits.[125]

Wells Fargo & Co. continued its interest in the route from Boise to the Columbia and down the river to Portland. The company was interested not only in carrying the mails and shipping express and treasure but also in handling freight. On June 16, Wells Fargo announced the renewal of a fast freight service from San Francisco, via Portland, into Boise, Idaho City, and Silver City. Rates from Portland to Boise were 23 cents a pound, 30 cents to Idaho City, and 33 cents to Silver City. An additional two cents was to be added for shipments coming all the way from San Francisco.[126]

Wells Fargo & Co. had more immediate problems with accidents and robberies on stage lines carrying its express and treasure. One of Hill Beachey's stages overturned near Wagontown, on Jordan Creek, a few miles from Silver City. Two Wells Fargo messengers, George W. French and H. C. Ward, were sitting on the outside next to the driver. As the stage turned over French was thrown against a cottonwood tree; his skull was crushed and he

[120]*Weekly Mountaineer*, February 15, 1868, p. 2, c. 1.

[121]*Owyhee Avalanche*, May 9, 1868, p. 1, c. 3, May 23, 1868, p. 1, c. 2 and 3; *Idaho Tri-Weekly Statesman*, May 23, 1868, p. 3, c. 2.

[122]*Owyhee Avalanche*, May 23, 1868, p. 1, c. 2 and 3.

[123]*Ibid.*, May 9, 1868, p. 2, c. 2, May 30, 1868, p. 2, c. 1, June 6, 1868, p. 3, c. 3, June 27, 1868, p. 2, c. 1. These reports were regularly reprinted in the *Idaho World*.

[124]*Ibid.*, August 1, 1868, p. 3, c. 1, September 5, 1868, p. 2, c. 3, September 12, 1868, p. 2, c. 3, September 26, 1868, p. 3, c. 3.

[125]*Ibid.*, July 11, 1868, p. 3, c. 5, July 15, 1868, p. 2, c. 5, July 18, 1868, p. 3, c. 1.

[126]*Idaho Tri-Weekly Statesman*, June 16, 1868, p. 3, c. 2; *Idaho World*, June 24, 1868, p. 2, c. 4.

died instantly. Ward was thrown in from between the wheel horses that were kicking furiously to extricate themselves. Although badly hurt, he saved his life by grasping the leg of one of the horses to prevent it from striking his head. Henry Greathouse was inside the stage with his wife and daughter, all of whom were unhurt. Everyone insisted that the driver, Charles Livermore, could not be blamed for the accident; he was moving slowly around a sharp bend in the road just before daylight when the accident occurred. Apparently on a narrow grade, the front wheels of the stage hit a small rock that kept the wheels from turning and caused the stage to run up the side of the bank so far that the stage was upset and rolled over one and a half times.[127]

Periodic stage robberies also received full coverage in the press. One traveler arrived in Boise from Virginia City, Montana, in May of 1868 and reported a holdup in Portneuf Canyon on the route between Salt Lake City and Helena in which the passengers were robbed and the Wells Fargo treasure box seized. It was empty. The highwaymen were reported to have fled the scene, passing through Boise on their way to Oregon.[128]

Then in August, 1868, one of John Hailey's stages en route from Boise to Umatilla was robbed in the Blue Mountains—creating a sensation. The Wells Fargo messenger had just laid down his gun and was in the process of striking a match on the bottom of his boot to light a cigarette when two men, one from either side of the road, stepped out and ordered the stage to stop. Four highwaymen marched the passengers (also four in number), the driver, and the messenger away from the stage for a distance of thirty feet. While two men kept them under guard, the other two robbers removed the Wells Fargo treasure chest along with the registered mail. The passengers were then permitted to return to the stage. After taking the "shooting irons" of the Wells Fargo messenger, the highwaymen unhitched the horses, taking them some distance before tying them to a tree. Their actions indicated they were experienced at the business. After an unusual delay, Wells Fargo announced a loss of $13,000 and offered a reward of $5,000.[129]

A month later, when three of the highwaymen had been captured by law-enforcement officers, Wells Fargo revealed the reason why the announcement of the loss had been so slow.

> It is now known that, by some means, the Agents of Wells, Fargo & Co. along the road in Union and Umatilla counties had an intimation that the robbery was intended, and accordingly loss of treasure was guarded against. The treasure was taken out at La Grande, and bags of shot and bars of lead and iron were substituted, and it was this valueless stuff that the robbers got from the treasure box the morning of the robbery. The real treasure went safely to its destination subsequently.[130]

Soon it was learned that remnants of the Plummer Gang who had not been rounded up by the vigilantes in Montana Territory were at work in Idaho, and in short order eleven men were captured and sent off to Portland in charge of federal marshals. While being transported by stage two of the culprits, named Wheeler and Savage, had jumped out of the stage not far from La Grande. Wheeler was captured three days later but Savage remained at large. A $200 reward was advertised for his capture.[131]

The robbers were brought to trial in Portland in November. There were eight of them, charged with either robbing the United States mails or aiding and abetting the act. The bill of indictment was complicated and the

[127] *Idaho Tri-Weekly Statesman*, September 26, 1868, p. 3, c. 2; *Idaho World*, September 26, 1868, p. 2, c. 2; *Idaho Tri-Weekly Statesman*, September 24, 1868, p. 3, c. 1; *Weekly Mountaineer*, October 2, 1868, p. 2, c. 4.

[128] *Idaho Tri-Weekly Statesman*, May 30, 1868, p. 3, c. 1, June 2, 1868, p. 3, c. 1. Oregon newspapers republished accounts. See *Weekly Oregonian*, June 6, 1868, supplement, p. 1, c. 5, and *Weekly Mountaineer*, June 6, 1868, p. 2, c. 5. The *Owyhee Avalanche* printed an abbreviated version.

[129] *Idaho Tri-Weekly Statesman*, August 6, 1868, p. 2, c. 2; *Weekly Mountaineer*, August 7, 1868, p. 2, c. 2; *Columbia Press*, August 8, 1868, p. 3, c. 1; *Weekly Oregonian*, August 8, 1868, p. 3, c. 2, August 15, 1868, p. 3, c. 2; *Idaho World*, August 8, 1868, p. 2, c. 1; *Owyhee Avalanche*, August 8, 1868, p. 2, c. 2.

[130] *Idaho World*, September 8, 1868, p. 2, c. 1.

[131] *Owyhee Avalanche*, September 5, 1868, p. 3, c. 3, September 12, 1868, p. 2, c. 1, September 19, 1868, p. 2, c. 1, September 26, 1868, p. 2, c. 2; *Weekly Oregonian*, September 5, 1868, p. 3, c. 3, September 12, 1868, p. 2, c. 1; *Weekly Mountaineer*, September 4, 1868, p. 2, c. 2; *Idaho World*, September 16, 1868, p. 2, c. 1; *Oregon State Journal* (Eugene), September 19, 1868, p. 2, c. 4.

charges serious because conviction for robbery of the United States mails and using deadly or dangerous weapons to do so made those accused subject to capital punishment. Sixty men were called to serve on the jury before twelve were selected. The trial turned out to be surprisingly brief; the culprits were found "guilty of robbing the mail, without putting the life of the carrier in jeopardy." Thus they were saved from the death penalty. Three were sentenced to ten years, two to seven years, and one to five years. Two were discharged. Others who were suspected of involvement in the crime had their cases held over until the next term of court.[132]

WELLS FARGO & Co. was used to dealing with such perennial problems as accidents on the road and stagecoach robberies. While they could not be anticipated precisely, they were part of the risk of the express and passenger business. But in the closing months of 1868 far more serious problems loomed for the company—including the possible loss of lucrative mail contracts and the establishment, with the encouragement of the railroad builders, of rival express companies in the West.

[132] *Weekly Oregonian*, November 14, 1868, p. 2, c. 3, December 5, 1868, p. 3, c. 2; *Idaho World*, November 26, 1868, p. 2, c. 3; *Weekly Mountaineer*, December 4, 1868, p. 2, c. 1.

The town of Silver City as it appeared in the late summer or early fall of 1868.

THE RAILROADS AND THE DEMISE OF STAGING

AS THE TRANSCONTINENTAL railroad neared completion, the directors of Wells Fargo & Co. recognized that it was essential to transfer their express service to the railroads. But the builders of the Central Pacific and the Union Pacific had other plans for the delivery of express—by companies controlled by the railroads. While the Central Pacific was struggling to cross the Sierra, two of its directors, Charles Crocker and Lloyd Tevis, organized the Pacific Union Express to compete with Wells Fargo. This rival company had filed a certificate of incorporation for the purpose of carrying on a general express, exchange, forwarding, collecting, and commission business in both the United States and foreign countries as early as December 18, 1867. The Pacific Union Express had a capital stock of $3,000,000 administered by trustees, many of whom were capitalists, bankers, and railroad executives; its managers on the Pacific coast were A. K. Grim and Lawrence W. Coe. Idaho residents learned of the incorporation in January of 1868, and the news was, quite naturally, welcomed: competition might mean lower prices for the delivery of express.[1]

Reports from California indicated that the Pacific Union Express was making arrangements to commence business on May 1, 1868.[2] Five days later, the eastern section of the Central Pacific Railroad, awaiting the joining of the two sections in the Sierra, had reached Lake's Crossing on the Truckee River at Truckee Meadows (soon to be renamed Reno). Hill Beachey established the interchange with his Railroad Stage Line at that point.[3] As an indication of future developments, the Pacific Union Express challenged Wells Fargo to races between Reno and Virginia City every time the train arrived. These symbolic races over a distance of thirty-two miles received publicity throughout the West, and Wells Fargo was regularly the winner.[4]

Soon the competition became more serious, when the Pacific Union Express announced in the western Nevada newspapers that the company's franked envelopes would be sold at $3 per hundred or five cents each for a lesser number. Wells Fargo, which had traditionally charged ten cents for an envelope, had previously reduced its price for individual envelopes to five and one-half cents. The public welcomed the lively competition, whose impact was soon felt in Idaho communities. In Silver City, for example, the Wells Fargo office was selling envelopes for $50 per thousand or five and one-half cents individually.[5] But rumors began to circulate that the Pacific Union

[1] *Idaho Tri-Weekly Statesman* (Boise), January 4, 1868, p. 2, c. 2; *Owyhee Avalanche* (Silver City), January 11, 1868, p. 2, c. 1.

[2] *Owyhee Avalanche*, May 9, 1868, p. 1, c. 2.

[3] Victor Goodwin, "William C. (Hill) Beachey: Nevada-California-Idaho Stagecoach King," *Nevada Historical Society Quarterly* (Spring, 1967), 10:33.

[4] W. Turrentine Jackson, "Racing from Reno to Virginia City by Wells Fargo and Pacific Union Expresses," *Nevada Historical Society Quarterly* (Summer, 1977), 20:76-92; *Owyhee Avalanche*, July 11, 1868, p. 3, c. 5.

[5] *Idaho Tri-Weekly Statesman*, August 13, 1868, p. 3, c. 2; *Owyhee Avalanche*, September 5, 1868, p. 2, c. 2.

Express was attempting to negotiate with the Central Pacific Railroad for an exclusive contract to carry express on the railroad. Any agreement of that nature could produce major repercussions in transportation and communication in Idaho Territory.

Progress on the construction of the Central Pacific Railroad was eagerly reported in the Idaho newspapers. Some 3,000 "Chinamen" were said to be shoveling snow from the railroad track and the connection between the two sections of the track in the Sierra was expected to be made toward the end of May or early June.[6] "Hurrah for the Cars," the *Avalanche* proclaimed, as the railroad shortened the distance from the Owyhee mining district in southwestern Idaho to San Francisco.[7]

As THE TIME approached for the renewal of mail contracts, rumors and speculations found their way to the columns of the newspapers in eastern Oregon and Idaho. When Postal Agent Quincy A. Brooks arrived at The Dalles to inspect the route to Canyon City, the *Mountaineer* was convinced that the through route to Boise City would be approved.[8] At the end of June, 1868, the *Avalanche* published a telegraphic dispatch to the effect that the contract for carrying the daily mail between Salt Lake City and The Dalles, via Canyon City, had been awarded to Lockwood & Co. At the same time, a telegraphic dispatch from Washington revealed that Wells Fargo & Co. was the highest bidder for carrying the overland mail between the termini of the Pacific railroads and therefore would not continue the service. It appeared that a Chicago man by the name of Carlton Spaides was the lowest bidder and had been awarded the contract for $1,000 a day.[9] In time, it was learned that Lockwood had indeed received the contract for mail deliveries between Salt Lake City and The Dalles. However, delivery was to be on the previously established route and not via Canyon City. Confusion continued to prevail over the contract between the railroad termini.

In Boise, under the heading of "New Line," the *Statesman* announced in early September that C. M. Lockwood, the new mail contractor, was en route to Oregon with a large band of horses and mules to stock the line between Boise and Salt Lake before undertaking to begin delivery of the United States mail on October 1. John Hailey was to continue as the subcontractor, just as he had been under Wells Fargo & Co., to carry the mail from Boise to The Dalles. "The fare will be materially reduced on this line, through tickets can be purchased at either terminus of the line, the accommodations will be as good as can be expected, and with opposition the fare and time will make it an inducement for eastward bound travelers," the editor suggested.[10] Wells Fargo met the competition on this route by racing to prove its speedier service. The *Idaho World* reported:

> In a late race from Salt Lake City to the Dalles, between Mr. Taylor, Road Superintendent of Wells, Fargo & Co., and C. M. Lockwood, of the Dalles, Lockwood made the whole trip through in seven days. Mr. Taylor fell sick on the way, but managed to have Dick Griffin, one of Hailey's Road Agents, to hasten on in his stead, and, fast as Lockwood would push ahead, Dick beat him to the Dalles about eight hours.[11]

Lockwood's contract, commencing on October 1, 1868, was to expire on June 30, 1870. "Wells, Fargo & Co. dispatched their last stage for Salt Lake City last Wednesday, their contract for carrying the mail on the route having expired. This evening the last stage will arrive in Salt Lake," the *Idaho Tri-Weekly Statesman* reported October 3, 1868.

> On Thursday Lockwood & Co. started the mail on their first regular trip. We understand it is their intention to keep the line up to the standard of efficiency to which Wells, Fargo & Co. have brought it. It will require good work to do that, for the time lately has been only about three days between Boise City and Salt Lake. The stage arrived yesterday 2¼ hours less than three days from Salt Lake.[12]

[6] *Idaho Tri-Weekly Statesman*, May 9, 1868, p. 2, c. 1.

[7] *Owyhee Avalanche*, June 27, 1868, p. 1, c. 2 and 3.

[8] *Weekly Mountaineer* (The Dalles), April 25, 1868, p. 2, c. 4, June 13, 1868, p. 2, c. 1.

[9] *Owyhee Avalanche*, June 27, 1868, p. 3, c. 2.

[10] *Idaho Tri-Weekly Statesman*, September 5, 1868, p. 3, c. 1.

[11] *Idaho World* (Idaho City), August 29, 1868, p. 2, c. 4.

[12] *Idaho Tri-Weekly Statesman*, October 3, 1868, p. 3, c. 2.

Three days later, under the heading "Gone From Our Gaze," the Boise newspaper reported the departure of Wells Fargo's division agents and drivers with the stages belonging to the company. "The old jerkies and coaches very much reminded us of an inland circus departing from a 'burg' after an unsuccessful exhibition," the editor observed. "We are indeed sorry to lose the association of these gentlemen, but hope that some future enterprise may bring them among us. We learn that they proceed to Salt Lake, and from thence to other fields of labor, which will be assigned them by the company."[13] According to John Hailey, Wells Fargo had hoped to make a deal with C. M. Lockwood to sell its live and rolling stock on the road but had not been able to do so.[14]

Hailey also remembered that the change "created some confusion for a while." At The Dalles, the *Weekly Mountaineer* stated that Hailey was running *daily* stages between there and Umatilla. Shortly a correction appeared to the effect that he was running a two-horse thoroughbrace wagon every other day, carrying the mail only, and alternating days with the steamer service of the Oregon Steam Navigation Company.[15] At this critical time, a serious accident occurred on John Hailey's line. As the stage was coming down John Day River Hill the brake gave way, the horses became frightened and unmanageable, the stage turned over at the bottom of the hill, and Thomas Turner, the driver, was killed.[16]

Hailey's Pioneer Stage Line between Boise and Umatilla, now bridging the distance in two and a half days, announced a reduction in passenger fares. From Boise City to Umatilla, the new rate was $30; to Baker City, $20; to La Grande, $25. Passengers for Portland could travel through for $45. Hailey's contract with Wells Fargo for carrying fast freight had now expired, and he announced that he would continue to carry it at sixteen cents a pound between Umatilla and Boise and to Idaho City for twenty-five cents.[17] Meanwhile, C. M. Lockwood & Co. advertised extensively in both the Salt Lake and Idaho newspapers.[18] Both Wells Fargo and C. M. Lockwood & Co. transferred personnel at this juncture: Wells Fargo's assistant clerk in Idaho City was transferred to Boise; Lockwood disposed of his interest in the Dalles and Canyon City Stage Line to Ad Edgar, and H. H. Wheeler, a stage driver, was transferred to Salt Lake City.[19]

The Cold Springs Ranch stage station, north of Glenns Ferry, in about 1918.

As THE CENTRAL Pacific continued construction across Nevada during the summer and fall of 1868, the Railroad Stage Line moved its western terminus. The rail service had reached Wadsworth, 194 miles from Sacramento, in July. The track had actually been laid to Oreana, 85 miles below Winnemucca, but the freight and passenger cars were not yet running to that point. Wells

[13] *Ibid.*, October 6, 1868, p. 3, c. 1.

[14] John Hailey, *The History of Idaho* (Boise: Syms-York Co., 1910), 125.

[15] *Weekly Mountaineer*, October 9, 1868, p. 2, c. 1, October 16, 1868, p. 2, c. 1.

[16] *Ibid.*, October 16, 1868, p. 2, c. 2, October 23, 1868, p. 2, c. 1; *Weekly Oregon Herald* (Portland), October 24, 1868, p. 4, c. 2.

[17] *Idaho World*, October 24, 1868, p. 3, c. 1.

[18] *Owyhee Avalanche*, October 17, 1868, p. 2, c. 4; *Salt Lake Daily Reporter*, October 28, 1868, p. 2, c. 4.

[19] *Idaho Tri-Weekly Statesman*, October 22, 1868, p. 3, c. 1; *Weekly Mountaineer*, November 20, 1868, p. 2, c. 1.

Fargo & Co. was using two messengers with its express on the stage line and Beachey provided a third, all "armed to the teeth."[20] By August, the Central Pacific was actually running to Oreana, further shortening the stage trip. Eugene Howard, Beachey's agent in Boise, regularly dispatched stages loaded to the brim for the 145-mile trip to the railroad terminus. The time of stagecoach departures and arrivals was scheduled to connect with the trains so passengers could go through to Sacramento or San Francisco in three days.[21]

Although there was great satisfaction with the passenger and express service on the Railroad Stage Line, there were complaints about the irregularity of the mails into Idaho City. The *Avalanche* immediately came to the line's defense. The government had inaugurated a system of delivery whereby all the mails went through under brass lock to Boise and from there were redistributed to Silver City and Idaho City, causing a slight delay. Even so, the mail arrived more quickly than that sent by the Columbia River. The *Statesman* in Boise was also offended by the criticism in the *Idaho World*. The Idaho City editor replied that he had criticized the mail service and not that of Hill Beachey. Moreover, he had considered it a public duty on occasions to criticize the Overland Mail service of both Wells Fargo and John Hailey's Pioneer Stage Line, yet both had continued to advertise in his columns; in contrast, Beachey's agent had offered to pay for favorable notices—an offer refused, as was a free pass on the stages—yet he had always praised the line that did not advertise in his columns.[22] Two months later the *Avalanche* was complaining about the ineffective mail service from California and Nevada. Apparently Idaho mails for California were tossed off the train at Reno, taken by stage to Virginia City, resorted, and then sent back to Reno and on to California points. No one blamed Beachey.[23]

The Central Pacific Railroad moved rapidly across Nevada. By the middle of August the tracks were at Brown's Station on the west shore of Humboldt Lake and late in the same month at a place known as Black Stage Station in Big Meadows operated by George Lovelock (a location whose name was changed by railroad officials to Lovelock). Early in September the interchange point for rail cars and stages was at Humboldt City station, forty-three miles below Winnemucca. Beachey's stages were coming into Silver City from the railroad in two days. By the middle of the month the rails were at Winnemucca and only forty hours of staging were required.[24] Now that the shortest route had been established, a "Table of Distances" was published for the 223-mile trip between Silver City and Winnemucca.

TABLE of stations and distances between Winnemucca and Silver City, I. T., as used by the Railroad Stage Line:

Stations.	Miles.
Toll House	10
Paradise	10
Cane Springs	14
Buffalo	7
Rebel Creek	8
Flat Creek	11½
Rock Creek	9
Quin's River	20
Ten Mile Creek	10
Jackson Creek	13
Summit Springs	5½
Battle Creek	9
Rattle Snake	14
Dry Creek	16
Sheep Ranch	11
Inskip's	12
Lockwood's	13
Tracy's	12
Wagontown	9
Silver City	9
Total	223[25]

W. C. Child, for a year or more the Wells Fargo agent at Walla Walla, was transferred to the new express office in Winnemucca.[26]

[20] *Idaho Tri-Weekly Statesman*, August 1, 1868, p. 3, c. 5; *Owyhee Avalanche*, August 8, 1868, p. 2, c. 2 and 4.

[21] *Idaho Tri-Weekly Statesman*, August 20, 1868, p. 3, c. 1, p. 2, c. 5, August 22, 1868, p. 3, c. 2, August 25, 1868, p. 3, c. 2.

[22] *Idaho World*, June 27, 1868, reprinted in issue of July 8, 1868, p. 2, c. 2 and 3; *Owyhee Avalanche*, July 4, 1868, p. 2, c. 2.

[23] *Owyhee Avalanche*, August 22, 1868, p. 2, c. 1.

[24] *Ibid.*, September 5, 1868, p. 2, c. 1, September 17, 1868, p. 2, c. 2.

[25] *Ibid.*, September 27, 1868, p. 4, c. 2.

[26] *The Weekly Oregon Herald* (Portland), September 12, 1868, p. 3, c. 2. Just as Owyhee County residents were primarily concerned about construction on the Central Pacific, Boise residents noted progress on the Union Pacific, which was within ninety miles of Green River. *Idaho Tri-Weekly Statesman*, August 29, 1868, p. 2, c. 1 and p. 2, c. 2.

In spite of being the highest bidder to carry the overland mail between the railroad termini, on October 1, 1868, Wells Fargo was authorized to continue the service. Spaides & Co. had offered to carry the mails for $335,000. Wells Fargo officials—realizing that between the time the bids for the overland mail service were requested and the actual letting of the contract, Congress was likely to amend the law to include not only letters but all the paper mail for delivery—had put in a bid for $1,300,000. When Spaides had been pressed to carry out his contract, he insisted that his offer had anticipated the carrying of only 640 pounds a day, with increases in compensation on a pro-rata basis for all above that. The volume of the overland mail had actually reached close to three tons a day, or nine times more than Spaides had offered to carry for $335,000, and he was in fact asking approximately two and a half times as much as Wells Fargo. The Post Office Department was obligated to deliver the mails; only Wells Fargo had the equipment and the experience to undertake the immediate responsibility. The terms of a new contract authorized the payment of $1,750,000 per annum for transporting the mails 800 miles between the railroads.[27]

Before the details of the agreement were publicized, both the new contract and the service performed by Wells Fargo came under bitter attack spearheaded by newspapers such as the *Frontier Index* at the Union Pacific terminal towns and the *Vedette* of Salt Lake City. More understanding of the overall problem appeared in the *Rocky Mountain News* of Denver. The *Idaho Tri-Weekly Statesman*, initially supportive of Wells Fargo, reprinted the *Rocky Mountain News* editorial suggesting that "our vote would be to give a good price for efficient service rather than any price, however small, for poor service."[28] The Salt Lake *News* also recognized the heavy load of mail matter that Wells Fargo

[27]*Rocky Mountain News* quoted in *Idaho Tri-Weekly Statesman*, November 3, 1868, p. 1, c. 5.

[28]*Ibid.*

The upper terminal of the Oregon Steam Navigation Company's portage railroad on the Washington Territory side of the Columbia. Photograph courtesy of the Oregon Historical Society.

The Bascomb-Stricker store at the Rock Creek Stage Station, as it appeared in 1978. The station was established in the 1860's to serve travelers on the Oregon Trail.

was suddenly called upon to carry. On the three days preceding October 22, the company's mail coaches had unloaded in Salt Lake City 13,000 pounds of mail matter from the east bound for the Pacific states and territories.[29]

By November, all three southwestern Idaho newspapers had adopted a negative attitude toward Wells Fargo, which no longer directly operated a stagecoach and mail service in the territory. Critical news stories and editorials appearing elsewhere were regularly reprinted. The *Avalanche* released an article from the *Sacramento Bee* claiming that Wells Fargo was refusing to transmit mails from the terminus of the Central Pacific Railroad until orders were received to do so. Rather than waiting patiently for a few days, the Sacramento editor suggested, the postmaster could send the mails to the east by sea until the railroad could be completed and the "old coaches" be superseded.[30] Although the editorship of the Silver City newspaper changed in early November, when W. J. Hill and H. W. Millard sold out to John McGonigle, the complaints about the overland mail continued. "Uncle Sam does pay for the transportation of the mail. He is a careless old coon about his employees," commented the new editor.[31]

The Pacific Union Express was causing a great deal of the confusion about deliveries over the Central Pacific and the overland mail. As early as August, newspapers in the Pacific Northwest had published reports that the Pacific Union Express had obtained the overland mail contract that had recently been let to the parties who underbid Wells Fargo. A. K. Grim, president of the former company, was reported to be in Salt Lake making arrangements to transport the mails.[32] (This report was, of course, false.) However, the Silver City newspaper welcomed an "Opposition Express" to Wells Fargo, the east-west transcontinental rail-stage route. The Pacific Union Express had also given a subcontract to Hoag & Ramsdell to operate from Silver City to the railroad to compete with Wells Fargo on Beachey's Railroad Stage Line. In November, E. L. James, the traveling agent for the Pacific Union Express, was in Silver City with the intention of establishing an express office there within thirty days. Soon the local editor's loyalty shifted from Beachey and Wells Fargo to Hoag and Ramsdell and the Pacific Union Express. "We are placed under obligations to the conductors of the 'Opposition Fast Freight' for California

[29]*Salt Lake News* quoted in *Idaho World*, October 31, 1868, p. 2, c. 1.

[30]*Owyhee Avalanche*, October 24, 1868, p. 4, c. 2.

[31]*Ibid.*, November 28, 1868, p. 2, c. 3.

[32]*Weekly Oregon Herald*, August 22, 1868, p. 3, c. 3; republished in *Owyhee Avalanche*, August 29, 1868, p. 2, c. 1.

papers in advance of the regular, or Wells, Fargo Line." In December, the newspaper again noted that the opposition line, via Flint, Three Forks, and Camp McDermitt, was making extraordinarily good time with careful and efficient drivers who were delivering both passengers and freight in good time and order.[33]

Henry Greathouse, another long-time stage operator on the important route between Boise and Idaho City, was like Hill Beachey experiencing competition. In July, John Buckley had established a passenger and freight line operating tri-weekly between the two Idaho communities, charging $5 in currency or one-fourth ounce of clean gold dust for passage. In September, Buckley sold out to Joe Mason, who operated the line on the same schedule.[34] There appeared to be sufficient business for both lines. Late in October, the *Statesman* observed that Joe Mason "comes down loaded to the guards, and in time quite as good if not better than the old line. Day before yesterday the opposition arrived in Boise an hour and a half or more ahead of Greathouse." This comment so angered Henry Greathouse that he refused to carry the *Statesman* on his stages. When Greathouse wrote the editor, "If the Opposition makes better time you had better send your papers that way," the editor replied, "That suits us exactly.... Mr. Greathouse is under no obligations to carry our papers in his way packet, nor we to furnish his drivers and office with papers for nothing. This is a free country, you see, and 'honors are even.'"

The feud continued, the *Statesman* encouraging competition by reporting the time of arrival of the rival stages and the number of passengers carried. Greathouse was now offering to carry passengers for one dollar from Idaho City, but travelers preferred to pay the full price of three dollars and a half to the opposition. "This is unusual in the history of oppositions, and argues one of two things: the superior management and accommodation of the opposition or the unpopularity of the old line."[35]

In November, the *Idaho World* reprinted a bitter attack upon Wells Fargo from the *Frontier Index*, suggesting that company agents were trying to cover up the fact that letters in the United States mails had been opened and the contents rifled.[36] Even the *Idaho Tri-Weekly Statesman* shifted away from its pro-Wells Fargo attitude and joined other Idaho journalists in criticism, suggesting that the company had the contract for carrying the mails between the railroad termini at their own price because the Postmaster General had no other choice. "The outrageous manner in which they are performing the service is becoming notorious," observed the editor. With little appreciation for the tremendous backlog that accumulated during the weeks when no delivery contract was in force and the great increase in the volume of mail and papers that had to be delivered under the 1868 contract, the Boise newspaper suggested that the company should provide two stages—and if they could not carry all the passengers and mails, then three or four could do so.[37] The Boise paper also reprinted an "explanation" of Spaides' failure to undertake the overland mail contract that had first appeared in the *Chicago Tribune*. According to this rationalization, the initial bidder did know about the additional mail to be carried under the new law, and the Post Office Department would not give him additional compensation for overload nor the necessary time to prepare for delivery. Moreover, A. H. Barney, president of Wells Fargo & Co., had offered a large sum of money to him and others interested in the contract to forfeit. Such libelous accusations were never proven.[38] It was eventually understood that Wells Fargo's contract provided only for a *maximum* of $1,750,000. The price for carrying the mail was to be reduced on a pro-rata basis of the distance remaining as each mile of the Pacific Railroad was completed. If the railroad

[33] *Owyhee Avalanche*, September 5, 1868, p. 2, c. 4, p. 3, c. 2, October 17, 1868, p. 2, c. 2, October 31, 1868, p. 2, c. 3, November 14, 1868, p. 3, c. 2, November 28, 1868, p. 2, c. 3.

[34] *Idaho Tri-Weekly Statesman*, July 9, 1868, p. 3, c. 1, July 28, 1868, p. 2, c. 5; *Idaho World*, July 15, 1868, p. 2, c. 4; *Idaho Tri-Weekly Statesman*, September 12, 1868, p. 1, c. 1, p. 3, c. 1.

[35] *Ibid.*, October 31, 1868, p. 2, c. 2, November 3, 1868, p. 2, c. 1, p. 2, c. 3, November 7, 1868, p. 2, c. 2.

[36] *Idaho World*, November 26, 1868, p. 2, c. 3.

[37] *Idaho Tri-Weekly Statesman*, November 24, 1868, p. 2, c. 1.

[38] *Ibid.*, December 5, 1868, p. 1, c. 5.

was finished by July, 1869, as expected, the contract would cost the government about $750,000.[39]

The Portland *Oregonian* and *Herald*, both concerned with the delivery of the overland mail into their city from Boise, exchanged comments on the terms of the contract and the possibility of mail delivery during the winter when the Columbia River was frozen over. The *Herald* initiated the exchange by stating that the United States paid "in the neighborhood of $300,000 annually" for the delivery of the mail from Salt Lake to Portland and expressed grave concern that Postal Agent Brooks offered no assurance of winter delivery. The *Oregonian* took exception by stating that the contract for carrying the mail from Salt Lake to The Dalles was $140,000 and from The Dalles to Portland $10,000—half the figure suggested. Moreover, Brooks had notified the Post Office Department about the importance of keeping communication open during the freeze-up period. By December, the *Herald* was ready to capitulate.

> Postal Agent Brooks says he has written to the Department saying that he would put on extra service in case the Columbia River closes on the overland route to Salt Lake City, unless forbid to do so. This is all right, and all we could expect or ask. Had Mr. Brooks informed us of this determination we should have made no reference to the matter, except to commend his action.

Even so, the most important question remained unanswered. Would the mail carried over the land route include the paper mail or just the letter mail, as had been the case the previous season?[40]

In spite of the criticism of Wells Fargo by the Idaho press, newspapers continued to accept and recognize services by the company's personnel. The editor of the *World* appreciated the receipt of newspapers all the way from Baltimore and Sacramento from his "good friends" Wells Fargo & Co. The Boise paper regularly expressed appreciation for California exchanges and added: "When the Statesman does not reciprocate, please let us know."[41]

Wells Fargo also continued to handle Idaho treasure. During the month of September, the company carried $146,043 from Silver City to San Francisco. Thos. F. Cole, Jr., & Co., Bankers, continued to handle these treasure shipments and conduct a banking business under the supervision of Wells Fargo. The *Avalanche* reported on November 14, 1868,

> Thos. F. Cole & Co., bankers, and Wells, Fargo & Co.'s offices have been removed from the old quarters to Messrs. Cole & Walbridge's fireproof granite building on the opposite side of the street. The office looks splendidly, and the appearance of their magnificent vault will produce a discouraging impression upon feloniously inclined.

Both Thos. Cole, Jr., and Webb & Myrick advertised their banking services in the Silver City newspaper at the close of the year.[42]

THE RAPID construction of both the Union Pacific and the Central Pacific in the closing months of 1868 necessitated repeated adjustments by stagecoach operators. By the first week in October, the Union Pacific railhead was at Green River; it was expected to be at Bryan (twelve miles farther west) by mid-month.[43] By early November, the Central Pacific track had moved on sixty miles farther to Argenta. Wells Fargo & Co.'s stagecoaches connected at that point, but Hill Beachey remained at Winnemucca as the rails headed on eastward.[44] Progress was also being made in the construction of the Union Pacific. In Boise, the *Statesman* reported:

> From our eastern exchanges we learn that the bridge is completed across the Green River and the track laid to Ham's Fork, twenty-one miles this side of Green River. Iron for ninety miles more is lying at different points near the end of the track. The three mile force of track-layers had been doubled, and they intend to lay six miles a day. The grading is so far advanced in Echo and Weber canyons that

[39] *Oregon State Journal* (Eugene), October 17, 1868, p. 4, c. 1.

[40] *Weekly Oregon Herald*, December 12, 1868, p. 3, c. 2, p. 4, c. 2, December 19, 1868, p. 3, c. 2, December 26, 1868, p. 4, c. 2; *Weekly Oregonian* (Portland), December 12, 1868, p. 3, c. 2.

[41] *Idaho World*, October 10, 1868, p. 2, c. 3, October 28, 1868, p. 2, c. 2; *Idaho Tri-Weekly Statesman*, October 24, 1868, p. 3, c. 1; *Owyhee Avalanche*, October 10, 1868, p. 3, c. 2.

[42] *Owyhee Avalanche*, November 14, 1868, p. 3, c. 1, December 19, 1868, p. 1, c. 2.

[43] *Salt Lake Daily Reporter*, October 3, 1868, p. 3, c. 1.

[44] *Owyhee Avalanche*, October 3, 1868, p. 2, c. 4, p. 3, c. 2, November 7, 1868, p. 2, c. 1; *Idaho Tri-Weekly Statesman*, October 29, 1868, p. 2, c. 1; *Salt Lake Daily Reporter*, November 6, 1868, p. 3, c. 2; *Weekly Mountaineer*, November 20, 1868, p. 2, c. 3.

it is proposed to make a temporary track around the tunnels and not wait for them to be completed.

Three days before Christmas, Salt Lake newspapers reported that Wells Fargo's stages were connecting with the railroad at Evanston, Wyoming, and running from there into Salt Lake City.[45]

At the end of 1868, Hill Beachey—still operating his stages between Boise and Winnemucca—decided that he should extend his service southward to the new mining district of White Pine, Nevada. Agents were dispatched to make the necessary arrangements, and Beachey promised that in a short time he would be ticketing passengers through from Boise to White Pine.[46]

On February 1, 1869, John Hailey obtained the mail contract on the Salt Lake City-Dalles route from C. M. Lockwood and purchased all the stock and equipment on the line. Hailey had previously delivered the mails on the route from Boise City to The Dalles by way of Umatilla, on a subcontract, and had also carried Wells Fargo & Co.'s express. Now he took over the entire line, and Wells Fargo's express was aboard all the way. Hailey immediately made a personal inspection of the new route and changed the name of his stagecoach service from the Pioneer Stage Line to the Boise City Stage Line.[47] The *Idaho World* reported that he hoped to connect with the railroad at Ogden about the first of May. "Passengers can then go through from Boise City to Chicago in seven days. Mr. Hailey has reduced the stage fare materially, and he will keep the road well stocked with fine American horses."[48]

As early as January, 1869, Wells Fargo was searching for a new route between the railroad termini to the north of the Great Salt Lake rather than to the south. Major Howard Egan was employed to locate a suitable stage route from Humboldt Wells to Bear River and north, and the next month he had succeeded in finding one by way of Meadow Creek, Duff Creek, and Promontory City, a distance of 209 miles. The road was reported to be well watered, with grass and timber most of the way and only a few tracts of desert.[49] The changes brought about by railroad construction were clearly illustrated when Wells Fargo started shipping bullion east by the railroad from the Reese River—treasure that had traditionally been carried west to San Francisco. When the first seven bars started on their journey on February 11, 1869, the *Idaho Tri-Weekly Statesman* observed: "This is a 'straw!'"[50]

Both Wells Fargo and John Hailey were frustrated by the periodic breakdown of service on the Central Pacific and Union Pacific between February and April, making their delivery service either late or erratic. Snow slides at several places in the Sierra Nevada during February meant that no California mail was received in Idaho. Wells Fargo managed to get express delivered by having it carried through the snowbanks by messengers on snowshoes.[51] The eastern mail did not arrive in Boise because of a snow blockade on the Union Pacific west of Laramie. Each issue of the *Salt Lake Daily Reporter* gave accounts of the blockage of the rail line. Wells Fargo sent out five extra stagecoaches to the Wasatch Mountains and managed on March 9 to bring them into Salt Lake City loaded with the mail and express matter, the first to reach Salt Lake City in three weeks. Even so, the Idaho mails were further delayed out of Salt Lake.[52]

The Union Pacific Railroad completed construction into Ogden on March 8, 1869. The company had laid out a town seven miles north of Ogden, at the crossing of the Bear River, that was expected to be the switching place for Montana and Idaho territories and therefore a

[45] *Idaho Tri-Weekly Statesman*, October 27, 1868, p. 2, c. 2; *Salt Lake Daily Reporter*, December 15, 1868, p. 3, c. 1, December 18, 1868, p. 3, c. 1, December 22, 1868, p. 3, c. 1.

[46] *Idaho Tri-Weekly Statesman*, December 31, 1868, p. 3, c. 1.

[47] Hailey, *Idaho*, 125; *Owyhee Avalanche*, February 6, 1869, p. 3, c. 1; *Salt Lake Daily Reporter*, February 7, 1869, p. 3, c. 2, February 16, 1869, p. 3, c. 3; *Idaho Tri-Weekly Statesman*, February 11, 1869, p. 3, c. 1.

[48] *Idaho World*, March 11, 1869, p. 2, c. 1.

[49] *Salt Lake Daily Reporter*, February 5, 1869, p. 3, c. 2; *Idaho Tri-Weekly Statesman*, February 13, 1869, p. 2, c. 4.

[50] *Idaho Tri-Weekly Statesman*, February 23, 1869, p. 2, c. 2.

[51] *Owyhee Avalanche*, February 20, 1869, p. 3, c. 1.

[52] *Salt Lake Daily Reporter*, March 3, 1869, p. 3, c. 1, March 5, 1869, p. 3, c. 2, March 7, 1869, p. 2, c. 2, March 16, 1869, p. 3, c. 1; *Idaho Tri-Weekly Statesman*, March 4, 1869, p. 2, c. 2, March 16, 1869, p. 3, c. 1.

place of considerable importance. The town was named Corinne, and by March 24 lots were being sold at auction.[53] Early in April, Wells Fargo was running its stagecoaches from Corinne to the end of the Central Pacific tracks.[54] Meanwhile, Ogden and Idaho residents were being told by John Hailey that they need not purchase tickets all the way into Salt Lake City if they were headed east because the railroad ran to the north of the lake. His stage road passed within fifteen miles of Monument, a railroad station on the Central Pacific eighty miles west of Ogden, and he expected to survey a road to that point shortly. Readers were also informed:

> From Ogden to Monument Point is where the contest lies between the Union Pacific and the Central Pacific Railroad companies. The Central Pacific Company, which starts at Sacramento, want to complete the line and make the connection at Ogden, while the Union Pacific want to come west as far as Monument Point. Each company have graded the line side by side between these two points, and each is striving to get the right of way, in order to secure that much more land granted as a subsidy by the United States. A compromise, however, is expected soon, and the entire road will probably be completed by the 15th or 20th of this month.[55]

On April 10, 1869, the *Idaho Tri-Weekly Statesman* expressed doubts concerning the location of Corinne as the capital of the Inland Empire. John Hailey also had reservations. He planned to survey the most direct route from Boise to the transcontinental railroad within the next sixty days, and there were indications that the point of connection with the railroad would be anywhere from twenty to fifty miles west of Corinne. One thing was clear: in the next eighteen months the passenger and freight business from Idaho communities to the railroad would equal that to Umatilla and the Columbia River. Hailey hoped to reduce the distance on the stage road from Boise to the railroad to two hundred miles.[56]

As the Central Pacific and Union Pacific railroads approached a junction, Wells Fargo worked to maintain mail deliveries. Throughout April, snowstorms continued to block the rail lines, alternating between the Sierra Nevada and the mountains east of Salt Lake City. Corinne remained the center of attention. The *Reporter* moved its base of operations there from Salt Lake and assumed a new title, *The Utah Reporter*. No postmaster had been appointed for the new town, and the residents found themselves without postal facilities, so the public turned to Wells Fargo for aid. "Wells, Fargo & Co. are still public benefactors," stated the *Utah Reporter*. "Their envelopes are transmitted with the utmost dispatch and cost but ten cents per envelope .... Those sending letters to Corinne should enclose them in Wells, Fargo & Co.'s envelopes."[57] Mail deliveries into Idaho seemed to improve toward the end of April, when the eastern stage brought ten sacks of mail weighing over one thousand pounds into Boise.[58]

Events now moved rapidly. Railroad officials began to gather in northern Utah by April 29, 1869. The Union Pacific and Central Pacific were joined on May 11 and official ceremonies were reported on May 12. The *Utah Reporter* noted: "The last run by Wells, Fargo & Co.'s stages between the termini of the two roads was made May 9, 1869. The distance, eight miles, was accomplished in forty minutes."[59]

While Wells Fargo established a base in Corinne for its stagecoach, express, and mail service into Montana Territory, Hailey looked elsewhere. Throughout May, he was surveying a road from Boise City to the railroad that crossed the Snake River below Salmon Falls, to connect with the rails at Indian Creek. At the beginning of the month he operated out of Corinne, then moved temporarily to Promontory Point and back to Corinne. By June 1, he had established his headquarters at Indian Creek. The trip there from Boise by stage was expected to take forty hours, but he allowed himself three additional hours to make

[53] *Salt Lake Daily Reporter*, March 10, 1869, p. 3, c. 2; *Idaho Tri-Weekly Statesman*, March 23, 1869, p. 3, c. 1.

[54] *Salt Lake Daily Reporter*, April 8, 1869, p. 3, c. 2.

[55] *Weekly Oregon Herald*, April 10, 1869, p. 3, c. 2.

[56] *Idaho Tri-Weekly Statesman*, April 10, 1869, p. 2, c. 2.

[57] *Salt Lake Daily Reporter*, March 16, 1869, p. 3, c. 1, March 19, 1869, p. 3, c. 2; *Utah Reporter* (Corinne), April 24, 1869, p. 2, c. 1.

[58] *Idaho Tri-Weekly Statesman*, April 24, 1869, p. 2, c. 1.

[59] *Utah Reporter*, April 29, 1869, p. 3, c. 1, May 11, 1869, p. 2, c. 2, May 12, 1869, p. 2, c. 1 and 2, p. 3, c. 3.

certain he connected with the train.[60] The *Utah Reporter* published an elaborate advertisement of John Hailey's service, now known as the Idaho and Oregon Stage Line, operating from Indian Creek through Idaho and eastern Oregon to Umatilla and thence by steamer into Portland.

IDAHO AND OREGON
STAGE LINE.
From and After JUNE 1st, the undersigned will run a
DAILY LINE OF COACHES
To and From the C. P. R. R. Company's Cars at
Indian Creek
THROUGH
IDAHO TERRITORY
AND
EASTERN PART OF OREGON,
CONNECTING WITH THE
OREGON STEAM NAVIGATION COMPANY'S
STEAMERS
On the Columbia River, at Umatilla City, for
Portland, Oregon.
RATES OF STAGE FARE (CURRENCY) AND TIME.

From			Time
Indian Creek to Boise City,	—	$ 60	2 days
" " Baker City,	—	85	3 "
" " Uniontown,	—	90	3 "
" " Lagrand,	—	95	3½ "
" " Walla Walla,	—	110	4 "
" " Umatilla,	—	110	4 "
" " Portland,	—	115	5½ "

JOHN HAILEY, Proprietor.[61]

In Boise, Hailey advertised his stage line and mail service under a different name: The Overland & Oregon Stage Line. E. S. Hubbell, his agent at an office adjoining the Overland Hotel, stated that the trip to Indian Creek would take forty hours, that to Umatilla forty-eight hours. The fare to Indian Creek was $60 in currency; to Umatilla, $40; to Portland, $50 in coin. Fast freight would be carried to the railhead for twenty cents a pound, currency, and to Portland for fifteen cents, coin. The editor of the *Statesman* noted that time and distance had been shortened and fares all along the route reduced. Hailey had made many moves along the railroad but had resolved, at least for the present, to keep his junction at Indian Creek, which was 240 miles from Boise.[62]

Hill Beachey had been extending his stage line from Boise and Silver City to the railroad and on south into the White Pine Mining Distrct, which was expected to boom by the spring of 1869. Service began in January. According to the Boise *Statesman*,

> Hill Beachey's railroad stage line has reduced the fare to White Pine, and also the time through. Their posters announce a few days since the time to be seven days. Agent [Eugene] Howard now informs us it is five days, and the fare is twenty dollars less. The road never was in better condition.[63]

Early in March, Beachey was making plans to shift his headquarters on the railroad from Winnemucca to Elko.[64] The expected White Pine boom had not materialized. In March, the *Statesman* noted:

> Travel is being reversed. All winter the stages went out from Boise loaded and came in light. Now they depart with the boot rocking high in the air and arrive loaded down. The railroad line last night brought nearly a full load of celestials.[65]

It appears that for a time Beachey ran stages between Silver City and Winnemucca and also between Elko and White Pine, with stages bridging the gap between the two Nevada railroad towns for Idaho passengers going to the new mining district. Wells Fargo continued its express and treasure transfer service not only on Hailey's network of stages throughout Idaho and eastern Oregon but also on Beachey's lines from Idaho to the railroad.

In April, 1869, Wells Fargo began making numerous personnel changes in the Pacific Northwest. Hugh W. McKee, agent in Pioneer City for the previous two years, was called back to San Francisco for reassignment. Edward Bromley, the delivery clerk in Silver City, soon followed him to California.[66] J. L. Smith, for some time the agent in Idaho City, was transferred to Silver City and James Henderson, who had served Wells Fargo as

[60]*Ibid.*, May 1, 1869, p. 3, c. 1; *Utah Weekly Reporter* (Corinne), May 22, 1869, p. 3, c. 2; *Weekly Oregonian*, May 29, 1869, p. 3, c. 4; *Idaho Tri-Weekly Statesman*, June 12, 1869, p. 3, c. 1.

[61]*Utah Reporter*, June 12, 1869, p. 3, c. 1.

[62]*Idaho Tri-Weekly Statesman*, June 24, 1869, p. 3, c. 1 and 3.

[63]*Ibid.*, January 16, 1869, p. 3, c. 1.

[64]*Owyhee Avalanche*, March 6, 1869, p. 3, c. 1.

[65]*Idaho Tri-Weekly Statesman*, March 23, 1869, p. 2, c. 1.

[66]*Idaho World*, April 1, 1869, p. 3, c. 1; *Owyhee Avalanche*, April 3, 1869, p. 3, c. 1.

agent in Canyon City, Lewiston, and most recently Walla Walla, was assigned to replace him. David F. Wagner, a clerk in the Boise office, took Henderson's place in Walla Walla. In announcing each of the personnel changes, Idaho newspaper editors paid glowing tributes to departing Wells Fargo employees.[67] When Henderson arrived in Idaho City, the editor of the *World* stated: "We regret to learn that he is an invalid, and that it is possible the onerous duties of the office here may prove to be more arduous than he can withstand in his enfeebled condition."[68] Scarcely had Henderson arrived when he requested a return to his old post at Walla Walla. The exchange was made and David Wagner returned to Boise.[69] Charles Woodward, the division agent for Wells Fargo, was back in Idaho by the end of May, having returned from a vacation with his family in Baltimore.[70]

Early in July, the Boise *Statesman* suggested:

There is now no reason why the entire overland travel from Oregon should not go up the Columbia river over Hailey's line to the railroad. It is the shortest, quickest, cheapest, and most comfortable route, and is in every way worthy of patronage.[71]

The Silver City *Tidal Wave* took vigorous exception and came to the defense of Beachey's line. The editor of the Boise paper responded with a long editorial that concluded:

We propose not to champion any routes as against the others, not for pay even, but to favor them all. The country needs them and the public service requires them, and no favors, no friendships or petty spites, nor any desire for notoriety or to be noticed in print, will be likely to influence us in the matter.[72]

Hostility and bitterness continued amongst the editors. The *Statesman* editor published the following excerpt from the Portland *Advocate:* "The Best Route—The O.S.N. Co. advertise to take passengers from Portland to Indian Creek on the Pacific Railroad, in six days, for $72.00 in coin. Fare from Indian Creek to New York $128.15 in currency." Then he added a postscript. "Pitch into him now, Mr. *Wave*. He didn't mention Silver and the 'scenery.' He's hostile. Go at him."[73]

Throughout the Northwest various newspapers noted the reduction in fares on Hailey's line. The Walla Walla *Union* reported that travelers could make the trip from Portland to New York in ten days for a fare of $166.83.[74] The *Statesman* called the attention of the public to the new $50 fare between Indian Creek and Boise and the charge of fifteen cents per pound for freight.[75] The quarrel between the editors of the *Idaho World* and *Idaho Tri-Weekly Statesman*, both of whom supported John Hailey's line, and the editors of the Silver City *Tidal Wave* and *Avalanche* continued. The crux of the continuing debate was which route would take travelers to Sacramento in the shortest time and for the cheapest fare. When all was said, the difference was minimal.[76] The Overland and Oregon Stage Line proprietor left the arguments to the editors and continued to operate the stages.

In July, 1869, both the travel time and the fare on Hill Beachey's Railroad Stage Line were reduced. The time to Winnemucca was now forty-four hours; to Elko, fifty; to Sacramento, sixty-four; and to San Francisco, sixty-eight. The fare from Boise to Silver City was advertised at $10, to Winnemucca $45, to Elko $56, and Sacramento $71, and to San Francisco $73.[77] The *Statesman* editor commented:

The time is shorter and the fare lower than on any schedule ever before published, and what is more the schedule is lived up to. Who can say the country is not making

[67] *Walla Walla Union*, May 8, 1869, p. 2, c. 5; *Idaho Tri-Weekly Statesman*, May 1, 1869, p. 3, c. 1; *Idaho World*, May 6, 1869, p. 3, c. 1.

[68] *Idaho World*, May 13, 1869, p. 2, c. 3.

[69] *Ibid.*, June 3, 1869, p. 3, c. 2, June 17, 1869, p. 3, c. 2; *Idaho Tri-Weekly Statesman*, June 5, 1869, p. 2, c. 1, June 10, 1869, p. 2, c. 2; *Walla Walla Union*, June 5, 1869, p. 3, c. 1.

[70] *Idaho Tri-Weekly Statesman*, May 25, 1869, p. 2, c. 2; *Idaho World*, June 3, 1869, p. 3, c. 1.

[71] *Idaho Tri-Weekly Statesman*, July 1, 1869, p. 2, c. 1.

[72] *Ibid.*, July 3, 1869, p. 2, c. 2 and 3. The articles in the *Wave* were quoted extensively.

[73] *Ibid.*, July 17, 1869, p. 2, c. 4.

[74] *Walla Walla Union*, July 24, 1869, p. 2, c. 4.

[75] *Idaho Tri-Weekly Statesman*, August 26, 1869, p. 2, c. 2.

[76] *Owyhee Avalanche*, September 25, 1869, p. 2, c. 3.

[77] *Idaho Tri-Weekly Statesman*, July 22, 1869, p. 2, c. 5.

progress. Less than a year ago it took four days to go to San Francisco with three days staging and fare ninety-five dollars.[78]

Later in the month reports were published that Beachey had plans to put on a new line of stages running from Silver City to Elko.[79] Throughout the summer, rumors were rampant about his plans to meet the competition from John Hailey. The Boise *Capital Chronicle* reported on August 14, 1869,

Hon. Merritt Kelly called on us yesterday. He has been exploring the country between this city and the railroad and hunting a more practicable stage route. Mr. Kelly informs us that a far better and shorter road was found and that Mr. Hailey will open the route next spring by running his stages on the new located road. As we understand Mr. Kelly, the route proposed leaves the present route at Cold Springs, runs direct south to Snake River, thence in a southwest direction and striking the railroad about half way between Elko and Indian Creek. The route cuts off mountain passes and is through a well watered and fine grazing country and shortens the distance, now traveled, to the railroad about fifty miles.[80]

Amidst the numerous changes in stagecoach service and mail deliveries in Idaho Territory, Wells Fargo & Co. continued to deliver express and to transport treasure. The company's activities centered on the Owyhee District. During February, 1869, from the company's office in Silver City, bullion worth $91,645.76 in coin and $122,194.34 in currency had been forwarded to San Francisco. The Rising Star Company was active in the mining district and in March, 1869, was making weekly shipments of $7,125 in coin by Wells Fargo, again to San Francisco.[81]

In March, the *Owyhee Avalanche* revealed that there were difficulties between Thos. Cole, Jr., banker, and the Rising Star. Cole had placed an attachment on the mining properties at Flint and had gone to San Francisco to consult with bankers there.[82] The community was shocked on May 1, 1869, when the newspaper reported that Thos. Cole, Jr. & Co. had failed.[83] The fact that this banking firm had the financial backing of Wells Fargo and represented the latter firm in Idaho was well known. The Boise *Statesman* explained that the Bank of California had called in one-fourth of its outstanding loan in the Owyhee District, and Wells Fargo had immediately requested that Cole settle an overdrawn account. Cole insisted that enough bullion was in transit to San Francisco to settle the account, but he was unable to come to a satisfactory understanding with Wells Fargo. The company president sailed for New York with instruction to protest Thos. Cole, Jr. & Co. drafts. Within a few hours protests and attachments closed up the business of the firm. The *Idaho World* expressed regret at the "very unhappy effect" the banking failure was having on business generally in Owyhee.[84]

Other banking firms stepped into the breach. Within a few weeks, Greathouse Bros. established a banking house with headquarters in Boise and branch agencies in both Idaho City and Silver City. The *Statesman*, in publishing an advertisement, commented: "These gentlemen have opened their establishment without noise and parade, which looks like business."[85] The *Idaho World* added a comment:

The Greathouse Brothers—George, Henry and Ridgely—have commenced a banking business in Idaho, with the chief house in Boise City, and Branch Agencies in Idaho City and Silver City. Unlike the late Thos. Cole, Jr., banking concern, which apparently ran on no capital, the Greathouse Brothers conduct their banking upon a sound gold basis, with the money in a bank, of their own, and not borrowed or contingent. Their correctness and fidelity as bankers in Yreka, California, a few years ago, made for them a handsome business and good reputation, and we have no doubt they will succeed equally in Idaho.[86]

Banking services were also being provided by the First National Bank of Idaho, based in Boise but with a strong agency in Idaho City engaged in a general banking business. The branch was located in a fireproof building on Main Street opposite Wells Fargo's office and was under the management of B. M. DuRell.[87]

[78] *Ibid.*, July 8, 1869, p. 3, c. 1.

[79] *Owyhee Avalanche*, July 24, 1869, p. 3, c. 1.

[80] *Capital Chronicle* (Boise), August 14, 1869, p. 2, c. 1.

[81] *Owyhee Avalanche*, March 6, 1869, p. 3, c. 1, March 27, 1869, p. 3, c. 1.

[82] *Ibid.*, March 6, 1869, p. 3, c. 1.

[83] *Ibid.*, May 1, 1869, p. 3, c. 1.

[84] *Idaho Tri-Weekly Statesman*, May 1, 1869, p. 2, c. 2; *Idaho World*, May 6, 1869, p. 2, c. 3.

[85] *Idaho Tri-Weekly Statesman*, May 25, 1869, p. 2, c. 2 and 4.

[86] *Idaho World*, June 3, 1869, p. 2, c. 4, p. 3, c. 1.

[87] *Ibid.*, May 20, 1869, p. 2, c. 3, p. 3, c. 1, May 27, 1869, p. 3, c. 2.

The First National Bank of Idaho utilized Wells Fargo's services in handling its treasure shipments. During the month of May the bank had forwarded gold bars and gold dust valued at $46,094 from Idaho City overland via Wells Fargo's express and thence by the Union Pacific Railroad to New York. This sum represented only the half-month's business since the opening of the agency.[88]

Silver City was left with very limited banking services upon the failure of Thos. Cole, Jr., & Co., but not for long. On July 3, 1869, Wells Fargo & Co. advertised that it was entering the banking business in the Owyhee community.

WELLS, FARGO & CO.
BANKERS,
SILVER CITY, IDAHO TERRITORY.
PURCHASE AND MAKE ADVANCES
ON
BULLION.
Buy and sell
CURRENCY.
Sell
EXCHANGE
on
Atlantic States and Europe.
Draw direct on
San Francisco and New York
Receive General and Special
DEPOSITS.
WELL, FARGO & CO.
J. L. SMITH, Agent.[89]

Within weeks, Wells Fargo had competition not only from Greathouse Brothers but also from the firm of Webb & Myrick.[90] Throughout Idaho Territory the various banking firms advertised extensively and rivalry was very keen.[91]

Although Wells Fargo & Co. faced stiff competition in the banking business in Idaho Territory, the company continued responsibility for transporting the accumulated bullion, treasure, and currency to the railroad on the stagecoaches operated by both John Hailey and Hill Beachey. The insured shipments than headed either east to New York or west to San Francisco. In Idaho City, B. M. DuRell instituted the practice of informing the *Idaho World* about the

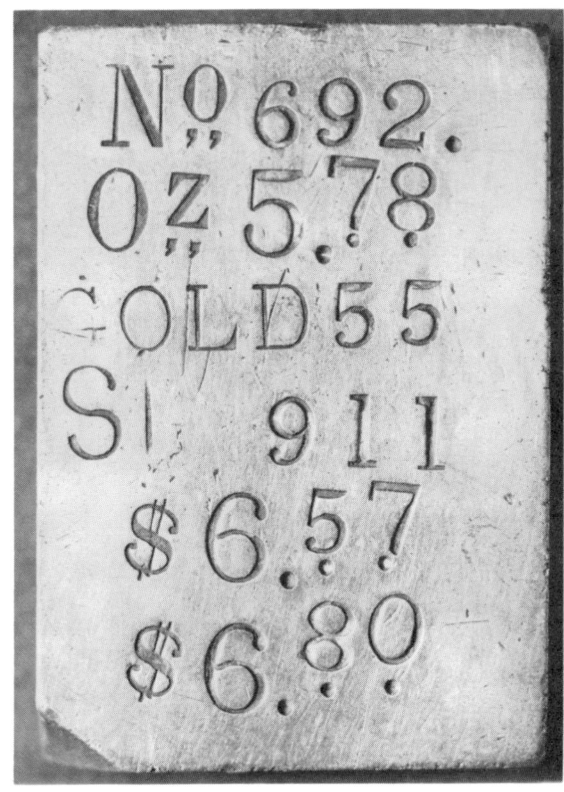

A silver ingot from the Boise City Assaying and Refining Works, established by B. M. DuRell.

shipments from the Idaho City agency of the First National Bank, and the other newspapers in Idaho reprinted the information. Weekly shipments in October amounted to between $16,000 and $17,000. For the entire month forty-four gold bars valued at $67,067 were forwarded to New York. It was estimated that $150,000 more was sent to California and Oregon. During the first ten days of November, gold bars worth $41,192 left Idaho City for New York, and the regular weekly shipments were worth just under $18,000.[92] Wells Fargo also continued its active role as a carrier of gold bullion and other treasure from

[88] *Ibid.*, June 3, 1869, p. 3, c. 2.

[89] *Owyhee Avalanche*, July 3, 1869, p. 2, c. 5. An identical advertisement appeared in the *Idaho World*, July 1, 1869, p. 2, c. 4.

[90] *Ibid.*, July 24, 1869, p. 3, c. 1.

[91] *Capital Chronicle*, August 4, 1869, p. 1, c. 2, p. 3, c. 1; *Idaho Tri-Weekly Statesman*, July 22, 1869, p. 3, c. 5, September 9, 1869, p. 1, c. 1; *Idaho World*, November 11, 1869, p. 4, c. 3.

[92] *Capital Chronicle*, October 23, 1869, p. 2, c. 2, quoting the *Idaho World* of October 21, November 6, 1869, quoting the *Idaho World* of November 4, November 13, 1869, p. 2, c. 2, November 6, 1869, p. 3, c. 2, November 20, 1869, p. 3, c. 2, November 27, 1869, p. 2, c. 2.

the Owyhee District and from White Pine. During June, the company shipped $96,320 in coin or $128,426 in currency from its office in Siver City.[93]

Equally important were the shipments from White Pine. The *Capital Chronicle* reported that fifteen bars of bullion worth $24,453.72 were consigned from that district to San Francisco via Elko on July 17, 1869. Between July 24 and 27, twenty-one additional bars were forwarded, valued at $127,707.34.[94] Then came the report that two tons of silver bullion had been sent to New York by railroad in charge of Wells Fargo, all of which had come from the Nevada mines in the last week of July.[95] Newspapers throughout the Northwest confirmed the fact that Wells Fargo & Co. was carrying bullion for numerous banks in both Idaho and California. The company was shipping bullion for both the First National Bank, to New York, and the Bank of California. During the week of September 10-17, 1869, Wells Fargo shipped over $30,000 to Portland from the Lewiston, Idaho, area and adjoining mines.[96]

THE BUSINESS OF transporting express and treasure from Idaho Territory and elsewhere in the West to the banking capitals in New York and San Francisco was often disrupted by thieves. Late in April, 1869, five masked men entered the office of Wells Fargo in Truckee in daylight while people were passing by on the sidewalk. They aimed cocked pistols at the company's employees and a patron. A clerk immediately seized a chair and struck one of the robbers over the head. The would-be thieves fired several shots, fortunately missing people each time. Alarmed that the noise might attract passers-by, they fled without obtaining the treaure in the company safe. The man who had been wounded in the head died confessing and implicating his associates, all of whom were soon captured.[97]

The summer and fall of 1869 witnessed a series of robberies that involved Wells Fargo's express and treasure on various stage lines in the Pacific Northwest. On July 12, Wells Fargo's coach was robbed thirty miles south of Virginia City, Montana. The treasure box, containing $7,200 in gold, was taken. The robbers fled to the mountains and as late as July 24 had not been arrested.[98] In August it was reported that on one occasion the stage between Boise and Umatilla was stopped and the driver requested to hand over the Wells Fargo box; but the horses, taking fright, bolted and ran, putting an end to the incident.[99] Later in the month a third holdup occurred, on the road between Elko and White Pine. Seven members of a gang of fifteen involved in the conspiracy to hold up the Wells Fargo stage had assumed the roles of ranchmen and stationkeepers along the road to better conceal their plans. However, H. L. Maize, a detective for Wells Fargo who joined the road agents, caused the arrest of the seven.[100]

On September 2, 1869, the details of a major robbery of the Wells Fargo stagecoach not far from Summit Station near Malad, Idaho, on the Salt Lake City-Helena run was reported. Four masked men, with three more nearby on picket duty, stopped the stage near midnight, forced the driver to throw out the light box from the front boot and then the heavier treasure chest, and demanded that he drive on. The ten passengers, who carried a sizable amount of dust and bullion, were not robbed.[101] Scarcely had the news of this robbery begun to circulate when another holdup occurred in the same area. This time there were four highwaymen, who demanded that the six male passengers and one Chinese woman throw their weapons out of the coach. Again the two express boxes were demanded. This time the passengers were forced out of the stage while the robbers broke open the treasure boxes, then systematically robbed all the passengers. One

[93] *Idaho Tri-Weekly Statesman*, July 3, 1869, p. 3, c. 1. This information also appeared in both the *Avalanche* and *Wave*.

[94] *Capital Chronicle*, August 4, 1869, p. 1, c. 3

[95] *Idaho World*, August 5, 1869, p. 2, c. 4, reprinting an article from the Elko *Independent*.

[96] *Walla Walla Union*, September 11, 1869, p. 2, c. 3 and 4; *Weekly Oregonian*, September 18, 1869, p. 3, c. 1.

[97] *Owyhee Avalanche*, May 1, 1869, p. 3, c. 2, May 8, 1869, p. 2, c. 3; *Walla Walla Union*, May 8, 1869, p. 2, c. 5.

[98] *Owyhee Avalanche*, July 24, 1869, p. 2, c. 3.

[99] *Capital Chronicle*, August 4, 1869, p. 3, c. 1.

[100] *Idaho World*, August 19, 1869, p. 2, c. 2, quoting from the *Owyhee Wave*.

[101] *Utah Reporter*, September 2, 1869, p. 3, c. 3.

The Inskip rock house on Ruby Ranch near Jordan Valley, on the stage route from Winnemucca, was used as both a stage station and a fort.

passenger asked for money enough for breakfast and the robbers complied. The travelers lost an aggregate amount of $1,600, most of their treasure having been consigned to the express. The treasure boxes were reported to be very heavy, one weighing approximately two hundred pounds. One of the robbers remarked that he was taking up a collection for the widows and orphans of the South.[102] Dan Robbins, the Wells Fargo divisional superintendent, led a posse (many of whose members were employees of the company) after the highwaymen. A shoot-out occurred in the mountains in the neighborhood of Devil's Gate. Robbins was shot in the breast and feared mortally wounded; one of the robbers was killed outright and another was dying. A single bar of gold worth $9,500 was recovered. Wells Fargo officials reported that over $50,000 had been stolen in this holdup and offered a reward of one-fourth of any of the money that was recovered as a reward.[103] By the end of the month all the highwaymen involved in the first robbery had been either arrested or killed. A different group of men, who brought off the second robbery, were captured and arrested near Winnemucca.[104] Several of their horses were found to be stolen from John Hailey's stage stations. The *Capital Chronicle* observed: "We think it is about time that highwaymen had ceased to interfere with W. F. & Co.'s treasure, for they invariably get caught."[105] Dan Robbins, better known to "old Californians" as "Curley Dan," died from his wounds.[106]

"The road agents seem to be after Wells, Fargo & Co. 'with a sharp stick,'" the editor of the *Owyhee Avalanche* commented toward the end of September. The week following the double robbery near Malad City, Hill Beachey's stages—carrying Wells Fargo's treasure from White Pine—were held up twice not far from Treasure City. On the first occasion the team became frightened and ran; the driver crawled down into the boot and managed to escape unhurt as the highwaymen fired at the stage. The following morning's holdup was a success: the robbers obtained Wells Fargo's treasure box and took the passengers' valuables.[107]

Another robbery in the fall occurred on John Hailey's Overland and Oregon Stage Line. The town of Kelton, Utah, on the Central Pacific

[102] *Ibid.*, September 8, 1869, p. 3, c. 1; *Idaho Tri-Weekly Statesman*, September 11, 1869, p. 3, c. 1.

[103] *Utah Reporter*, September 11, 1869, p. 3, c. 1; *Idaho Tri-Weekly Statesman*, September 14, 1869, p. 2, c. 1, p. 3, c. 1; *Idaho World*, September 16, 1869, p. 2, c. 1; *Owyhee Avalanche*, September 18, 1869, p. 2, c. 6.

[104] *Capital Chronicle*, September 25, 1869, p. 3, c. 1. This account was also published in the *Oregon State Journal*, October 9, 1869, p. 4, c. 1.

[105] *Capital Chronicle*, September 25, 1869, p. 3, c. 1.

[106] *Idaho World*, September 30, 1869, p. 2, c. 3.

[107] *Owyhee Avalanche*, September 25, 1869, p. 2, c. 3.

Railroad had been designed by the Post Office Department as the terminus of his route, and the Salt Lake end of the route was discontinued. Kelton immediately became a town of some importance, comparable to Corinne. A telegraph station was located there and mails could be delivered by the United States Postal Service or by Wells Fargo express between the town and Boise.[108] Late in September it was discovered that the Wells Fargo & Co. treasure box was missing near the Snake River from the stage running from Boise to Kelton. It contained approximately $3,000 in dust and bars. Employees of the stage and express companies went to work to ferret out the robber, who was finally arrested in Boise; nearly all the money was recovered. At the time of the robbery, the culprit had been currying horses at the Snake River Station.[109]

WHEN WELLS FARGO lost the mail contract between Salt Lake City and The Dalles in July, 1868, the company had ordered thirty or more stagecoaches from Abbott-Downing Company in Concord, New Hampshire. Some of these were sold to John Hailey, who took over the stage-mail route from the contractor that had underbid Wells Fargo. On August 14, 1869, the *Utah Reporter* at Corinne noted:

> Yesterday afternoon five elegant new overland coaches passed through the city for the Boise Stage Line, running from Idaho and Oregon to the C.P.R.R. cars at Indian Creek. These coaches were manufactured in the East for Wells, Fargo & Co., and have lately been operated by them, but a short time since were bought for this stage line. They are well made and furnished with every appointment for the traveler's comfort. We understand that Wells, Fargo & Co. have ordered for the line operating between here and Helena a number of new coaches which will soon arrive.[110]

The new stagecoaches were to be used both on the Montana route and in Colorado Territory.

On September 2, the press announced that Messrs. Salisbury & Gilmer had purchased Wells Fargo's stage line from Corinne to Helena.[111] A few days later the *Avalanche* reported a rumor that Wells Fargo & Co. was withdrawing not only from the stagecoach business but from express service as well.[112] The rumor was false: the decision to withdraw from stagecoach operations had been made by the company's board of directors in New York, but the basic express business would continue for years to come.

During the season of 1869, when the White Pine mining boom was at its height, Wells Fargo operated its own stagecoach service from Treasure City and Hamilton in that mining district to the Central Pacific Railroad. At one time there were as many as six stagecoach operators on the route. However, by the fall of the year the excitement was largely over and the *Avalanche* informed its readers:

> Wells, Fargo & Co. have hauled off their coaches from the Elko and White Pine stage, and hereafter Hill Beachey "goes it alone," assuming Wells, Fargo & Co.'s contract with the United States for carrying the mail. He also carries their express matter, as well as that of the Pacific Union Express Company.

Thus Beachey could turn his energies to the Nevada route as the competition with John Hailey reduced the importance of the Railroad Stage Line in Idaho Territory. Three weeks later, another change was announced: Beachey had consolidated his White Pine operations with those of Len Wines, in a firm known as Beachey, Wines & Co. Wines was to superintend the road.[113]

Idaho readers learned that a "grand express war" had broken out in September, 1869. Wells Fargo & Co. was notified by the Central Pacific Railroad to quit transmitting express on the 15th of the month. A new company known as the Pacific Express was to have a monopoly on the Central Pacific to Promontory Point, the Continental Express Co. thence to Omaha. In Boise, the editor of the *Statesman* suggested:

> It is hardly to be supposed that W. F. & Co. will give up their vast and lucrative business without a struggle. If they get "froze out" of the Central railroad line it is not

[108] *Idaho Tri-Weekly Statesman*, September 16, 1869, p. 2, c. 1.

[109] *Ibid.*, October 9, 1869, p. 3, c. 2.

[110] *Utah Reporter*, August 14, 1869, p. 3, c. 1.

[111] *Ibid.*, September 2, 1869, p. 3, c. 3; *Idaho Tri-Weekly Statesman*, September 7, 1869, p. 1, c. 5. For a full discussion, see W. Turrentine Jackson, *Wells Fargo Stagecoaching in Montana Territory* (Helena: Montana Historical Society Press, 1979).

[112] *Owyhee Avalanche*, September 25, 1869, p. 3, c. 4.

[113] *Ibid.*, October 9, 1869, p. 2, c. 1, October 23, 1869, p. 2, c. 5; *Idaho World*, October 14, 1869, p. 2, c. 3.

improbable that the company will throw their influence for the southern route, obtain a monopoly of it and hasten its construction. By the way, does it not sound a little queer that these railroads which have received so much aid from government and have really been built with the people's money, should be granting exclusive privileges to express freight over their roads? What right have they to sell the exclusive privilege to send fast freight and messengers to take care of it, to any company to the exclusion of all others, any more than they have to sell one man a passage ticket and exclude everyone else? If we are not mistaken this subject will be brought to the notice of congress at any early date.[114]

Newspapers and residents expressed a great deal of interest in what was happening. It was generally recognized that the owners of the Central Pacific Railroad were financing the Pacific Express and the Union Pacific the Continental Express. With surprising bitterness, the *Avalanche*, in reporting the fact that Wells Fargo was being driven off the railroad, stated: "We are glad to hear it. The latter company has monopolized the business until it has grown fat and despicably mean. It is hoped that the new company will extend a branch of its business this way."[115]

Newspapers throughout the West reported that Wells Fargo & Co., Adams & Co., American Express Co., and United States Express Co. were organizing for a fight. Meanwhile, the Pacific Union Express was reported to be taking no active part in the struggle, but it was expected that this company might well be incorporated into the Pacific Express at an early date.

The contest will be of gigantic proportions, involving all the express companies and many of the leading railroads; it will create a great sensation in financial and commercial circles, and may open the eyes of the public to many things of general interest connected with the express business.[116]

Tremendous confusion existed in the newspaper accounts between September 15 and October 1, 1869, as tension mounted. Apparently for a time the United States Express had decided to challenge Wells Fargo by attempting to negotiate an exclusive right to the Pacific railroads. Wells Fargo was reported to have set aside a million and a half dollars to meet losses in the projected competition. The United States Express apparently decided it was cheaper to compromise than to fight, and arrangements were reported whereby Wells Fargo would retain all its business west of Salt Lake City and perform the services of the United States Express between there and the Missouri River through Wells Fargo agents.[117]

All of the conflicting interests came to terms in the "Omaha Agreement," a merger of express companies and the railroad interests in a company to be known as Wells Fargo & Co. The capital stock of the company was increased from $10,000,000 to $15,000,000, largely to purchase the railroad's interest in the recently incorporated Pacific Express Company. The decision did not meet with enthusiasm from all of the stockholders at the company meeting in New York City, but the resolve of the directors prevailed. One casualty of the agreement was the Pacific Union Express. In mid-December, it was announced:

The Pacific Union Express Company have suspended business on this coast. Arrangements have been made whereby Wells, Fargo & Co. will complete all unfinished business and will carry all franked envelopes in the hands of the public. The Pacific Union Express was a great benefit to the people as a means of effecting a cheaper carriage, the rivalry between it and Wells, Fargo & Co. being very spirited. This rivalry resulted in a reduction of rates to figures ruinous to the new company, which is reported to have sunk lately from $15,000 to $20,000 per month. About two hundred employees will be thrown out of work by the suspension of business.[118]

Thus the Pacific Union Express Company was forced to abandon the express business. Competition from Wells Fargo was not the only reason; the railroad interests decided to make a more serious challenge to Wells Fargo's business through the Pacific and Continental expresses prior to compromise and merger, thereby freezing out the Pacific Union Express.

[114]*Idaho Tri-Weekly Statesman*, September 11, 1869, p. 2, c. 1. Additional information is available in W. Turrentine Jackson, *Treasure Hill: Portrait of a Silver Mining Camp* (Tucson: University of Arizona Press, 1963).

[115]*Owyhee Avalanche*, September 18, 1869, p. 1, c. 1.

[116]*Weekly Oregonian*, September 18, 1869, p. 1, c. 1, republishing an article from the *Commercial Herald* of San Francisco. A brief version also appeared in the *Walla Walla Union*, September 18, 1869, p. 2, c. 3.

[117]*Weekly Oregonian*, October 30, 1869, p. 3, c. 2.

[118]*Capital Chronicle*, November 27, 1869, p. 2, c. 3; *Walla Walla Union*, December 4, 1869, p. 2, c. 6, December 18, 1869, p. 2, c. 2.

THE 1870's AND BEYOND

Alturas Gold, Limited.

$ Rocky Bar, Idaho, 188

WELLS FARGO & CO'S BANK

SALT LAKE CITY, UTAH.

Pay to or order

Dollars.

ALTURAS GOLD, LIMITED,

No 1272 By

SUPERINTENDENT.

Western B.N.& Engraving Co. Chicago

AFTER THE Pacific Railroad was opened for transcontinental traffic on May 10, 1869, several new stage and freight routes were established to connect southwestern Idaho with the Central Pacific. The termini of these routes were, from east to west, Kelton in Utah and Toano, Elko, and Winnemucca in Nevada. As early as 1863 freighters out of Salt Lake had opened a route via the site of Kelton to Boise, so the way was generally known when John Hailey transferred his stages there. Kelton was destined to become the main shipping point on the Central Pacific in 1870: the community received all the passenger and express business conducted by Hailey's stage line, including shipments by Wells Fargo & Co.

Hailey operated a 42-hour stage service between Kelton and Boise, with nineteen stage stations on the 232-mile road:

Black's Creek (15 miles from Boise)
Baylock (13 miles)
Canyon Creek (12 miles)
Rattlesnake (8 miles)
Cold Springs (12 miles)
King Hill (10 miles)
Clover Creek (11 miles)
Malad (11 miles)
Sand Springs (11 miles)
Snake River at Clark's Ferry (10 miles)
Desert (12 miles)
Rock Creek (13 miles)
Mountain Meadows (14 miles)
Oakley Meadows (12 miles)
Goose Creek Summit (11 miles)
City of Rocks (11 miles)
Raft River (12 miles)
Clear Creek (12 miles)
Crystal Springs (10 miles)
Kelton (12 miles)[1]

In March of 1870, the *Capital Chronicle* of Boise reported that pack trains had already started to Kelton with loads of spring freight, and small trains of wagons were also moving out on the road.[2] A key location on the route was Clark's Ferry, where the freight wagons and stages crossed the Snake River; from there

[1] Larry Jones, "Kelton Road," Reference Series, No. 74 (Boise: Idaho State Historical Society, 1972).

[2] *Capital Chronicle* (Boise), March 5, 1870, p. 3, c. 1.

The Overland Hotel in Boise.

it was approximately 125 miles to the railroad at Kelton.[3]

John Hailey recorded that he continued to run the line from Kelton via Boise and Walla Walla to The Dalles until July, 1870, when his contract for carrying the mail expired. He reported that he sold his stock, wagons, and stations to the Northwestern Stage Company, which had the mail contract over this route for the next four years.[4] Idaho newspapers reported that the operation of the freight and stage lines and the awarding of new mail contracts was somewhat more complicated. Speculation concerning the awarding of new mail contracts had begun as early as March, 1870.

Rumor has it that none of the veteran and efficient mail contractors of this Territory will receive a contract, all having been underbid by John Gilmore, who, we presume, is the same man who but a few years ago was in the employ of Wells, Fargo & Co. as division agent from Green river to Salt Lake. It is said that his bid from Boise City to Winnemucca was for $10,000, where some $70,000 has heretofore been paid. The rates of his bid on John Hailey's line to the Dalles and to Kelton is equally as low. Wells Fargo once before obtained one million dollars for carrying the overland mail when bids for one fourth the amount had been put in by some kind of legerdemain, but the parties could not be found, when the contracts were let. We may be mistaken but this looks a little as if the same thing was to be tried over again by them. We confess that it is unwise in the Post Office Department to tolerate any thing of the kind. We know that Hill Beachy [sic], John Hailey and Mr. Pinkham have carried the mails as low as they can afford, and no contractors on the Pacific Coast were ever more faithful in performing their duty.[5]

The editor was mistaken. Long after Wells Fargo's unique service and carefully supervised compensation for carrying the mails between the ever closer railroad termini in the crucial months before the completion of the track were public knowledge, the belief that the company had exploited the situation and unduly profited thereby lingered on in some quarters.

All the routes northward from the railroad stops at Kelton, Toano, Elko, and Winnemucca were to be affected, for better or worse, by the mail-contract negotiations of 1870. The *Idaho World* announced:

We learn from a private source that Messrs. Gilmore & Saulsbury who own the stage line from Corinne to Virginia City, Montana, have secured the mail contracts over the routes from Kelton to Umatilla, and from Winnemucca to Boise City. We do not know what the amounts of their bids were, but are sorry to know that Beachey and John Hailey were underbid, as they have heretofore carried the mails with such regularity and in a manner seldom, if ever equalled in a country of such a nature through which their routes ran. The new contractors will have to be about the best stage men to be found anywhere if they can perform their contracts with as much satisfaction to the people for less money.[6]

The Corinne *Reporter* confirmed—perhaps with unwarranted optimism:

The mail contracts have been awarded to our enterprising fellow citizens, Messrs. Gilmer & Saulsbury. The mails for all parts of Montana and Idaho are to be carried out from Corinne, all other routes, and proposed routes, having been rejected by the Postoffice Department. The stages of G. & S. leave here daily with U. S. mails and overland express for Virginia City, Helena, and from no other point on the Pacific Railway.[7]

John Hailey did not sit idle while the maneuvering over mail contracts was going on. C. W. Lockwood, the well-known government contractor, stock dealer, and stagecoach operator, purchased a half interest in the stock, stages, and equipment of Hailey's Overland and Oregon Stage Line from Kelton to Umatilla. The *Avalanche* editor thought:

The firm of Hailey & Lockwood is a strong one, both in wealth and ability, and the company that successfully competes with it will have to bring to the task an amount of money, energy, and economical management that the signs of the times do not by any means warrant. The members of the new firm are both men of great stage experience, and established integrity, having the confidence of everybody, which gives them great advantages both in running the stages and purchasing supplies.[8]

Other newspapers agreed: "even if they don't have the mail contracts they will make it warm for the individual and company who has, and if

[3]*Owyhee Avalanche* (Silver City), March 19, 1870, p. 2, c. 2.

[4]John Hailey, *History of Idaho* (Boise: Syms-York Co., 1910), 125.

[5]*Capital Chronicle*, March 23, 1870, p. 3, c. 2. Reprinted in the *Statesman* (Walla Walla), April 2, 1870, p. 1, c. 7.

[6]*Idaho World* (Idaho City), March 24, 1870, p. 2, c. 2.

[7]*Corinne Reporter* quoted in *Owyhee Avalanche*, April 2, 1870, p. 2, c. 2.

[8]*Owyhee Avalanche*, April 9, 1870, p. 2, c. 2.

they don't run 'em off the track we will quit prophesying."[9]

Hill Beachey had also been making adjustments in his transportation services. In May, he transferred his stages to what was designated the Cope Road, running into Elko, and dispatched his division agent Joe Jones to supervise the transfer. The *Avalanche* reported:

From what we can learn, it appears probable that both the Winnemucca and Kelton mail routes to Boise City will be discontinued and one mail line be established from Elko to the Columbia river. In this case we opine that Beachey, Hailey, and other stage men interested, will join together and do the most extraordinary staging on the continent.[10]

Then in July came the news that Hill Beachey has sold his stage line from Elko to Silver City.[11] Hailey & Lockwood had also disposed of its stage company between Kelton and Umatilla. The name of the purchaser was not immediately known, but it was rumored that Kansas capitalists had bought out both firms along with John Early's line from Silver City into Boise. In a short time the purchaser was reported to be the Western Stage Company; the price paid to Hailey & Lockwood, $130,000.[12] Apparently Gilmore & Salisbury had sold its mail contracts to the Northwestern Stage Company, which was to undertake the integration of all the remaining stage routes in the Pacific Northwest. John Hailey summarized the situation in retrospect:

The same company got the contract for carrying the mail from Boise City via Silver City to Winnemucca, Nevada, which route had been run by John Earley and Hill Beachey. This company bought them out.... This was an eastern company. The first proprietors were Owen Teller, Bradley Barlow and J. W. Parker. Later the firm changed to C. C. Hundley and Bradley Barlow. They ran these routes, carrying U. S. mail, Wells, Fargo & Co. express, and passengers for eight years, until July 1st, 1878, when another change was made.[13]

Idaho residents were concerned about John Hailey's future plans. In Walla Walla, it was rumored that he would buy a farm in the valley and make his home there, a welcome citizen. Soon Boise sources reported that he was keeping a meat market in that community.[14]

THE NORTHWESTERN STAGE Line had selected Elko from among the various towns on the Central Pacific Railroad as the starting point for its lines into Idaho. It advertised as follows:

NORTH WESTERN
STAGE LINE
FROM ELKO TO IDAHO!

Carrying Wells, Fargo & Co.'s Express and the United States Mails.

STAGES LEAVE ELKO DAILY UPON THE arrival of the Western Train, arriving at Mountain City the following morning; leaving Mountain City at ten o'clock, A.M., and arriving at Silver City at six o'clock, A.M. the following day; leaving Silver City at seven o'clock A.M. and arriving at Boise City at six o'clock P.M. same day. Returning from Boise City to Elko on same time schedule.

RATES OF FARE:

From Elko to Mountain City	$15
From Mountain City to Silver City	25
From Silver City to Boise City	10

For further information inquire of the following named Agents: E. S. Hubbell, Boise City; C. M. Hays, Silver City; L. Fisk, Mountain City; and W. C. Beachey, Elko.

O. R. JOHNSON, Superintendent

Silver City, I.T., June 16, 1870.[15]

Although it was not as affected by mail contracts and stage operations as were other terminal towns on the Central Pacific Railroad, Toano began to flourish in the late months of 1870. The town had served the Nevada mines as far south as Pioche before undertaking to gain a portion of the Idaho trade as well. When Payne's ferry across the Snake River at Thousand Springs began service at the beginning of October, the Toano route gained a good connection to the already established stage road north of the Snake, and freight began to move over the road in the fall of 1870. The route continued to be used by freighters in the 1870's but not for stages and mail.[16]

[9] *Idaho World*, April 7, 1870, p. 2, c. 2.

[10] *Owyhee Avalanche*, May 21, 1870, p. 3, c. 4.

[11] *Ibid.*, July 16, 1870, p. 2, c. 2. Reprinted in the *Idaho World*, July 21, 1870, p. 2, c. 4.

[12] *Capital Chronicle*, July 9, 1870, p. 3, c. 2; *Statesman*, July 30, 1870, p. 3, c. 1, August 13, 1870, p. 2, c. 1.

[13] Hailey, *History of Idaho*, 125-126.

[14] *Statesman*, July 30, 1870, p. 3, c. 1; *Owyhee Avalanche*, August 27, 1870, p. 2, c. 2, summarizing "Boise sources."

[15] *Ibid.*, November 5, 1870, p. 3, c. 5.

[16] Victor Goodwin, "The Toano Route," Reference Series No. 75 (Boise: Idaho State Historical Society, 1964, 1967).

John Hailey also recalled that the Northwestern Stage Company bought out the route operated by Ebenezer and Joseph Pinkham within the Boise Basin, but this change came somewhat later. Henry Greathouse, by now a banker in Boise and Idaho City, was the successful bidder for the 1870 mail contract between Boise City and Placerville, and he immediately began improvements on a new road via Warm Springs and thence up Sheep Gulch to Mores Creek, to strike the road at Stringham's Toll Gate. The editor of the *Idaho World* thought: "This would be quite an improvement on the present road, and it will avoid crossing the divide at the head of the Fort Canyon."[17] In July, Greathouse purchased the interests of the Pinkham brothers in the stage line running between Boise and Idaho City, at the time the only line between the two places carrying the United States mails and Wells Fargo & Co.'s express. The Pinkham brothers were to retain their line throughout the Basin and, as subcontractors to Greathouse, were to carry the mails and express, making connections at Idaho City with the Greathouse line into Boise.[18] The Greathouse Stage Line advertised both routes and charged passengers on the daily line between Boise and Idaho City $3.00 in gold coin. By December, 1870, the fare had been doubled to $6.00.[19]

Wells Fargo & Co.'s express and treasure were carried on all these stage routes in Nevada and Idaho. On January 1, 1870, Wells Fargo had announced a reduction of the tariff on express freight.

Reduction of Tariff
ON
EXPRESS FREIGHT.

FROM AND AFTER THE FIRST OF January, 1870, until further notice, Wells, Fargo & Co. will charge as follows on Express freight, per hundred pounds:

Boise City, to San Francisco *via*	
Central Pacific Railroad	$20.00
Boise City to Ogden (Utah)	15.00
Boise City to Kelton (Utah)	13.00

WELLS, FARGO & CO.[20]

The company continued to carry treasure on the various stage lines, with the final destination of San Francisco, Chicago, or New York over the railroad. These shipments, noted in every issue of the Idaho newspapers, were from two sources: the eastern Nevada mining camps and the Owyhee District of Idaho. The total value of the bullion shipped by Wells Fargo from the White Pine District for 1869 had been $1,938,888.44. Of this amount $605,088.24 had been sent east, the rest to San Francisco.[21] By summer, treasure was flowing to the railroad at Elko from both north and south. For the month that ended July 10, 1870, the Wells Fargo office there handled $161,276 from Idaho, $135,417 from White Pine, and $22,088 from Cope, a new Nevada district.[22] By midsummer, the weekly shipments indicated that Idaho was providing two-thirds to three-fourths of the treasure that was arriving at Elko. Shipments continued to decline, however, from both Idaho and White Pine.[23] Early in September, a week's shipment from Idaho totaled only $57,289; from White Pine, $40,905.[24]

From the Owyhee District, Wells Fargo had shipped $835,181.07 worth of bullion, coin value, for the year 1869. With unwarranted optimism, the *Avalanche* commented:

> The total product of our mines for '69 may safely be put down at a million dollars in coin, as the aggregate carried away in private hands would easily bring it up to that amount. This, be it remembered, is from only two or three mines and most of the time but two mills were in operation. We challenge the mining camps of the world to equal this under the same circumstances. We confidently look forward to the time, believing it not far distant, when our bullion shipments will foot up a million a month, instead of a year. Our mountains contain umlimited treasure, which must soon be added to the metallic currency of the world.[25]

Never a week passed that the paper did not report on shipments of treasure, and the other

[17] *Idaho World*, May 31, 1870, p. 1, c. 5.

[18] *Ibid.*, July 21, 1870, p. 3, c. 1; *Capital Chronicle*, July 16, 1870, p. 3, c. 1.

[19] *Idaho World*, July 7, 1870, p. 2, c. 5; *Capital Chronicle*, July 23, 1870, p. 2, c. 3; *Idaho Democrat* (Boise), December 24, 1870, p. 3, c. 5.

[20] *Capital Chronicle*, January 12, 1870, p. 3, c. 5; *Idaho World*, January 6, 1870, p. 2, c. 5.

[21] *Capital Chronicle*, January 26, 1870, p. 3, c. 2.

[22] *Ibid.*, July 20, 1870, p. 2, c. 2.

[23] *Ibid.*, July 27, 1870, p. 2, c. 1, August 31, 1870, p. 1, c. 5; *Owyhee Avalanche*, July 23, 1870, p. 2, c. 4, August 27, 1870, p. 2, c. 1; *Idaho World*, July 28, 1870, p. 2, c. 1.

[24] *Owyhee Avalanche*, September 17, 1870, p. 4, c. 2, September 24, 1870, p. 1, c. 4.

[25] *Ibid.*, March 5, 1870, p. 3, c. 4. Noted in the *Idaho World*, March 10, 1870, p. 3, c. 1.

Thirty Concord coaches ordered by Wells Fargo and shipped west by rail. Photograph courtesy Wells Fargo Bank.

Idaho newspapers regularly reprinted the statistics. Wells Fargo treasure shipments for July were reported to be $100,000, moved as bars of bullion.[26] Between August and October, the weekly shipment was anywhere from ten to fifteen bars of silver with a total value of from $20,000 to $30,000. At the close of 1870, the *Avalanche* published a summary statement of bullion shipments for the year.

> Owyhee Bullion Shipment for 1870.
>
> We herewith publish a statement of the number and coin value of bullion bars shipped from here by Wells, Fargo & Co. during the year 1870. By comparison it will be seen that the monthly shipments have steadily increased in value since May, at which time the mills were undergoing repairs and the roads broken up. This shows well for the growing prosperity of our camp. . . .

	Bars.		Value.
January	18		$ 51,469.12
February	19		48,484.19
March	29		51,458.16
April	19		35,891.91
May	2		3,621.28
June	23		46,329.81
July	43		77,048.49
August	40		73,388.73
September	40		93,910.76
October	43		86,471.79
November	56		114,256.89
December	63		123,743.36
Total	391	[sic]	$806,074.49[27]

There had actually been a slight decline in the amount of treasure handled by Wells Fargo in 1870 from that of the previous year.

As long as Wells, Fargo & Co. moved treasure on stagecoaches, highwaymen were determined to intercept the coaches and obtain treasure boxes. The first week in August, 1870, two stage robberies were reported in Idaho Territory. One stage was stopped on the Cope Road between Silver City and Elko and the Wells Fargo treasure box taken. The company offered a $3,000 reward for the capture of the robbers. The second robbery took place in the eastern part of the territory on the route between Corinne, Utah, and Helena, Montana, when six men stopped the stage at the Snake River and took the Wells Fargo treasure box, for which the company offered a $6,000 reward. The editor of the *Idaho World*, in reporting such incidents, commented: "Wells, Fargo & Co. never 'lets up' on these road agents, and we hope the scoundrels will be captured and dealt with to the extreme penalty provided by law."[28]

The Umatilla stage, on its way down to Boise, was held up on August 17, 1870, in the neighborhood of Pendleton, Oregon. As originally reported in the press, only two robbers were involved in taking a Wells Fargo treasure box that was thought to contain $10,000. The agent at Umatilla telegraphed

[26] *Owyhee Avalanche*, July 9, 1870, p. 2, c. 2. Reprinted in the *Capital Chronicle*, July 13, 1870, p. 2, c. 2, and the *Idaho World*, July 14, 1870, p. 2, c. 4.

[27] *Owyhee Avalanche*, December 31, 1870, p. 2, c. 3.

[28] *Idaho World*, August 11, 1870, p. 2, c. 3.

James Henderson, agent in Walla Walla, who immediately had two suspicious characters who had arrived from Spokane placed under arrest. After a preliminary hearing they produced satisfactory alibis and were released. The Walla Walla *Statesman* suggested:

Crime should be at all times investigated and punished, but it seems hard that innocent individuals should be arrested and incarcerated on light suspicions. The energy and activity of Wells, Fargo & Co. in bringing these highwaymen to justice, has, indeed been a wholesome lesson and we trust that these freebooters will be yet apprehended.[29]

In reporting the facts, the editor of the *Idaho World* agreed:

The depredations of these cavaliers of the road are becoming too frequent, and the success attending them of late will probably embolden them to make other attempts, when we hope parties who are on the lookout for them will accommodate them with a little lead instead of gold.[30]

The news of the robbery spread rapidly; as it did, the facts about the incident became confused and more details were supplied in good western-legend fashion. The scene was sometimes described as three miles from Umatilla or near the Umatilla Landing; the highwaymen sometimes numbered three rather than two; the amount taken was between $1,000 and $1,500 rather than $10,000. The apparent leader was reported as saying, "I'm Patrick Brown, the man who killed that s-n of a b---h in the Blue Mountains, and you had better hand over the treasure box without any of your gab." Brown had just escaped from the penitentiary in Salem, Oregon. One Professor Plummer, a caricaturist, was a passenger on the stage and had about $2,000 in his possession—"the proceeds of his drollery and wit." He passed himself off as a preacher of the

[29] *Statesman*, August 20, 1870, p. 3, c. 2.

[30] *Idaho World*, August 25, 1870, p. 3, c. 2.

Clawson's toll gate on the Idaho City road, as drawn for Elliott's History of Idaho Territory *(1884).*

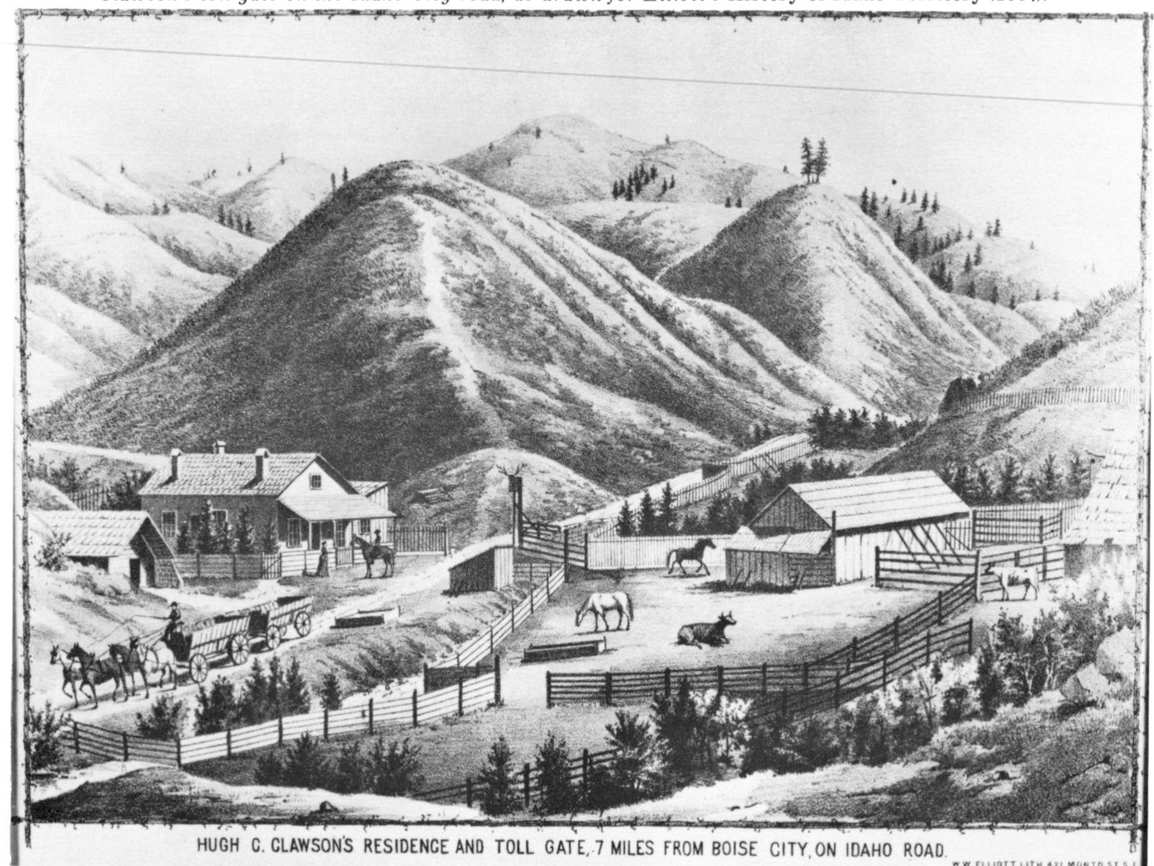

"Hard-Shell persuasion" at the time of the hold-up. He furnished the press with a long and detailed account of the incident as he recalled it. Only one thing was certain: Wells Fargo issued a handbill offering a reward of $1,000 for the detection of the robbers.[31]

Idaho residents soon learned of the next robbery of Wells Fargo & Co.'s treasure box, this time on the Central Pacific Railroad at the Verdi station, eight miles west of Reno, on the night of November 4. Three robbers jumped up on the express car and knocked down and gagged the messenger. Three others held the engineer at pistol point while others uncoupled the passenger cars. Then they ran the engine with the express and mail cars for a distance of four miles down the track and there robbed Wells Fargo of approximately $41,000 in gold coin. The silver, too heavy to carry, was scattered about the floor of the express car. Later reports revealed that eight to a dozen highwaymen were involved, many of them passengers on the train. The brakeman, conductor, and fireman had fought valiantly to protect the train, one attempting to use a hatchet—no match for the pistols of the robbers. Apparently the highwaymen were not satisfied; the same train was again held up at Independence, twenty-two miles west of Toano, where it was taking on water. Four men again uncoupled the train from the engine and express car, rode fifteen miles down the track, and robbed the express of several thousand dollars more. Wells Fargo immediately offered a $5,000 reward for the capture of the thieves and the railroad company agreed to pay $1,000 for the arrest and conviction of each man connected with the robberies.[32] The highwaymen had readily transferred their activities from stagecoaches to the express car on the railroads.

WELLS FARGO & CO. continued to be a major banking house in Silver City, located on Washington Street. The company purchased and made advances on bullion, bought and sold currency, sold exchange on the Atlantic states and Europe, drew direct on San Francisco and New York, and received both general and special deposits.[33] The route for the delivery of express and treasure from Owyhee to the railroad was in flux. As noted earlier, Hill Beachey had abandoned his old route to Winnemucca and transferred his stages to a new line into Elko. Immediately, an "Opposition Line" to Winnemucca was proposed. A. T. Clark began running a semi-weekly service from that community to Idaho and announced that if there were sufficient support from the public he would put on a tri-weekly or even a daily service. "The Winnemucca people are doing their utmost to make their town the depot for Idaho," noted the editor of the *World*. "They may succeed as far as freight is concerned, but at present no stage line from the railroad can be sustained without the aid of a mail contract."[34] Toward the end of July, the Winnemucca newspaper announced that Thomas Early had made arrangements to establish a fast-freight and passenger line of stages from there to Silver City. Early was out stocking the road and expected to run tri-weekly stages before the end of the month.[35]

In August, the *Capital Chronicle* of Boise announced: "Wells, Fargo & Co. have removed their office from the upper end of Main street down to the building formerly occupied by G. Kohlberg & Co., opposite the Overland Hotel in the Oriental block."[36] W. W. Atlee, long-time Wells Fargo agent, continued to supply the Boise newspaper with the latest news exchanges.[37]

Wells Fargo agents in Idaho City also maintained the tradition of good relations with the press. The *Idaho World* repeatedly expressed appreciation for the exchanges provided by D. F. Wagner, "the gentlemanly and accommodating agent" of the company.

[31] *Capital Chronicle*, August 24, 1870, p. 3, c. 2, August 27, 1870, p. 2, c. 1; *Owyhee Avalanche*, August 27, 1870, p. 3, c. 2; *Oregon State Journal* (Eugene), August 27, 1870, p. 2, c. 4; *Weekly Oregon Herald* (Portland), August 27, 1870, p. 2, c. 4 and 5; *Statesman*, August 27, 1870, p. 1, c. 2.

[32] *Idaho World*, November 10, 1870, p. 2, c. 5; *Owyhee Avalanche*, November 12, 1870, p. 2, c. 2; *Statesman*, November 12, 1870, p. 2, c. 1.

[33] *Owyhee Avalanche*, February 26, 1870, p. 1, c. 6.

[34] *Ibid.*, July 2, 1870, p. 2, c. 3.

[35] *Ibid.*, July 23, 1870, p. 1, c. 5.

[36] *Capital Chronicle*, August 6, 1870, p. 2, c. 3, August 10, 1870, p. 3, c. 1. The building was at the corner of Eighth and Main.

[37] *Ibid.*, August 31, 1870, p. 2, c. 2.

Messengers also brought the latest news concerning the Franco-Prussian War, and the company's employees made the practice of forwarding the latest telegrams if they contained any news of interest.[38]

Wells Fargo's services to outlying districts were often noted in the newspapers. In March, 1870, the company established an office in Mountain City in the Cope Mining District at approximately the same time a post office was established there, so the newest mining camp had both express and mail service. The next month, Wells Fargo was making plans to start an express from Baker City to El Dorado and all the adjoining camps.[39]

The year also brought changes in the assignments of Wells Fargo personnel in Idaho Territory. J. L. Smith, who had served as agent in Idaho City for many years and more recently in Silver City, resigned his position with plans to retire to California. His replacement, in March, 1870, was A. W. Buchanan. The Owyhee newspaper reported:

> Mr. Buchanan has been in the employ of Wells, Fargo & Co. for sixteen years. He now hails from the Dalles, where he has been agent of that Company during the last seven years. Capable through long experience, he is eminently qualified for the important position he occupies. He is affable, obliging, and a very pleasant gentleman withal. Silver bids him welcome.[40]

In April, Mrs. Buchanan arrived to join her husband and the press took note: "Buck looks like a new man."[41]

The *Owyhee Avalanche* reported that Wells Fargo was conducting all the express business of the community with the exception of Knapp & Co.'s express to the nearly Loon Creek diggings.[42] In May, D. C. Field, who had been an accountant for many firms in Silver City, and most recently for Wells Fargo & Co., was called to the San Francisco headquarters to assume a position in the banking department there.[43] Another well-known employee of the company, Joe Jones, who served as messenger on the Railroad Stage Line between Silver City and Elko, always delivered the newspaper exchanges; when he was injured as a stage overturned, great concern was expressed.[44]

In the communities along the Columbia River, Wells Fargo's activities were no longer featured in the news as they had been in the decade of the 1860's. Other concerns remained much the same. The Oregon Steam Navigation Company was accused of charging too much for freight and passenger fare. The mail service was deemed inadequate. Railroad construction was progressing in Oregon along the banks of the Columbia River and north and south through the Willamette Valley.[45] The Columbia River froze in winter, shutting down communication; when summer came, the

Northwestern

STAGE COMPANY

—o—

COACHES LEAVE BOISE CITY daily for all points North, South, East and West.

Great Reduction

IN FARE TO THE EAST.

Rates of Fare:

BOISE CITY to Kelton, Utah,....	$ 50 00	currency.
" " Silver City, Idaho,..	10 00	coin.
" " Mountain City, Nev.	40 00	"
" " Elko, Nevada,......	50 00	"
" " OMAHA, via Kelton,	111 50	currency.
" " CHICAGO, do do,	129 50	"
" " Baker City, Oregon,	23 00	coin.
" " La Grande. Oregon,	30 00	"
" " Walla Walla, W. T.,	40 00	"
" " Umatilla, Oregon,...	40 00	"
" " Portland, do	50 00	"

THROUGH TICKETS

To Omaha and Chicago

Can be purchased at all our offices.

☞Parties purchasing Through Tickets to Chicago can go by either the Chicago & Northwestern, the Chicago, Burlington & Quincy, or the Chicago, Rock Island & Pacific Railroads.

THEO. V. MATTHEWS,

June 1, '71tf. Assistant Gen'l Supt.

[38] *Idaho World*, March 10, 1870, p. 3, c. 1, September 22, 1870, p. 2, c. 5.

[39] *Capital Chronicle*, March 26, 1870, p. 2, c. 3, April 9, 1870, p. 4, c. 4.

[40] *Owyhee Avalanche*, March 12, 1870, p. 3, c. 4.

[41] *Ibid.*, April 16, 1870, p. 3, c. 2.

[42] *Ibid.*, April 30, 1870, p. 3, c. 4.

[43] *Ibid.*, May 7, 1870, p. 3, c. 3.

[44] *Ibid.*, July 30, 1870, p. 3, c. 2, August 6, 1870, p. 3, c. 2.

[45] *Statesman*, March 5, 1870, p. 3, c. 2, March 26, 1870, p. 2, c. 6, August 13, 1870, p. 3, c. 2, May 7, 1870, p. 1, c. 2, December 17, 1870, p. 3, c. 1, December 31, 1870, p. 1, c. 2.

steamers ran all the way to Lewiston—resulting in a lull of business in Walla Walla. The Wells Fargo agents retained great respect in Walla Walla.

E. L. James, Esq., a pioneer agent for Wells, Fargo & Co.'s express, arrived here by Saturday's stage, looking well and hearty, and glad to be back on his old stamping ground. Our acquaintance with him dates back so many years we are afraid to name them lest we both be suspected of growing old; but this we can say, that during the whole time we have known him as a true gentleman and whole-hearted friend.[46]

Farther down the Columbia at The Dalles, C. M. Lockwood was finally awarded the contract in April, 1870, to carry the United States mail once a week to Boise City via Canyon City for $20,000 a year.[47]

In April, 1871, the Northwestern Stage Line, running between Elko and Boise and carrying the United States mails and Wells Fargo & Co.'s express, advertised its schedule and charges in the Silver City paper and elsewhere:

NORTH WESTERN
STAGE LINE
FROM ELKO TO IDAHO!

Carrying Wells, Fargo & Co.'s Express and the United States Mails.

STAGES LEAVE ELKO DAILY UPON THE arrival of the Western Train, arriving at Mountain City the following morning; leaving Mountain City at ten o'clock, A.M., and arriving at Silver City at six o'clock, A.M. the following day; leaving Silver City at seven o'clock, A.M. and arriving at Boise City at six o'clock P.M. same day. Returning from Boise City to Elko on same time schedule.

RATES OF FARE:

From Elko to Mountain City	$15
From Mountain City to Silver City	25
From Silver City to Boise City	10

THROUGH TICKETS:

From Silver City to Omaha, coin	$134.35
From " Chicago, "	152.35

Office—Idaho Hotel, C.M. HAYS, Agent.
Silver City, I. T., April 8, 1871.[48]

The line, more popularly known as the Northwestern Stage Company, was rumored to be making plans to withdraw its stages from the Umatilla route and place them on the road between Walla Walla and Boise. The Walla Walla paper commented: "this will prove to be the case we have no doubt."[49]

The company soon posted fares on the line from the Columbia River through eastern Oregon to Boise City and Silver City and on to the railroad by either the Elko or the Kelton route. Through tickets all the way to Omaha or Chicago were available in Walla Walla.

North-Western Stage
COMPANY.
GREAT
Reduction in Fare to the East.
RATES OF FARE:

	Coin.
Walla Walla to La Grande, Oregon	$ 12.00
Walla Walla to Union, Oregon	14.00
Walla Walla to Baker City, Oregon	20.00
Walla Walla to Boise City, Idaho	40.00
Walla Walla to Silver City, Idaho	50.00
Walla Walla to Kelton, Utah, C.P.R.R.	75.00
Walla Walla to Elko, Utah, [sic] C.P.R.R.	75.00
Walla Walla to Omaha, Neb., 1st Class	131.50
Walla Walla to Omaha, Neb., 2d Class	124.00
Walla Walla to Chicago, Ills., 1st Class	149.50
Walla Walla to Chicago, Ills., 2d Class	137.00

THROUGH TICKETS
TO
OMAHA AND CHICAGO

Can be purchased at all our offices.

Parties purchasing Through Tickets to Chicago can go either by the Chicago & North-Western, the Chicago, Burlington & Quincy, or the Chicago, Rock Island & Pacific Railroad.

Office of the Northwestern Stage Company at the Oriental Hotel, Walla Walla, W. T.

ADAM E. SMITH, General Superintendent
J. B. DEXTER, Agent.
Walla Walla, May 28, 1871.[50]

The next step in the company's plan to establish an integrated network of stage services was the purchase of Henry Greathouse's Boise and Idaho Stage Line by Theodore V. Mathews of the firm, which expected to deliver both passenger and mails between Boise and the Basin. The *Democrat* commented:

While we regret to lose Mr. Greathouse, who has been in the stage business for years in Idaho, we are pleased to announce that Mr. Mathews is to be his successor. We

[46] *Ibid.*, June 18, 1870, p. 1, c. 2.

[47] *Daily Oregon Herald* (Portland), April 13, 1870, p. 3, c. 1.

[48] *Owyhee Avalanche*, April 8, 1871, p. 2, c. 3.

[49] *Statesman*, April 29, 1871, p. 1, c. 5.

[50] *Ibid.*, May 20, 1871, p. 2, c. 7.

predict Mr. Mathews will meet with the same success and become as popular among the traveling public as his predecessor.[51]

Henry Greathouse's decision to withdraw from the staging business after so many years was prompted by personal reasons. His brother, Ridgely, had become seriously ill and left for Mexico in hopes of regaining his health. He was accompanied by George, Henry's son, whose destination was San Jose, California, where he expected to complete his college studies. The third brother, also named George, had recently been ill, and he also left Idaho for California.[52] On May 27, 1871, the *Idaho Democrat* announced that Greathouse Bros. had closed their banking business in Boise and elsewhere in the territory.[53] A younger generation was taking over the stage business. The Northwestern Stage Company employed W. C. Beachey, a nephew of the "indefatigable Hill Beachey," to work in its offices in Boise.[54] Also at this time, C. C. Hundley, for a long time a stage man in Montana, had purchased an interest in the Northwestern Stage Company.[55] According to the local press, the one line not controlled by the Northwestern Stage Company in May, 1871, was that of the Pinkham brothers in the Boise Basin between Idaho City and Placerville, which had even extended service three miles further to Quartzburg.[56] John Hailey suggests that their independence did not last long: Ebenezer and Joseph Pinkham were soon bought out.[57]

By June, Theodore Mathews was on the scene in Idaho, working to integrate the service on the Boise and Idaho Stage Line with that of the Northwestern Stage Company between Boise and Elko, a section of which he was the assistant general superintendent. The *Idaho World* reported that he was introducing

[51] *Idaho Democrat*, May 10, 1871, p. 3, c. 1.

[52] *Ibid.*, January 28, 1871, p. 3, c. 1.

[53] *Ibid.*, May 27, 1871, p. 3, c. 2.

[54] *Ibid.*, May 6, 1871, p. 3, c. 1.

[55] *Owyhee Avalanche*, May 13, 1871, p. 2, c. 1.

[56] *Idaho Democrat*, May 6, 1871, p. 3, c. 1.

[57] Hailey, *History of Idaho*, 125-126.

An oil painting of Payne's Ferry, near Thousand Springs on the Snake River. From the Idaho State Historical Society's collection.

new stock, coaches, and drivers and that the entire line between the Columbia River and Central Pacific Railroad would be under his management. The editor commented:

After this, persons paying their fare will not be required to walk half the way, nor will they be required to assist spavined, broken-winded old stage plugs to get the empty stage up any of the hills, as has been the case too often heretofore. Mathews understands his "bis," and intends that travelers over his line shall have nothing to complain of.[58]

Services between the two communities were advertised.

At the Boise end of the line, connections could be made for all points in all directions.

The Northwestern Stage Company also consolidated its position at each end of its stage network. First it purchased Abbott's short line between Walla Walla and Wallula, on the banks of the Columbia.[59] Then came the report that the company would abandon the Elko route and return to Winnemucca.

NORTH WESTERN
STAGE LINE

From Winnemucca, Nevada, to Silver City and Boise City, Idaho. Carrying Wells, Fargo & Co.'s Express and the United States Mails.

Through to Silver City in
36 HOURS!

STAGE LEAVES WINNEMUCCA DAILY, at 9 ½ o'clock, A.M., upon the arrival of the Western Train, arriving at Silver City at about 10 ¼ o'clock, P.M., the second day.

Leaves Silver City daily at 5 o'clock A.M. arriving at Boise City at 4 o'clock P.M. the same day.

RETURNING—Leaves Boise City daily at 3 o'clock A.M., arriving in Silver City at 3 o'clock P.M., connecting with Winnemucca stage which leaves at 5 o'clock, P.M. same day.

RATES OF FARE:

Winnemucca to Silver City or vice versa $40.00
Silver City to Boise City, " " 10.00
Office—Idaho Hotel

C. M. HAYS, Agent.

Silver City, I. T., July 14, 1871.[60]

The change in route was made necessary by a new mail contract. The *Winnemucca Register* reported with some pride:

The Northwestern Stage Company commenced running and carrying the U. S. mails and Wells, Fargo & Co.'s Express on the Winnemucca route to Silver and Boise City on the first of last month. This Company is now a fixed institution of Winnemucca, and their fine Concord coaches, prancing steeds and gentlemanly business agents connected therewith, have already given a lively air and healthy appearance to business in our flourishing little city. The coaches depart from this place for the North every morning at 9 ½ o'clock, and arrive at 1 ½ P.M. daily; their early arrival affords passengers two and a half hours rest before the arrival of the 4 p.m. west-bound passenger Express for the Bay. Their time from Winnemucca to Silver is made in 36 hours, and to Boise in 48 hours. This we consider remarkably good time.[61]

Although the Toano route from the transcontinental railroad was not used by stages, and that from Kelton only for a brief period, freighters continued to use both. Major improvements were made on the Kelton Road, and freighters could make the trip between Boise and Kelton in nineteen days. One freighter reported that there was not a grade on the new route where a wagon could not stand without blocking, and the route was superior to the other roads into southwestern Idaho.[62] A Toano freighter who had promoted the Toano Road to Idaho reported that by September, 1871, he had shipped 45,000 pounds of freight to Boise. At that point the great Pioche fire disrupted the Idaho traffic from Toano because freighters were diverted carrying goods for the rebuilding of that Nevada community.[63]

As winter approached, the few remaining independent and short stage lines in Idaho began to shut down. The proprietor of the Rocky Bar line notified the *Idaho Herald* in Boise the first week of November that after two or three more trips he would withdraw his stages from Rocky Bar to Rattlesnake, where a junction was made with the overland line. The proprietor planned to run stages from Boise to Rattlesnake as long as the traffic required the service, and from the overland road to Rocky Bar he would use pack animals until cut off by snow.[64] At The Dalles, the *Mountaineer* announced that a tri-weekly mail service would

[58]*Idaho World*, June 1, 1871, p. 3, c. 1.

[59]*Owyhee Avalanche*, June 3, 1871, p. 3, c. 3.

[60]*Ibid.*, July 8, 1871, p. 2, c. 4.

[61]Quoted in *ibid.*, August 6, 1871, p. 1, c. 4.

[62]"Kelton Road."

[63]"The Toano Route."

[64]*Idaho Herald* (Boise), November 8, 1871, p. 3, c. 1.

be put on the route between The Dalles and Boise City by way of Canyon City. Ad. Edgar, the proprietor of the Dalles-Canyon City route, had gone to San Francisco to purchase new stages.[65] Evidence suggests that his was one of the few stage routes in Idaho and eastern Oregon that the Northwestern Stage Company did not control.

Late in July, the Northwestern Stage Company had advertised a material reduction in rates of fare from the Columbia River communities to Omaha, Chicago, and other points in the Atlantic states. The stages were making connections with the railroad at Kelton.[66] Apparently, the Northwestern Stage Company operated dual routes: one to Winnemucca for passengers and mails destined for California and another to Kelton for those headed east. At the close of 1871, the company was still advertising its reduced rates.

North-Western Stage Co.
GREAT
Reduction in Fare to the East.

THROUGH TICKETS TO OMAHA, CHICAGO, St. Louis, Kansas City, via Kelton and Boise City, the short direct route East, we now offer at reduced rates over the lines of the North-Western Stage Company.

New coaches, good stock, skilled drivers, and reliable performance of service on time are special features of the Company.

Office—At Oriental Hotel, Walla Walla, Washington Territory.

W. H. P. BRYAN, Agent.

WM. B. MORRIS, Gen'l Sup't.[67]

WELLS FARGO & CO.'S express was carried on all the stages operated by the Northwestern Stage Company, a fact well advertised throughout Idaho Territory. In July of 1871, the office of the Idaho and Boise Stage Line, integrated with the larger stage company, was changed from the Luna House in Idaho City to Wells Fargo & Co.'s express office, at the corner of Main and Commercial streets. D. F. Wagner, the Wells Fargo agent, attended to the business of both firms.[68]

Bullion shipments from the Owyhee District were handled by Wells Fargo throughout 1871. The newspaper carried announcements of each weekly shipment. In January, the total shipments amounted to $116,185.40.[69] February witnessed weekly shipments of from ten to nineteen bars of silver valued at approximately $26,000 to $39,000.[70] The weekly shipments of May were slightly lower, anywhere from five to fifteen bars with a value of between $14,000 and $17,000.[71] The *Avalanche* published a summary of the shipments of treasure by Wells Fargo from Silver City for 1871.

Gold Dust and Bullion for 1871.

We herewith append a statement of the gold dust and bullion (coin value) shipped by Wells, Fargo & Co., from this place during the year ending December 31st, 1871.

	Dust.	Bullion.
January	$ 2,790.00	$150,375.39
February	2,136.63	147,564.46
March	2,500.84	93,270.47
April	2,990.00	44,819.64
May	3,480.50	86,170.06
June	4,310.00	66,438.86
July	6,470.00	92,773.58
August	4,350.00	77,285.23
September	3,640.00	53,781.15
October	4,903.58	46,734.51
November	4,517.66	32,218.02
December	3,038.67	44,803.00
	$45,128.38 [sic]	$936,234.37
Total		$981,362.75.

This amount exceeds the treasure shipments for 1870 by $175,288.26. . . . From present prospects, 1872 will foot up at least two millions, and no telling how much more, if the South Mountain mines should be worked, as they most assuredly will.[72]

A significant change occurred in Wells Fargo's handling of bullion when it began to ship Nevada treasure east to New York rather than west to San Francisco. The amount of bullion received at the Wells Fargo office in Salt Lake City from Pioche during the single month of February, 1871, was 159 bars

[65] *Ibid.*, November 17, 1871, p. 3, c. 2.

[66] *Statesman*, July 29, 1871, p. 2, c. 6.

[67] *Ibid.*, December 2, 1871, p. 2, c. 7.

[68] *Idaho World*, July 20, 1871, p. 3, c. 1.

[69] *Idaho Democrat*, January 11, 1871, p. 3, c. 2, quoting the *Owyhee Avalanche*, February 1, 1871, p. 2, c. 1, February 8, 1871, p. 2, c. 3. The same statistics appeared in the *Idaho World*, February 2, 1871, p. 2, c. 1, February 9, 1871, p. 2, c. 5.

[70] *Idaho Democrat*, February 15, 1871, p. 4, c. 1, February 25, 1871, p. 2, c. 3, March 1, 1871, p. 1, c. 5.

[71] *Ibid.*, May 10, 1871, p. 2, c. 1, May 17, 1871, p. 2, c. 2, May 24, 1871, p. 2, c. 3.

[72] *Owyhee Avalanche*, January 6, 1871, p. 2, c. 2.

weighing 16,998 pounds, valued at $226,776 in coin. It was all consigned to a New York firm.[73]

In the struggle between Elko and Winnemucca to become the terminus of the mail route from Idaho Territory, Wells Fargo was convinced that the latter community would be the ultimate winner. As early as February, 1871, the company had curtailed its operations in Elko by appointing M. P. Freeman & Co. as its agents there. Freeman & Co. were to carry on a banking business as usual, but Wells Fargo & Co. discontinued the drawing of checks at the community.[74]

Although the completion of the Central Pacific-Union Pacific Railroad necessitated Wells Fargo & Co.'s decision that express, treasure, and fast-freight services from Idaho Territory should head in that direction, the company by no means abandoned its services along the Columbia River. The Walla Walla *Statesman* revealed early in February, 1871, that Wells Fargo had made a reduction of from 25 to 33 per cent on its rates for "Fast Freight" from Portland to various points in Idaho and Washington territories and eastern Oregon.[75]

In April, Wells Fargo & Co. Bank in Silver City advertised:

> $20,000 Legal Tenders
> For Sale
> at
> WELLS, FARGO & CO.'S[76]

The company was still active in the banking business at the year's close. The editor of the *Avalanche* noted: "Banking—Wells, Fargo & Co.—When Buck pulls his mustache it is all right, but when he goes after his eyebrows, look out for breakers."[77]

A significant personnel change was made in Boise City in June, 1871. W. A. Atlee, the popular and efficient long-time agent, was transferred to Portland to take charge of the office there and George Greathouse took charge of the Boise City office.[78] Soon thereafter Jack Shepard, the Wells Fargo messenger who for years had supplied the Idaho newspapers with exchanges, was promoted by the company to take charge of the agency in Winnemucca, Nevada. He was also to be the agent for the Northwestern Stage Company. The editor of the *Idaho World* wrote: "We congratulate him on his good fortune, and the two companies could not have made a better selection, as he is thoroughly qualified, a genial and whole-souled gentleman, and has a host of friends wherever he is known."[79] The friendship between the editor and the agent was obvious. "We return thanks to our friend Capt. Jack Shepard, Wells, Fargo & Co.'s attentive and gentlemanly agent in Winnemucca, for special favors in the way of late news by telegraph and otherwise," the editor soon noted. "'Shep,' may your shadow never grow less."[80]

There were important differences between the United States mail and the express service in Idaho. The Silver City newspaper explained to its readers in July:

> All persons desiring to send letters by way packet from Silver City to Boise and Winnemucca, or any way station on the road to either place, or to any house or persons between those two places, are hereby notified that the same must be enclosed in Wells, Fargo & Co.'s express envelopes or in prepaid stamped envelopes, and unless this rule is complied with the agent will not receive them, as the Postal Law prohibits mail carriers from doing otherwise than stated above in relation to carrying way letters.[81]

The Walla Walla *Statesman* also provided information about the difference in the way treasure was handled by the mails and express between San Francisco and the east.

> It is a fact not generally known that all gold sent East from San Francisco now goes through the mail bags. It is put up in small boxes, weighing two or three pounds, and each box is sent as a registered letter. In this way the cost of transportation is about one per cent., while the express companies charge five. One hundred thousand dollars thus passes daily through the Omaha postoffice.[82]

[73] *Idaho World*, March 23, 1871, p. 3, c. 1.

[74] *Owyhee Avalanche*, February 25, 1871, p. 2, c. 3.

[75] *Statesman*, February 11, 1871, p. 2, c. 5. Reprinted in the *Idaho World*, February 23, 1871, p. 2, c. 5.

[76] *Owyhee Avalanche*, April 15, 1871, p. 3, c. 3.

[77] *Ibid.*, December 30, 1871, p. 2, c. 3.

[78] *Idaho World*, June 15, 1871, p. 2, c. 5.

[79] *Ibid.*, August 31, 1871, p. 3, c. 2.

[80] *Ibid.*, September 28, 1871, p. 3, c. 2.

[81] *Owyhee Avalanche*, July 8, 1871, p. 3, c. 2.

[82] *Statesman*, September 23, 1871, p. 3, c. 3.

There was a further explanation of the difference between sending freight by express and sending it by stage.

A Mistaken Idea—Many of our people entertain the idea that they can get freight much cheaper and just as quick by having it come in care of the Northwestern Stage Company, as they can by express. In this they are mistaken. Wells, Fargo & Co. charge the same rates from Winnemucca, as do the stage company; and the express freight always takes precedence and *must* come through, though all other freight and even passengers can be left behind. This will serve to explain the cause of the frequent delays of packages and freight which have been ordered by stage instead of express.[83]

Wells Fargo also announced a reduction in express charges from San Francisco into the Idaho communities in October of 1871. Freight to Silver City was reduced from twenty-five to sixteen cents a pound; from Winnemucca to Silver City, it was only ten cents a pound. The *Avalanche* believed this would "enable merchants and others to get light and valuable freight promptly by express rather than trusting ox-teams, or the tender mercies of a blundering stage company."[84] The general reduction in rates was publicized throughout the northwest. Emphasis was placed upon the new rate from California to Boise, nineteen cents rather than twenty-five.[85]

The year did not pass without a stage holdup. On October 2, 1871, the stage running between Umatilla and Boise was stopped by two road agents about two miles south of Old's Ferry. The highwaymen thrust the muzzles of their shotguns into the face of the driver and demanded the Wells Fargo treasure box. After consulting the passengers, he decided to hand it over to the robbers. "Then they inquired how many passengers were aboard; and were told three. 'Have you any Jews along?' 'No.' 'Then drive on quick.'" The next day the box was found, smashed open and its mail contents scattered promiscuously in the road. The manifests were within the box and it was not known just how much treasure had been lost—perhaps not more than $75. The stagecoach of the previous day had carried thousands of dollars. The three passengers on board considered themselves fortunate in not being molested. The sheriff of Boise City had gone in search of the culprits.[86] The road agents usually paid a price for their folly: three months later the two culprits were sentenced to fifteen years in the territorial prison.[87]

THE NORTHWESTERN STAGE Company expanded its influence throughout Idaho Territory during 1872. In January, the Pinkham brothers finally sold out their Boise Basin line to Theodore V. Mathews. The *Idaho World* commented:

The new proprietor has reduced his rates to a greenback basis, both on passengers and freight tariff, which is not only a great convenience to the public, but a sensible move on the part of Mr. Mathews, who is not only an agreeable and courteous gentleman, but seems to understand the business.

Concerning the previous proprietors, the editor said:

We regret to part with the old proprietors, who have for four or five years past managed the stage business in the basin in a manner highly satisfactory to the traveling public. Ever accommodating, and prompt and attentive to the requirements and comfort of those who travel over their line, we believe that we but express the sentiments of all the people when we say that we regret to hear of their relinquishment of the stage business in this section.[88]

In the spring, W. C. Tatro, proprietor of the Rocky Bar Stage Line, announced that he had made arrangements with the Northwestern Stage Company to transport its mails, freight, and passengers to and from Rattlesnake Station, there to connect with his line to and from Rocky Bar. The *Idaho Standard* of Boise noted: "In all transactions during the course of several years, Mr. Tatro has given general satisfaction as a prompt and reliable businessman" from his office on Main Street.[89]

[83] *Owyhee Avalanche*, October 21, 1871, p. 3, c. 3.

[84] *Ibid.*, October 28, 1871, p. 3, c. 3.

[85] *Idaho World*, November 9, 1871, p. 2, c. 4; *Idaho Herald*, November 8, 1871, p. 3, c. 2.

[86] *Statesman*, October 14, 1871, p. 2, c. 6; *Owyhee Avalanche*, October 7, 1871, p. 2, c. 3.

[87] *Owyhee Avalanche*, December 30, 1871, p. 2, c. 3.

[88] *Idaho World*, January 18, 1872, p. 3, c. 1 and 2.

[89] *Idaho Standard* (Boise), May 15, 1872, p. 3, c. 1.

The *Idaho Standard* also published a timetable for the operation of the stages of the Northwestern Stage Company out of Boise.

TIME TABLE OF THE NORTH
WESTERN STAGE COMPANY.

Boise City, Idaho,
May 23, 1872.

Umatilla Stages,—Due at Boise City daily at ....6 A.M.
Leaves Boise City daily at ....4 P.M.
Kelton Stage.—Due at Boise City daily at ....1 A.M.
Leaves Boise City daily at ....4 P.M.
Winnemucca Stages.—Due at Boise City daily at ....5 P.M.
Leaves Boise City daily at ....5 A.M.

Stages from Willow Creek Mines, Canyon and Dalles City arrive every Saturday and leave every Monday at 3 A.M.

Time through to Kelton ....2 days.
Time through to Walla Walla ....2 days.
Time through to Umatilla ....2 days.
Time through to Portland ....4 days.
Time through to Winnemucca ....2 days.

Close connections at Winnemucca and Kelton with trains East and West.

Umatilla Stages leaving Boise on Fridays and Mondays make close connection with the O.S.N. Company's steamers leaving Umatilla Mondays and Thursdays.

WM. B. MORRIS,
Superintendent.

Boise City, May 23, 1872.[90]

Thus the Northwestern Stage Company continued its double termini on the railroad at Kelton and Winnemucca; at the northern end, its line ran into Walla Walla and on to the Columbia at Umatilla.

TELEGRAPH CONSTRUCTION WAS another topic of national concern in the early 1870's. There was debate as to whether the "national system" should be owned and operated by the government or by private enterprise. The editor of the *Avalanche* favored a postal telegraph system operated by the government, comparable to the United States mails, and wrote a long editorial defending his position and countering the arguments of private business. The outcome of the debate affected the interests of both the express and the telegraph companies.

The Government carries letters, treasure and packages of all sorts through the mails. The same business is followed to a large extent by our express companies. Now, it is not an invasion of Wells, Fargo & Co.'s rights for the Government to carry letters and treasure, though Wells, Fargo & Co. are in the same business. Then why should it be deemed an interference with the rights of Western Union Telegraph Company for the Government to transmit intelligence for the people by telegraph? What is the difference in principle, between transmitting it by telegraph or by mail? The Government will not compete with private enterprise in one case more than in the other.[91]

At the end of March, Wells Fargo announced that A. W. Buchanan, its agent in Silver City, had been relieved of his duties there and recalled to San Francisco. Soon the reason for his departure became known: Wells Fargo had decided to give up its banking business in Silver City, and its new agent, J. L. Gardner, Jr., was to take over the firm's operations in that area. On April 1, 1872, the public was officially notified:

THE BANKING BUSINESS HERETOFORE conducted in this place under the name and style and for account of Wells, Fargo & Co. has this day been transferred to Mr. J. L. Gardner, Jr., with all the good will, emoluments, risks, and responsibilities. All parties holding certificates of deposit, open accounts, pass-books, checks, or other evidence of indebtedness against this office, will please call and have them paid, or transferred to Mr. Gardner's accounts. Mr. Gardner being well recommended is therefore commended to the confidence and good will of the community.

CHAS. E. McLANE,
Supt. Banking Dept.
By A. W. BUCHANAN,
Agent.

Dated, Silver City,
I. T., April 1st, 1872.

To the Public

MR. J. L. GARDNER, Jr., HAS been appointed Agent for Wells, Fargo & Co.'s Express, and will transact for account and risk of Wells, Fargo & Co., all legitimate Express business.

JNO. J. VALENTINE,
Genl. Supt.

April 1st, 1872.[92]

Wells Fargo & Co. remained active in the express business in northern Idaho. In January, 1872, the *Lewiston Journal* reported: "W. F. & Co.'s Express leaves by every steamer and the Walla Walla stage."[93] However, the service from Portland into Idaho remained uncertain. Telegraphic dispatches periodically reported the departure of

[90] *Ibid.*, July 17, 1872, p. 3, c. 2.

[91] *Owyhee Avalanche*, March 9, 1872, p. 2, c. 1.

[92] *Ibid.*, March 20, 1872, p. 3, c. 2, April 6, 1872, p. 2, c. 3.

[93] *The Lewiston Journal*, January 13, 1872, p. 1, c. 5.

steamers with both the mails and Wells Fargo's express on board, but they were a long while reaching their destination in the winter months. The Lewiston editor remarked: "The amount of mail matter that has accumulated here is perfectly astonishing. We are rather surprised that the people of Portland are so indifferent to their mail communication. It is a pity that they have so little enterprise."[94]

Three stage lines ran out of Lewiston in 1872: to Walla Walla, to Pierce City, and to Elk City. The most important of these was the Lewiston & Walla Walla Stage Line, which advertised:

LEWISTON & WALLA WALLA
STAGE LINE,
CARRYING
U. S. MAIL
AND
Wells, Fargo & Co.'s Express
MAKES
Regular Tri-Weekly Trips
to and from the above named points. Leaving Lewiston on MONDAYS, WEDNESDAYS and FRIDAYS, at 7 o'clock A.M. Leaving Walla Walla the same hour on alternate days.

FARE:

From Lewiston to Pataha	$ 2.50
" " " Tucanon	5.00
" " " Waitsburg	7.50
" " " Walla Walla	10.00

This line is now provided with good Coaches, the best of Animals, and employ careful and accommodating Drivers.
OFFICE at Lewiston, Hotel De France.
CHAS. LE FRANCOIS, Agent.
OFFICE at Walla Walla, Oriental Hotel.
J. D. COOK, Agent
MATTHEW FETTIS,
Proprietor.

The North Idaho Stage Company was taking the United States mails and its own express to Pierce City.

NORTH IDAHO
STAGE COMPANY,
CAPPS Brothers, Proprietors,
carry, by Stage, the U. S. MAIL and their EXPRESS and PASSENGERS to and from Lewiston and Pierce City.

FARE THROUGH, $15

Lewiston to Lapwai	$ 1.50
" " Cold Spring	2.50
" " Reed's Ferry	10.00

The Capps Brothers are Expressmen, and attend to all matters which are included in that line of business.
INCLUDING COLLECTIONS.

They have the privilege to refer to Levi Ankeny, merchant, Lewiston, I. T. and Thos. Charman, merchant, Oregon City, Ogn.

The Lewiston and Elk City Express was another local line that made connections with Wells Fargo in Lewiston.

LEWISTON and ELK CITY
EXPRESS
BAIRD BROS., Proprietors,
CONNECTING WITH WELLS, FARGO & CO. Office at LEVI ANKENY'S store, Northwest corner of Third and D streets.[95]

Throughout 1874 and 1875 the Lewiston and Walla Walla Stage Line continued to advertise its service in *The Northerner.* The Lewiston and Warren's Express that had been started by the Baird brothers in 1867 also continued, making connections with Wells Fargo's express in Lewiston.

LEWISTON
AND
WARREN'S
EXPRESS,
BAIRD BROS.————————Prop's.
THE PROPRIETORS ANNOUNCE THAT they will run a WEEKLY EXPRESS to and from the above named points, and also from
LEWISTON TO ELK CITY.
These Expresses both make close connections at Lewiston with WELLS, FARGO & CO.
Office at LOEWENBERG BROS.[96]

On July 1, 1878, the Northwestern Stage Company lost the contract for carrying the United States mails. John Hailey joined Gilmer & Salisbury of Salt Lake, who had succeeded Wells Fargo & Co. in Montana, to form the Utah, Idaho and Oregon Stage Company. Hailey and his associates took over the contracts both for the mails and for the transportation of Wells Fargo & Co.'s express, with Hailey as superintendent.[97] The Utah, Idaho, and Oregon Stage Company ran from Hailey to Kelton and also to Boise City, Silver

[94] *Ibid.,* p. 2, c. 2.

[95] *Ibid.,* p. 4, c. 2 and 3.

[96] *The Northerner,* September 12, 1874, p. 4, c. 4, June 5, 1875, p. 2, c. 7.

[97] "Idaho Express" collection, Idaho State Historical Society, Boise.

City, and Winnemucca. The rate from Hailey to Kelton was $25.00, from Hailey to Boise $22.50. In June, 1881, the company advertised that it was handling Wells Fargo's express.[98] The company had started using the Glenn's Ferry route on the Kelton Road as early as 1879, and a new stage station at Salmon Falls replaced the Malad Station as a result of this change.[99]

When the transcontinental railroad reached Idaho in 1883, Wells Fargo had seventy offices in the territory.[100] The impact of railroad construction was producing many adjustments. L. A. Hall, special agent for Wells Fargo's express, arrived in the Wood River area toward the close of February to shut down the company's offices in Hailey, Bellevue, and Ketchum; the Oregon Short Line was carrying the Pacific Express, and Wells Fargo was unable to compete.[101] In the same month, the Oregon Short Line reached Shoshone. Kelton was soon replaced as the major supply-distribution point for the southern part of Idaho. By March 1, 1883, all stage express, mail, and freight traffic from Kelton had been transferred to the advancing Oregon Short Line terminus. By July, 1884, a traveler noted that grass was growing over the ruts in the old Kelton Road.[102] The competition from the railroad forced the Utah, Idaho and Oregon Stage Company to liquidate in 1886.[103]

Scarcely had the railroad replaced the stages in Idaho Territory when historians and writers began to reminisce about the past. In 1884, the authors of the first comprehensive

[98] *Wood River Times*, January 15, 1881, p. 3, c. 6.

[99] "Kelton Road."

[100] "Wells Fargo Offices in Idaho" citation, newspaper index, Idaho State Historical Society.

[101] *Wood River Times*, March 1, 1883, p. 3, c. 4.

[102] "Kelton Road."

[103] "Idaho Express."

City of Rocks, a major landmark on the California Trail and freight routes from Utah northward.

History of Idaho Territory turned to the 1864 directory for information about the agencies of Wells Fargo & Co. in Boise County and quoted the following:

Bannock [Idaho] City is the county seat; no post-office; agent Wells, Fargo & Co., C. T. Blake; 190 miles southeast of Lewiston. Population, 5,000. . . .

Centerville has no post-office; agent Wells, Fargo & Co., P. W. Johnson; seven miles northwest of Bannock City, population 1,500. . . .

Pioneer has no post-office; agent, Wells, Fargo & Co., A. Slocum; 14 miles northerly from Bannock City. . . .

Placerville has no post-office; agent W., F. & Co., W. A. Atlee; fourteen miles northwest of Bannock City. Population, 1,500.

Wells Fargo's role in delivering the mails in the absence of an adequate federal postal service was also described.

There was at this time no mail facilities. The post-office department sent mail from Great Salt Lake through Boise to Walla Walla, in Washington Territory. Letters were carried by Wells, Fargo & Co. The charge on these letters when carried any distance to mining camps was usually twenty-five cents each in gold dust. Oftentimes letters would accumulate on account of the lack of facilities, and would follow a miner from point to point, he having left his name at the express office, for mail to be forwarded.

On one occasion a miner had moved from place to place without hearing from home for fourteen months, when he was informed that a quantity of mail awaited him at the express office. Sure enough, on arrival, there was handed to him twenty-one letters from folks at home, the charges on which were forty cents each, in all $8.40, which he cheerfully paid in gold-dust, and eagerly devoured the news from loved ones at home.[104]

Thus Wells Fargo & Co. was already finding a place in the recorded history of the American West.

By 1920, Wells Fargo's historic role as a carrier of mail, express, and gold dust—including the constant risk from highwaymen who sought the treasure box—was an established chapter in the history of Idaho. With some exaggeration, a standard history of the state paid tribute to the company.

The Wells-Fargo Express

One of the great institutions of the early days of California was the express business. Several companies came into existence in the early '50's, of the larger companies the Wells-Fargo Company being the only survivor. After gold was discovered in Idaho that Company extended its operations into this jurisdiction. After stage lines came into existence, a ready method of taking out gold dust and of bringing in valuable articles was opened to this company. The risk from highwaymen was great and the charges for taking the dust out to the San Francisco mint or to banking institutions in the larger cities of the coast were high. The Wells-Fargo Express cut a very important figure in the early history of the mining sections.

Mail Facilities

In the very early days of the mining camps, no arrangements were made for bringing in mail and the Wells-Fargo Express carried most of the letters. Charges for this service varied greatly, running as high as one dollar for bringing in or sending out an ordinary letter, but finally being reduced as regular mails were established to fifty cents and twenty-five cents per letter. For years many of the business houses in the larger mining camps sent their important communications by express, believing it to be a safer method of communication.[105]

Wells Fargo's early history was in the news again in April, 1952, when its old building in Idaho City collapsed. The *Idaho Statesman* ran pictures of how the structure, built in 1867, looked and told the following story:

Old Landmark Falls in Heap
At Idaho City
Wells Fargo Building
Collapses With Thud
Under Weight of Years

The old Wells Fargo building and corner saloon collapsed with a thud Monday night. No, it wasn't the atomic bomb. Just old age and too much snow on its roof last winter, between three and five feet.

The crash brought all the townspeople running. No one was hurt as the large brick building was unoccupied. Several weeks ago the near wall had caved in. The furniture, including a long bar and mirror and Wells Fargo safe, had been removed.

Now just a rubble of bricks and broken glass, the building had been a showplace of pioneer architecture, with fan-shaped windows and ornate brick work. For 85 years it had stood on the north-west corner of Main and Wall streets, the busiest corner in the gold rush town in the 1860's and one of the busiest corners in the West in its time. . . .

An item from the Idaho World of Oct. 9, 1867, states the building was near completion at a cost of around $16,000. . . . Nearly 160,000 bricks were required to build the structure, 32 by 36 feet, which contained a cellar 42 feet long. . . . Enough gold dust passed through its doors to have filled Fort Knox.[106]

[104] *History of Idaho Territory, Showing Its Resources and Advantages . . .* (San Francisco: Wallace W. Elliott & Co., 1884), 200, 201.

[105] James H. Hawley, editor, *History of Idaho: The Gem of the Mountains* (Chicago: S. J. Clarke Publishing Co., 1920), 129-130.

[106] *The Idaho Statesman* (Boise), April 23, 1952.